W9-CKE-330

Time Pioneers

Time Pioneers

*Flexible Working Time and
New Lifestyles*

KARL H. HÖRNING,
ANETTE GERHARD
MATTHIAS MICHAILOW

Translated by Anthony Williams

Polity Press

English translation © Polity Press 1995

First published in German as *Zeitpioniere: flexible Arbeitszeiten – neuer Lebensstil*
© Suhrkamp Verlag Frankfurt am Main, 1990

Published with the financial support of Inter Nationes, Bonn

This translation first published in 1995 by Polity Press in association with
Blackwell Publishers Ltd

2468107531

Editorial office:
Polity Press
65 Bridge Street
Cambridge CB2 1UR, UK

Marketing and production:
Blackwell Publishers Ltd
108 Cowley Road
Oxford OX4 1JF, UK

Blackwell Publishers Inc.
238 Main Street
Cambridge, MA 02142, USA

ISBN–0–7456–10765

A CIP catalogue record for this book is available from the British Library and the
Library of Congress

Typeset in Sabon on 10.5/12 pt by Colset Pte Ltd, Singapore
Printed in Great Britain by TJ Press Ltd, Padstow, Cornwall

This book is printed on acid-free paper

Contents

     and Time**   **99**
    4.1 The complex role of reduced income   100
    4.2 The reorganization of household management   104
    *4.3 Dissociation from the dominant dictates of money and
          time*   110
    *4.4 The resistance to change of ingrained consumption
          models*   115

5   **The Time Structures of the New Lifestyle**   **119**
    5.1 Restructuring everyday time patterns   120
    5.2 Changed time allocation techniques   126
    5.3 The time pioneers' perception of time   135
    5.4 The gain in temporal affluence   143

6   **The Dynamic of the New Lifestyle**   **147**

7   **Future Prospects**   **156**

    Notes   170
    Bibliography   176
    Index   190

Foreword to the English Edition

Many stories are told about time. Those told by men are frequently different from those told by women, those told by managers different from those told by blue-collar workers, those told by philosophers different from those told by sociologists. This book describes a system of time as perceived and contested by a group of our contemporaries. The curious features of the German debate on working time may surprise English-speaking readers, but beyond these peculiarities, they will quickly realize that they are familiar with the cultural backdrop against which the debate is taking place. Like all good stories, this one has no ending: its heroes are distrustful of visions and utopias. All their attention is focused on the present. The flexibilization of their working time is intended to secure them the maximum degree of flexibility at this point in time. They have no desire to arrange and plan everything; on the contrary, they wish to be able to react swiftly to changing circumstances. To this end, they want to 'have more time'. Thus, this book focuses on the 'presence of time'. For those who perceive that the main problem with time lies in 'time' and orientate themselves accordingly, the timescale of activity is the present.

However, although the book is about pioneers, it is not an heroic story. Their actions are directed against a life model which promises to elevate to the status of 'master of all things' those who, via a process of rationalization, achieve an heroic victory over time and the 'wastage' of time. In the eyes of the time pioneers, this is a futile struggle, since the sum total of that which has been achieved this century is not more, but less time. The time system which, following a great deal of effort, obtains today is characterized by a scarcity rather than a surplus of time. And as, so to speak, a 'perverse' side effect of equality between the sexes, this 'lack of time' also affects women.

Thus, it is not time control which becomes the key issue for the – male and female – time pioneers, but rather careful and independent time management. The flexibilization of working time is an essential prerequisite of such time management, yet on its own it is far from adequate, since the time gained can easily result in boredom. Although new forms of working time flexibility augment the dispositional freedom of the individual, they also abrogate certain collective rhythms of the time system which for so many people are a source of guidance and support.

It is possible to relax the rigid time systems of social life. Whether or not the resulting opportunities are exploited depends on the ability of individuals to develop time systems of their own which are able to overcome the exacerbated problems of coordination and self-discipline. This is due to the fact that in post-industrial society the task of constructing a life over time and in time is becoming increasingly complex and imposes great demands upon the individual.

One of the most puzzling findings of this sociological study is that the time pioneers do not (wish to) know what to do with the increased amount of free time on their hands. The purpose of their struggle was not to obtain more time off work, but more free time. They secured greater room for manoueuvre for the purpose of managing their time and themselves more effectively. They do not regard free time as a vacuum calling for rapid utilization and occupation. They wish to 'disencumber' time, not pack it full of activities again. Ultimately, they take the view that time should be utilized for the purpose of shaping their own lives.

The fact that time thus becomes a problem and an issue for individuals means that they begin to reflect upon time references: they gradually develop a 'reflexive time consciousness'. Thus, they are constantly aware of 'time'. They utilize the time which they have gained as a result of the flexibilization of their working time for the purpose of intitiating a process of time management, and thus of self-management. Therefore, they are not simply time pioneers, but also pioneers of self-centred time. They take the time to reflect upon time, and thus also upon themselves in time, and to discuss the matter with others.

In so doing, they not only seek to escape the perils of harassment and lack of time, but also to learn more about themselves. Whether or not they will be successful in this quest is rather uncertain. The experiment is underway: some are in the process of abandoning it, others are in the process of telling new stories.

K. H. H., A. G. and M. M.

Acknowledgements

Our thanks are due to a great many people. However, we are particularly indebted to Theo Bardmann, who was instrumental in originating this project. Susanne Bode-Weissenberg provided assistance during the revision of the manuscript.

K. H. H., A. G. and M. M.
Aachen, May 1990

Introduction

In human experience, time is a scarce commodity, and this scarcity of time is a millstone around our necks. Indeed, everyone complains of having too little time. Though not exactly egoists, nor heroes, people who consciously appropriate some time *for themselves* are something akin to explorers. Such people set their own time standards, while others, possessing no such standards, squander time because they do not realize that they actually have any time in the first place. These explorers adopt a different approach towards time management, and thus they are pioneers who, possessing time, have less need for other possessions.

Studies of the contemporary world consistently reveal that an independent approach towards time management would seem set to become one of the major questions of our age, and one which has already been the object of much theoretical deliberation and speculation. However, hitherto the actual opportunities for and possible forms of such an approach to time management have been largely ignored. 'Time pioneers' are people who strive to realize their conceptions of time at work and in their everyday private lives, in the process of which they confront obstacles and interruptions and develop independent forms of time management. On the one hand, they endeavour to introduce some degree of flexibility into their working time, thus distancing themselves from the ideals of the employment society. On the other, they couple these aspirations to flexibility with demands 'for more time for themselves', thus bringing into play the entire fabric of the way in which they fashion their lives.

The point of departure for our analysis is the flexibilization of working time. This was secured by the personal efforts of the time pioneers. They work much shorter hours and, where possible, gear their working time towards their own preferences. However, for the time pioneers, the additional time which this creates is not simply leisure time – it is 'free' time, time which they endeavour to manage as prudently as possible in order that it should not become immediately reoccupied with responsibilities and commitments. It is our hypothesis that, during the course of their independent struggle against the prevailing time structures, the behavioural and interpretive practices of the time pioneers increasingly assume the characteristics of an independent lifestyle.

In this respect, our analysis is fundamentally different from previous empirical studies. Such studies either investigate the problems of flexible working time to the exclusion of the accompanying social changes in the structures of working and private time, or they concentrate exclusively upon the question of changed attitudes towards time, time preferences, thus losing sight of the formative social force represented by changes in awareness. In contrast, we pose the question of how certain radical changes in the social conditions of work and time are absorbed by the time pioneers and become assimilated in their behavioural and interpretive practices. It is our opinion that these upheavals become particularly concentrated in the lifestyle of the time pioneers.

A full appreciation of this viewpoint requires the abandonment of conventional interpretive schemata inadequate to the task of explaining the processes of change which this analysis identifies, indeed, which portray such processes in the wrong light. A case in point is the fundamental question of the changing importance of work. Studies of the contemporary world are too precipitate in excluding from the work- and achievement-orientated society people whose 'only' ambition is to change it rather than to reject it outright. The time pioneers do not at all regard employment as a necessary evil. Quite the contrary: in fulfilling their responsibilities, they display motivation, willingness and commitment. Nevertheless, in order to avoid becoming appropriated by the demands imposed upon them by their employers, they harbour their own concepts with regard to the organization of their work. Their interest lies in gaining more time for themselves by adopting certain methods of organizing their working and private lives, rather than in the separation, overlapping and compensation of working and free time. In rejecting the established working time standard, they adopt a position outside the universally accepted cultural model of the conduct of life.

To some degree, this study is an examination of a new stage in the conflicts over working time policy. Employees are rebelling against the unreasonable behavioural expectations imposed by inflexible, standardized working time. They are consciously and deliberately adopting an independent position and opposing such expectations with their own concepts of the relationship between 'work and living'. However, as a result, they now find themselves 'between the devil and the deep blue sea', sandwiched between the great antipodes. As yet, working time policy has no place for them. Employers are only willing to sanction flexibilization on their own terms, and the trade unions, fearful of employees forfeiting any employment protection rights, have hitherto consistently rejected flexibilization on this basis. Thus, the time pioneers are left to their own resources. They acquire their free time at the cost of a plurality of disadvantages, primarily labour intensification. Thus do opportunities and risks become personalized!

We encountered time pioneers in a wide variety of occupations and positions. They are middle-income salaried employees in commercial, administrative, engineering, social and teaching professions. Our target group comprises men and women in approximately equal numbers; a small proportion of them live alone, and a third have non-adult children. Their work is altogether different from that associated with typical part-time employment.

We conducted a detailed study into the motives behind the desire for changes in working time, how individuals secured the flexibilization of their working time and the consequences which they faced at the workplace as a result. It became apparent that the primary obstacle to the practical implementation of new working time arrangements are traditional conceptions of employment in the enterprise. The dispute concerning flexible working time is exposed as a cultural conflict at the workplace, a clash of incompatible cultural perspectives between employer and employee. We discovered that the cultural paradigm of the employment society, the paradigm with which the time pioneers are at loggerheads, still remains very strong.

This situation poses a serious dilemma for the time pioneers: from the standpoint of job content, they take their work seriously and approach the performance of their tasks with commitment, but they have no desire to become appropriated by the temporal, organizational, and particularly normative, demands of their employers. This attitude brings obvious disadvantages and assessment deficits in its train. Employers are not so easily persuaded to accept such a rejection of the prevailing cultural paradigm of the employment society. The time pioneers do not adopt an instrumental attitude towards work: in other words, they do not constitute the drop-outs of a leisure and consumer society for whom employment is nothing more than an end to a private means. However, in the interpretive schemata of the time pioneers, the meaning of life is linked to certain forms of work: through the restructuring of the relationship between work and life, time assumes central thematic importance. Time pioneers desire interesting and skilled work, but also more time for themselves. However, it is not their intention that such free time should immediately become recongested with other tasks and commitments. It becomes quite clear that their reorientation is not governed by 'another side', such as free time. New priorities are evolving *vis-à-vis* the way in which people conduct their lives, priorities which envisage a changed balance between work and life, thus undermining the strict segregation that exists between work and free time. These incipient independent interpretive schemata reveal some of the central elements of an independent 'lifestyle'.

This lifestyle is primarily characterized by two typical changes: the changed relationship between time and money, and the reordering of daily time schemata. Consequent upon their changed working time, involving in many cases a reduction in hours of up to 50 per cent *vis-à-vis* full-time employment, time pioneers suffer a drop in income level. They make strenuous efforts to determine for themselves the correct relationship between certain income levels and the time which is gained. They make no attempt to compensate for loss of income – in order to maintain living standards – by intensifying their levels of involvement in domestic work, consumption-related work or the black economy. Inveterate consumption patterns militate against the implementation of changes in the way in which they conduct their lives necessitated by the reductions in their income levels. From this perspective, time pioneers scrutinize and re-evaluate the role of money and consumption. Time enters into competition with money: it is employed as a means of increasing affluence; and, from a certain standard of living upwards, temporal affluence competes against material affluence. This is an attempt on the part of the time pioneers to distance themselves from the money–time dictate prevailing in the economic sector.

Our empirical analysis of the reordering of daily time schemata breaks new ground. Hitherto, the debate on working time has completely failed to examine this question, and the burgeoning number of time theories also avoids testing them empirically. In contrast, our analysis focuses upon the changed time allocation practices and the changed interpretive schemata of time. By reorganizing everyday life in terms of time, the time pioneers acquire the ability to assume sole responsibility for time management, and thus opportunities to develop a new awareness of time. This is primarily geared towards achieving a lifestyle predicated upon flexible and disposable time structures in order to create 'more time for themselves'.

In turn, the availability of disposable time triggers a self-reflective process in the time pioneers: they now have the time on their hands to reflect upon time. The result is judicious time management, the foremost objective of which is the avoidance from the outset of occupying time or allowing it to be occupied. The time pioneers are convinced that this will facilitate the realization of their subjective aspirations in life. The new time management techniques and interpretive schemata largely bear the hallmark of this subject-centring.

Our analysis extends far beyond the issue of the flexibilization of working time. It is our opinion that far-reaching changes are discernible in the lifestyle of the time pioneers, changes which are particularly manifested in the problem of structuring time: time is now representative of something more. 'Time' symbolizes a different lifestyle, a lifestyle which is less subordinate to the unilaterally imposed demands of the industrial society and makes greater efforts to establish independent patterns.

Using the flexibilization of working time, this study introduces a research perspective which analyses the specific conceptions of life behind these changes. Without such an examination of these lifestyles, which exert so much formative influence and hence are themselves subject to such influence, it is impossible to fathom the underlying processes of this social change. Flexible forms of working are an expression of the upheavals occurring in the world of work and its industrial time regime. Our interest in forms of working time secured on an individual basis points beyond the narrow confines of flexibilization to the existence of an enhanced level of awareness of the phenomenon of time *per se*. The lifestyle of the time pioneers demonstrates that within the framework of the socio-cultural environment conceptions of life develop in whose interpretive schemata the problem of time is identified as a central theme. The time pioneers adopt an independently critical stance towards the prevailing time relations, which are manifested as scarcity and shortage of time and are concentrated in the characteristic topos of a 'society with no time'.

They react to society's surplus production of temporal demands, they keep these temporal directives in check and they endeavour to enhance the level of harmony between different time references.

By the manner in which the time pioneers assimilate certain upheavals in social time structures and develop changed time management techniques, they acquire a perception of time which ultimately fosters a lifestyle based on 'temporal affluence'. They still retain a 'pioneering' reputation as individualists and outsiders, and this reputation is repeatedly subject to confirmation and reinforcement, particularly in their working lives. However, in their own eyes, they are distinguished from the overwhelming majority of their colleagues less by being special or different in any way than by the conviction that the way in which they organize their lives constitutes an improvement in the quality of life over that which they enjoyed prior to securing flexibilization.

They prove themselves to be true pioneers by virtue of the fact that, in the face of great opposition, they establish new schemata in respect of the relationship between work and living, discover ways out of the crisis of the employment society via their form of participation in employment and gear the way in which they organize their lives, and their interpretive schemata, towards the constructive reappropriation of time for themselves.

1 Lifestyles and Time Relations in Flux

A different approach to time management is not the sole distinguishing feature of the time pioneers at the centre of this study: their lifestyle also provides a particularly striking indication of the radical changes currently taking place in modern society. In terms of numbers, the time pioneers are still rather thin on the ground, and can be investigated only by means of a systematic case study. Nevertheless, it is beyond question that they perform a pioneering role. Their participation in employment is marked by a flexible attitude towards time. This attitude can serve as a model in which changed aspirations and new interpretations, open to adequate explanation only against the backdrop of a general process of social transformation, assume definite shape.

Sociology is reluctant to provide the appropriate analytical tools which such an explanation requires. For this reason, the following chapter is devoted to expounding the theoretical and empirical basis of our study, and introducing the context of working time policy which is of such crucial importance.

1.1 The abandonment of old thought models

Sociology professes to investigate social reality by means of theoretically sound categories. This claim is being increasingly called into question by the realization that central sociological thought models no longer permit an adequate grasp of significant changes in modern society. Sociology is harbouring growing doubts about the validity of some massive concepts from its nineteenth-century traditions. In problematizing 'work' and the 'employment society', for example, sociology has challenged the validity of a social model in which employment was crucial as the central category and the driving force behind a dynamic process of development. Modern research into inequality is similarly casting serious doubt upon the analytical explanatory power of the class and strata model.

All this has undermined key sociological categories which hitherto have spearheaded the analysis of social differentiation and integration almost as a matter of course. Widespread theoretical uncertainty is generating numerous exploratory attempts. The preliminary results of such attempts are still somewhat unsatisfactory, and it is therefore essential to examine them critically and to develop our own theoretical frame of reference as a basis for this study.

At the beginning of the 1980s, the category of 'work' was toppled from the pedestal upon which it had stood largely unchallenged for more than a century. This process initiated a debate on the 'crisis of the employment society', during the course of which employment forfeited its status as the structural centre of society, to which it had long been automatically assigned. For sociology, work was the axis about which all else revolved: from this standpoint, each and every sphere of life was organized in accordance with the requirements of employment; work overshadowed everything else, and its 'long arm' reached into every last nook and cranny of society.

Industrial sociologists were particularly disconcerted by this collapse. They found it hard to have to recognize the existence of social changes which fundamentally questioned the decisive influence of employment. Their analytical tools were not geared towards adequately recording forms of experience and sociation other than work, nor towards relating these forms to employment. Thus the claims about the 'decline in the significance of work' came as a serious shock to their system, and it was some time before they were in a position to redefine their research subjects (Hörning 1989).

Claus Offe (1983) in particular had appointed himself advocate of the 'crisis of the employment society'. He assembled a large number of indicators pointing towards the fact that employment had forfeited some of its determining force. In opposition to the concept of a standard form of employment, Offe maintains that individual employment circumstances are subject to such variation in respect of earnings, qualifications, security, social visibility and recognition, workload, promotion prospects, communication opportunities and autonomy that salaried employment as such can no longer claim 'precise and shared significance for those in work for the perception of their social interests, for their consciousness or for their organizational and political behaviour' (Offe 1983: 45). 'It has now become practically [impossible]' for employee status 'as such to become the starting point for the formation of cultural, organizational and political aggregates and collective interpretation' (1983: 45). The validity of the concept of a standard form of work has been negated by important structural changes, such as the segmentation of the labour market, the dualization of work into a formal and an informal sector, and the growing difference between the organization of work in the manufacturing and service industries, and such concepts should therefore be abandoned.

Posing the question of the 'subjective valency and centrality of work for the employee' increases the doubts about the dominant significance of work. Ralf Dahrendorf regards our society as having reached the end of an era in which 'work as the radiating force of life cemented together the remaining aspects of the social construction of life' (Dahrendorf 1980: 756) and, similarly, Claus Offe takes as his point of departure the 'decentralization of the sphere of work vis-à-vis other aspects of life' (1983: 50). The theory of the dominant significance of paid work is no longer tenable at the level of either social or system integration.

In Offe's view, the status of work both as a moral obligation and as a structural necessity has undergone a transformation. Most work situations no longer allow 'employees to act, to function, to affirm themselves, or to achieve recognition as people acting morally as bearers of responsibilities' (1983: 51). The 'de-professionalization of work' is leading to the disappearance of the occupational ethos and of pride in production, and to a decline in occupational responsibilities and aspirations. Offe attributes the 'moral alienation and subjective meaninglessness of the sphere of work' to the dissolution of specifically proletarian social milieus (1983: 52). Further causal factors for Offe are discontinuous employment histories and a reduction in the proportion of adult life engaged in work, both of which reduce the subjective centrality of work. Under these circumstances, work becomes one concern among many others, thus forfeiting its function as the sole point of orientation for the development of personal and social identities.

The second major theme developed out of research into inequality. This research emphasizes the fact that the unilinear and vertical class structure based on work and occupational category is declining in relevance and is becoming increasingly unsuited for capturing modern relations of social inequality. Although it is true that, despite all efforts and all reforming impulses based on the welfare state, the class and stratification system of the Federal Republic of Germany is distinguished by a relatively high level of stability (Beck 1983: 35; Hradil 1987: 28; Kreckel 1983), nevertheless, this chiefly applies to the level of distribution. The fact that, despite the continued existence of clear distributional inequality, political conflicts have declined is attributable to social changes, which Ulrich Beck terms individualization processes (1983). According to Beck, shifts in social living standards and subjective aspirations have initiated 'a process of social and cultural erosion' which 'is dissolving the sub-cultural existential basis of class in terms of reality and experience' (1983: 53) and resulting in the diversification and individualization of life situations and ways of life. Consequent upon changed living conditions, which exercise a correspondingly formative influence upon subjective frames of reference and social and biographical starting points, the basis in the lifeworld for experiencing class- and stratum-specific relations of inequality (Berger 1987; Mooser 1983; Zapf et al. 1987) subsequently dissolves. This process is caused by greater economic prosperity and the security provided by welfare state benefits, by mobility, by increases in the length of vocational training courses, the creation of internal company hierarchies, the intensification of competitive pressure, and particularly by the dynamics of the labour market.

According to this viewpoint, the labour market processes in democratic welfare states in particular have set in motion historically specific processes of individualization. There 'is a tendency towards the emergence of individualized forms and bases of existence which in turn – for the sake of their own survival – are now compelled to place themselves ever more emphatically and exclusively at the centre of their own planning and conduct of life' (Beck 1983: 41). In this context, Beck regards individualization as a historically specific contradictory process of sociation: 'individualization is taking place under the conditions of the organized labour market based on the principle of the welfare state, and in this sense it is thus the product of social conditions, and in turn results in a specific conflictual method of sociation, in other words, in a collectively individualized form of existence' (1983: 42).

According to this interpretation, these fundamental social changes assume the character of a double and apparently paradoxical process: the homogenization of situations in life on the one hand, and the individualization of forms of existence on the other. On the one side, social welfare benefits and economic prosperity have become firmly established; on the other, and this represents the reverse side of the coin, the price of these increases in living standards is not only that the individual member of society becomes dependent upon these welfare benefits, but also the fact that the social, non-bureaucratic institutions of social welfare become de-functionalized. Risks and potential dangers exercise a more direct and immediate effect on the individual life situations.

Without wishing to dispute the importance of the socio-structural and labour market processes established by Beck, the fact remains that at core his arguments are too narrowly defined. His attempt at interpreting the above-mentioned processes of social transformation by means of the theory of individualization results in the scenario of a completely atomized society in which the individual becomes both the largest and the smallest sociation unit, and in which individualization in the shape of growing fragmentation into isolated individual existence becomes absolute. Beck's individualization theory prevents him from recognizing the existence of intermediate forms of sociation. He abandons, so to speak, the individual who has been liberated from traditional social ties, without being able to recognize any new forms of sociation. In concentrating his attention on structural processes, Beck embarks upon a one-sided expansion of the theoretical diagnosis of individualization, which he precipitately regards as *the* sociation model *per se*. He must therefore stand accused of employing a one-sided, namely, a structural-determinist concept of individualization which, in the sense of de-traditionalization, ultimately and inevitably results in the atomization of the individual.

Both themes clearly demonstrate that although class differences undoubtedly persist, they no longer constitute the central component of the identity of this society. Membership of a class-related, economically conditioned group is no longer the determining factor in shaping the conduct of life. Similarly, it is no longer possible to regard work and its social organization as the model of integration governing everything else. In consequence a sociation of individuals supporting the social structure has also become a problem, the analysis of which requires a correspondingly different frame of reference categories.

In conclusion, we can state, firstly, that the importance of employment as the analytical focal point of our society is increasingly being undermined. Secondly, although it is true that the dissolution of milieu-bound classes is being forced apace by processes of individualization, this does not imply that society is disintegrating, as in Beck's interpretation. For this reason, the next section develops the analytical concept of 'lifestyle', by means of which we conceptualize a method of sociation capable of the integration of the individual.

1.2 Lifestyle as an analytical concept

If taken seriously, the breach in the well-established conceptual structure of sociology consequent upon social development poses new and serious theoretical problems, notably with the assertion that the centrality of employment is declining. This mainly affects the problem of sociation. How is social integration to be sociologically comprehended if concepts of the social organization of employment, social integration through the division of labour, and sociation through work (on this point, see Beck 1984; Dahrendorf 1980, 1983) are no longer sustainable? We attempt to find an answer to this question by means of the analytical concept of 'lifestyle'. However, an explanation of some basic assumptions of differentiation theory is required in order to facilitate the adequate development of this concept.

In contrast to the social model of the 'employment society', in which society 'revolves' around work, from the standpoint of differentiation theory, it is necessary to start by assuming that in modern society no social functional system is able to lay claim to a position exceeding the scope of its own function. Each functional system operates in relative autonomy, though, as a result of the emphasis on addressing one particular social problem only, it is dependent upon the successful performance of the other functional systems. In this case, the claims to dominance of, for example, the economy, politics, science or religion can simply be regarded as the self-hypostatization of the individual functional systems. From this standpoint, the 'crisis of the employment society' can be seen as a by-product of functional social differentiation revealing the absolutist pretensions on the part of the economic system to be a case of self-overreach (Luhmann 1988).

From the standpoint of differentiation theory, individualization processes also appear in a different light. Functional specialization increases the susceptibility of the functional system to malfunction, and intensifies its need to exclude personality. The result is the growing independence and differentiation of the individual *vis-à-vis* the social systems, in other words, individualization. In the wake of functional differentiation, value and orientation models binding on the whole of society become de-functionalized. The individual experiences this process as the pluralization and relativization of values. Therefore, for individuals, social differentiation entails the problem that they no longer receive unilinear instruction, such as by means of generalized values or of processes of institutionalization binding on the whole of society. Instead, they are compelled to assume a relative degree of self-responsibility for the management of their own lives. They are now forced to pursue the selective utilization of the opportunities, rationality precepts and orientational facilities of different functional systems, for whose consistency there is no guarantee. These processes of differentiation ensure greater scope for individual development and impose varied selectivity in respect of the functional systems, and in consequence the subjective component available to individuals in the shaping of their own lives is increased. Members of society increasingly appear as the sole centre of their life planning.

However, differentiation can be seen not only at the level of system structures, but also at the level of socio-cultural processes, of the differentiation of lifeworlds.[1] For this reason, we believe that the system perspective can only be made sociologically fruitful if the problems which this system makes apparent are afforded adequate consideration from the standpoint of their socio-cultural integration and articulation. At the level of socio-cultural processes, problem formulas are generated which cannot be reduced to problems of the system. System differentiation and pluralization of lifeworlds produce disparate and unique specific situations. This alters the approach to the problem of sociation. Our alternative theory for the interpretation of social changes and structural upheavals in modern society is not individualization in the sense of isolation – as propounded by Beck's individualization thesis (Beck 1983) – but *sociation via specific situations*.

If processes of social differentiation compel individuals to utilize and arrange the creative opportunities and latitude which are placed at their disposal by means of accepting personal selectional responsibility, then the mechanisms of sociation also undergo a transformation: increasingly they become unique and self-related. This is sociation via specific situations, adopting specific thematic forms around crystallizing points related not only to socio-cultural starting positions, but also to current problem situations of both an individual and a collective nature. In the case of the sociation mechanisms, the starting point should be social integration, which is systematically incorporated into the structurally diversified specific situations. The form of sociation which can be distinguished at this level is lifestyle.

Lifestyles constitute a systematic configuration of specific situations incorporating conditions, problem situations and prioritizations. Life-style is geared towards individual themes grouped around crystallizing points. The thematic cores are manifold, and not at all restricted to certain functional areas. Individual lifestyles subject them to different degrees of emphasis and problematization.

As an analytical concept, lifestyle affords consideration to the increased amount of scope (made available by the social differentiation process) for making subjective prioritizations and forming subjective interpretations of structural standards. As a result, the analytical perspective is able to focus upon the scope available for shaping the conduct of life, rather than concentrating upon structurally determined restrictions. Given the fact that the general debilitation of the structural social determination of lifestyle and awareness enhances the status of the interpretive schemata and prioritizations of individual members of society, they are themselves incorporated into the systematic configuration of life as structural data.

This is a form of sociation which – to a far greater extent than is taken into account by the conceptions of stratification sociology – is dependent upon collective interpretive schemata and subjective prioritizations. We credit lifestyles with an inherently valuable reference niveau of social integration. They obtain a force of their own that has an intrinsic quality which is not the sole product of structural social conditions. This touches upon a sociological approach which stands in marked contrast to the conventional conceptions of lifestyle.

1 This interpretation of lifestyle as a form of social integration requires the term to be distinguished from its usage in everyday parlance in the sense of an individual existence technique ('healthy', 'reasonable' lifestyle). Instead, it should be regarded as a personal life-style which individuals demonstrate in public or during their leisure-time pursuits via consumer goods, or as an individual technique for coping with life such as those life management techniques at the centre of the 'Lifestyle Analysis' studies which take their point of departure from the individual psychologist Alfred Adler (for an overview, see Ansbacher 1967; Gilbert 1960; Gushurst 1971).

2 The sociology of leisure time equates lifestyle with leisure-time style (Attias-Donfut 1978; Tokarski and Uttitz 1985; Tokarski and Schmitz-Scherzer 1985: 251ff). In contrast, the objective of our concept of lifestyle is to overcome the classical dichotomy between

working time and leisure time prevailing in industrial and leisure-time sociology by means of thematizing the status of work or the type of leisure-time availability as a specific lifestyle issue.

3 In the assumption that as the 'best indicator', consumption can be deployed as a means of classifying lifestyles 'as they are observed in everyday life', commercial lifestyle research picks up the thread of the sociology of consumerism and similarly bestows upon lifestyle the narrow definition of consumer style (see Hörning 1970: 92–126).

4 Neither should lifestyle be regarded as the outcome of the arrangement of social indicators (such as occupational status, income, age, household type, time budget, or value orientations, etc.). Although these indicators are capable of achieving high levels of intensification, they ignore the constitutive processes of lifestyle (see Becker and Nowak 1982; Gluchowski 1987; Zapf et al. 1987).

5 From our standpoint, the most interesting approach is that developed by Bourdieu (1984). However, it is our opinion that Bourdieu's lifestyle analyses are subject to economic determinism, since ultimately he affords priority to the distinctive character of practical forms over economic capital (see Bourdieu 1983: 181). As a theoretical building-block, the 'habitus', which as the code incorporated into the meaning of action generates the practical forms and the classification schemata, is also tailored towards this priority assignation in that it continually harks back to the derivative relations of the class situation whose indelible stamp it bears. For this reason, we believe that we should develop a more open conceptual framework.

In contrast to other forms of sociation such as milieu, clan, class or subculture, lifestyles are much more flexible in the face of social changes, and approach different problem situations and definitional scope with a far greater degree of perceptual focus and sensitivity. In this context, lifestyles are not communalizations of relatively homogeneous milieus (with good claims to conformity and homogeneity), but rather sociations of particular problem situations. In contrast to milieu-related communalizations, lifestyles are shorter-lived and more particularized, and can therefore absorb social changes more rapidly. They are dynamic processes.

Against the backdrop of extensive processes of social differentiation, lifestyles are geared towards the growing need on the part of individuals to be able to shape their own lives in a manner which will preserve their individuality and identity. Lifestyle has recourse to the achievements of social sub-sectors, though it is not compelled to adopt the logic of such sub-sectors. Instead, in turn, lifestyles access various areas and spheres of life, and produce independent passions, shapes and stylizations.

Each lifestyle is fashioned differently and in isolation from other lifestyles. Thus it is a question of 'comparison', and particularly of the establishment of differences. In the face of increasing social differentiation and particularization, the growing contingent experience of individuals is enjoining them to adopt a plurality of stances. At this juncture, lifestyle assumes the guise of a selective authority which filters, interprets and thematizes the meanings offered by society. Lifestyle becomes a force for the production of social differences. As a result, the requirement for gradual stylization, or for stylization capable of undergoing intensification by any means whatever, becomes generalized, and symbolizations increase in stature. Symbols and stylization principles of lifestyles function as identification and dissociation symbols indicating social affiliations. In modern society, the call for a plurality of relations on the part of the individual member of society goes hand in hand with the enhancement of the status of the expressive components of personality representation. The identifiable symbolizations of lifestyles facilitate the attainment of social recognition and the social categorization of the individual (for a continuation of this theme, see Hörning and Michailow 1990).

It is not only on account of the dynamism of the labour market and the other structural social processes to which Beck (1983) refers that individuals are increasingly left to their own resources. The greater degree of formative scope at the disposal of individuals forces them to pursue the planning and shaping of their lives ever more actively. However, the greater degree of reference to the self on the part of individuals in the shaping of their lives should not only be regarded as an opportunity for individual members of society. There is a concomitant increase in the demands made upon their own subjective prioritizations and characteristics. The functional systems of society are no longer able to supply any universally valid meaning systems, or provide support for the subjective reality constructions of the individual. The insecurity and contingency which are produced by society not only provide a powerful boost to the affirmation of personal identity but also continually impose excessive demands upon it. The 'management of personal identity', the process on the part of individuals of ensuring that they lead 'correct' lives, is left largely to the individual; it becomes a private affair (see Berger and Luckmann 1983).

Our concept of lifestyle absorbs the growing importance of time references in the conduct of modern life. The development of subjective elements in the constitution of identity is accompanied by a greater personal requirement for time. 'Individual cultivation', individualization processes and 'identity management' require time, not simply as a quantum, as a sufficient amount of time, but also in the qualitative sense, as subjectively meaningful time. Individualization in the form of differentiation between the individual and the social system also implies differentiation between personal time options and social-system time standards. Members of society become increasingly more aware of their subjective time, which cannot be reduced to the system times of the functional systems. They see themselves as people who each have their own past and future, their own present, their own ways and means of handling future opportunities, their own forms of experience of time, and their own forms of time management.

To the extent to which individualization processes also result in the serious exacerbation of problems of time for the individual, questions of time management emerge as a theme of crucial significance, lifestyle becomes responsible for addressing questions of time, developing interpretive alternatives in respect of time which are specific to lifestyle, and thus for differentiating between time and the demands which social sub-systems make upon time. Against this particular background, the issue at stake now not only becomes that of addressing lifestyle as a form of sociation, but also that of analysing it as a 'chronotope', in other words, of focusing attention upon the time structures which are of specific relevance to lifestyle. Conceiving lifestyle as a 'chronotope' means grasping the fact that lifestyle is an independent form of network of various different time structures. The lifestyle chronotope characterizes the specific techniques of time management, formulates shortages of time, provides for the elongation and consolidation of time, prepares temporal ascriptions of meaning and future horizons, develops daily schedules and life plans, and formulates schemata of biographization. Not only is participation in various spheres of life and social circles determined by lifestyle, but also the degree of time identification: the extent to which time standards and perspectives are incorporated into the subjective experience of time, therefore becoming subjective temporality.

1.3 Time as the thematic core of lifestyle

The objective of this study is to employ the analytical dimension of time in order to penetrate the rich variety of arrangements for the conduct of life. Thus, ultimately, the study is based upon the fundamental premise of the sociology of time that time is not a concrete quality which has always been present in material and natural reality, and which, as such, only needs to be discovered by people. Rather, time is a *dimension of meaning*, a dimension which has been conceived by people, and via which they attempt to come to terms with their natural and social environment. Sociological interest in time commences at the point where time differences are not 'inconsequential' to people, but rather indicative of behavioural differences, where time attains a social identity, is formulated in terms of expectation and experiential form, and where time is condensed into semantic categories and accompanies life as an interpretive schema.

Since Emile Durkheim (1976) at least, sociology has been at pains to highlight the social character of time (see Bergmann 1983; Heinemann and Ludes 1978). It emphasizes the fact that time is relatively independent of individual awareness, and in so doing, sociology stresses the independence of social time. Social time is a reflection of social life, and time indicators are qualified by mores and customs, by rituals and routines, and by forms of interaction and ways of life (Wendorff 1980).

In its social dimension, time is *made* in order that people can find their temporal bearings and orient themselves in the meaningful construction of their lifeworld. Time does not only fulfil the function of an orientational guide in the lifeworld. Time expectations are also made in order that sociality does not break off at the interactively animated barriers of space ('out of sight, out of mind'), but rather that communication remains integrated and synchronized over space. Time is also made in order to draw individuals into the social system, to civilize them; as sociologists also stress, time is made for the purpose of exercising authority, control and discipline. The making of time does not proceed in an arbitrary fashion. On the contrary, it proceeds in conformity with specific conditions, and thus interests, the discovery of which is a focal point of sociological interest. What people think of 'their time' can only be expressed as a manifestation of social time which has been formulated and organized against the background of shared group living.[2]

In his observations on the theory of time, Norbert Elias (1982) emphasizes that behind these time concepts and time systems lurks the human endeavour to solve specific problems, and that all forms of time calculation are linked to historically changing social requirements. He makes clear that time as implied in the substantivist utilization of the term does not exist at all: time is neither palpable nor visible. The substantive 'time' produces the 'myth of time' which conspires to steer all trains of thought towards the objective of achieving mathematically precise calculations of time as if it were a matter of measuring the dimensions of an object. For the purposes of obtaining a sociological comprehension of time, it is helpful to replace the substantive 'time' by a verb such as 'to time'. At first glance, this verb appears somewhat unsettling, but nevertheless it expresses the fact that time represents a social symbol with which people designate their calculation of time, their 'times' and their 'time-making'. Timing, or rather time-making, is a synthesis, a process of interrelating various sequences of events: at least two continual sequences are compared with each other, and one of them is standardized as a reference sequence for the purpose of functioning as a yardstick against which to gauge and determine other sequences. Depending upon the relevant social requirements, approximate natural cycles such as the transition from night to day, low tide and high tide, the phases of the moon, and the seasons may serve this purpose. Alternatively, more sophisticated processes may be required such as the filtering of sand through an hour-glass. Ultimately, absolutely precise reference sequences appear necessary, such as the frequencies which control the most advanced clocks. By referring to the symbolic character of time, Elias argues for understanding human endeavours to calculate time in the context of contemporary historical and cultural problem-contexts, and of acquiring a (self-)critical problem awareness with respect to time-making.

These fundamental premises of sociological thought on the subject of time form the basis for developing both criticism of and distance from the prevailing chronometric perception of time, particularly as manifested in the form of physico-astronomic time. 'Objective' standard time, which is perceived in purely quantitative terms, is relativized as one, but only one, form of social time. Sociologists emphasize as forcefully as possible that no matter how accurately a time of day is calculated, it is incapable of revealing the nature of time sufficiently for a sociological analysis.

As a rule, sociological analyses of time restricted to the quantitative-numerical level are criticized as too myopic. Drastic examples of this can be found in the field of time budget research (see Blass 1980;

Kössler 1984; Krüsselberg et al. 1986), for which the issue at stake is achieving the most precise measurement possible of the quantitative extent of activity times. The sociological criticism of the approaches and findings of research into time budgets is not directed at the precision of the measuring methods or results, but at the premise that it is possible to obtain sufficiently accurate measurements of time using pure chronometry. Gert Eichler criticizes this assumption as the 'ontologization of time' which culminates in 'the indifferent concatenation of forms of time utilization treated as equivalent in content' (Eichler 1979: 64). It is not possible to reveal the contents or the qualitative aspects of associations of time utilization by adopting a purely arithmetical approach to accessing time. Following Elias, it would be possible to accuse arithmetical analysts of time that, as a result of their blind faith in standard time, they had allowed themselves to be led down the garden path by the 'fetishist character' of socially institutionalized 'objective' time (see Elias 1982: 1004), and that their reductionist approach to time as a 'yardstick' had made them blind to questions of the social quality of time.

The central argument against time budget analyses which are based solely upon chronometry boils down to the claim that as delimited units of time (hour, day, week, etc.), not all time quanta are equal in quality. Before it is even possible to arrive at an appropriate interpretation of a statement to the effect that someone has four hours of pure free time at their disposal per day, it is first necessary to obtain information on the length of the sub-stretches involved and then on the juncture of the day at which they occur. Only then is it possible to draw any conclusions as to the quality of the time quantum in question (see Müller-Wichmann 1984). The idea behind this is that time only assumes a qualitative character from certain quantities onwards, that time is qualified by scope for action, and that in turn, time quanta render activities possible or impossible.

Within the context of the debate on working time,[3] sociologists are now emphasizing the fact that in the case of reductions in working time, it is also invariably a question of gauging the quality of the time which is gained against the scope which it allows for pursuing personal interests and attending to personal needs. According to this view, the quality of time becomes evident from the type of activities which it involves, from the intended and possible occurrences which it involves, and from the use to which it is put.

However, such claims are insufficient to substantiate the definition of time as a qualitative dimension of meaning. The reason for this is that in attempting to equate the quality of time with opportunities for meaningful action, the arguments focus upon calls for the improvement of hitherto 'incurable' time systems. In this regard, improvements are usually gauged against subjective life interests. An attempt is made to provide an answer to the question of the quality of time by referring to the scope for action which it entails, though this loses sight of the perception of time, a variable which itself requires analysis. Sociological studies of time which investigate the question of quality over and above that of quantity while adopting a conventional perception of time and equating increases in quality solely with an increase in the scope for action do not exhaust all the avenues of analysis at their disposal.

The objective of this study is not simply to identify new forms of time allocation and ask whether they are beneficial or detrimental to the quality of life. Rather, it also entails establishing the extent to which they are indicative of specific structures of time awareness, particularly of forms of the social perception of time. This investigation into the question of the quality of time is intended to be radical in the sense that we prevent our analysis of time from becoming an information-gathering exercise on scope for action at too early a stage in the proceedings, and take as our point of departure the examination of the social structure of time and of awareness of this. Sociologists of time (such as Rinderspacher 1985; Deutschmann 1983) repeatedly stress the fact that the departure from natural time rhythms, the loss of orientation towards tasks and activities within the context of time awareness, were important factors in generating changes in the quality of time. Thus, for example, E. P. Thompson (1991) demonstrates how task-oriented time allocation in the agricultural sector retreats in the face of the orientation on the part of industrial working methods towards abstract time of neutral content, such as that displayed on clocks. Industrial capitalism required people to rethink their approach to the subject of time, requiring them to learn to find their bearings in an abstract time schema of neutral content instead of in 'natural' task-related time schemata (Laermann 1975; Zoll 1982). It is emphasized that this equates to a redefinition of the abstractness of the quality of time. However, no matter how important and correct it might be to point to the abstractness of time in the modern age, from the standpoint of sociologists of time, it is wholly inadequate for the purpose of grasping the concept of time. This is because the abstraction of time implies the abstraction of time from its content. However, insofar as notions of time become divorced from human actions, social cycles and natural rhythms, they can find their purpose only within themselves. The 'history of time' is the history of the de-substantialization of time, during the course of which time divests itself of all vestiges of content, and begins to relate to itself: *time becomes reflexive*. The reflexivity of time primarily involves

> relating the time horizons of past and future to the present; grasping that these time horizons are different for each present, initially from a purely chronometric standpoint, but subsequently also from the standpoint of the past and the future which they make appear relevant to the present; and finally, the additional complication that past and future presents (and thus, not simply past and future objects) appear in the past and the future of every present, to which in turn the maxim applies that they have already had, or will have, their own time horizons. (Luhmann 1980a: 294)

The question of the quality of time points not only to abstraction but also, at the structural level, to reflexivity. It is this which facilitates the characterization of time as a dimension of meaning, since it is the reflexive structure of time, in the sense that it finds its references of purpose within itself, that facilitates independence. However, identifying reflexivity as the structurally qualitative core of time also implies exploding the current linearity notions of time and their typical metaphors of movement, chain and flux, and understanding notions of time as contingent, as having other possible forms. For our analysis of lifestyles from the standpoint of the theory of time, this involves searching for time schemata which go hand in hand with specific methods of time management, and which are possible within the framework of structurally reflexive time.

It is our assumption that lifestyles develop time structures of their own, in the process of which they become adjusted to different time structures obtaining in their environment and thus reflect these as their own alternative times. The temporality of a lifestyle contains three inter-linked time references: those of social time (1), those of sub-system times (2), and those of subjective time (3).

(1) By *social* time, we mean two different time references which are relevant to lifestyle: the socially historical perception of time on the one hand, and standardized normal working time (as an objectivized medium of synchronization, this is also known as 'world time'), on the other. This system theory is based on the assumption that, as a comprehensive social system, society is subdivided into a plurality of differentiated sub-systems, each of which observes its own selectivity, thus ruling out the possibility of the reproduction of a common

history or the projection of a common future. Each of the social sub-systems has its own future and past constructions and develops its own time management methods. Social time is a specific form of time and, being the highest authority for the reduction of complexity levels, it is to social time that the responsibility falls for integrating the different sub-sector temporalities and, from the standpoint of time, effecting the utilitarian integration of the various system times into a society of the present.

The time structures in force in modern society are characterized by a linearization of time (see Rammstedt 1975: 50), though the time horizons themselves are temporalized: history loses its model character (Koselleck 1967: 206), is itself understood as something which has always been historical (historization of history), and serves the present as an indication of horizons of opportunity which past presents failed to exploit, but which the current present can assume to be realizable. In modern society, history is devalued in relation to the future. To modern society, the future is no longer simply the extension of the past beyond the present: in more than one respect, the future can be regarded as a radically different future present, thus imposing upon the present a sensitivity towards time whose centre is the reflexivity of time itself: it compels the present to effect the temporalization of time notions. It converts the time awareness of the present from a closed to an open future. In the form of (positive or negative) utopia, the open future can be conceived as a completely different future present, and held up to the current present as a criticism (see Luhmann 1976); as an open future, it can be de-futurized by means of planning and technology, and deprived of its openness and uncertainty by visualizing future objectives which treat current, systematic action as the past of the future present (see Bergmann 1981: 243ff). It is possible to counter the open future with safety precautions. The implementation of measures which absorb uncertainties minimizes the imponderability of the future in the present (see Kaufmann 1970). In modern society, historization of history, orientation towards an open future, and de-futurization of the future are equivalent to a 'radicalization of the historicity of the present' (Deutschmann 1983: 497). The present is reduced to the status of the turning-point in the process of deciding, or even the location of the decision, between extremely different pasts and futures (Luhmann 1977: 45). It is itself temporalized.

The prevailing social perception of time is manifested in abstract, homogeneous standard time of neutral content. Standard time becomes the system time of world society owing to the fact that it is the only form of time which is able to sustain the variety and inter-dependence of functional system times.

> As the coordinating factor of generalization, world time must ensure:
> 1. homogeneity, in other words, independence from movements and speeds, both of world time and of other times; 2. reversibility, in other words, reverse mental calculability, the irreversibility of the course of time notwithstanding; 3. determinability via dating and causality; and 4. transitivity as a condition of comparisons between time stretches of different times. (Luhmann 1975: 111)

World time ensures that the various system times can be compared with each other.

In social terms, it is essential that the differences between inner-social time structures are capable of at least symbolic mutual compari-son; a time schema becomes socially necessary in order to facilitate reciprocity and compatibility across the boundaries of the sub-systems. 'Objective time', standardized normal time, 'serves the purpose of smoothing, levelling, and equalizing time relations which in them-selves are extremely complicated' (Luhmann 1975: 115). Standar-dized normal time surmounts the relative isolation of the local time of each social system. It is more abstract, more generalized than any social system time. The standardization of time ensues in a chronological form. A chronological conception of world time faci-litates orientation towards a concatenation of junctures which is independent of system-specific experiences of time (Bergmann 1981: 101f). Social systems utilize this schema for the purpose of effec-ting beyond their own specific system times self-temporalization which is recognizable to other environmental systems. They translate their own system time into the 'language of normal time'. This faci-litates the comparison between and collocation of those factors which had been dissociated from each other by means of system differentiation. Social systems are distinguished from each other by virtue of their different selectivity and their correspondingly different selections, and their mutual integration is effected via standardized normal time.

(2) Thus attention is now focused upon the second time reference of lifestyle: *industrial time as a form of sub-system and organizational time*. Each of the time demands made by the time structures of the sub-systems has a special niche in the temporality of lifestyles. We emphasize the importance of the time structures of the economic

system, though – in contrast to the usual approach – without equating them with social time. As a result, the analytical force of our study is considerably enhanced.

The system time of the capitalist economic system, industrial time, primarily makes its presence felt in the way people conduct their lives via the stipulation of factory/office hours and working hours, and their arrangement within labour organizations (see Deutschmann 1983; Heinemann 1982). By virtue of their decision-making programmes, labour organizations exercise a profound influence upon personal behaviour, and bestow upon the selectivity of the economy practical relevance for the conduct of life (see Bardmann 1986: 176ff; Rinderspacher 1988). For this reason, any analysis of lifestyle should afford special consideration to the relationship between lifestyle and organizational times, particularly working time, one of those forms of organizational time which exercises the most sustained influence upon the conduct of life.

The logic of time which is typically conveyed here is the logic of money, in accordance with which the future horizon is open and the time quanta are subject to both extensive and intensive exploitation. Like money, in labour organizations, time also is owned: via their contract of employment, employees place their working time at the disposal of the company management, their time programmes and their regulatory decisions. It is in the industrial working environment that employees are confronted by the 'industrialization of time' (see Olk et al. 1979). The working environment promotes rational time management, economic time budgeting, time saving, punctuality, synchronization, and consistency, etc.; it is here that employees become aware of the separation of lifetime into the time blocks of working time and free time, and that time limits and time markers are formalized and imposed upon private life.

We can add two important observations to these statements. For the first of these, we fall back upon our explanations concerning social time as the abstract form of time of neutral content, and highlight the difference between this time reference and economic time in the form of industrial organizational time. This difference is usually completely overlooked. However, failure to recognize this difference results in the disappearance from view of the various problem backdrops which these two time references introduce into the conduct of life. Whereas organized factory/office hours are problematized as 'forms of economic coercion', 'the time terror of the industrial and labour system', 'the dictatorship of the stopwatch', and 'capitalist and pathogenic time harassment', the abstractness of social time is problematized by the fact that it has become dissociated from content interpretations, has ceased providing any orientational guidance, no longer provides any pointers as to 'correct behaviour' and unreasonably expects that in the conduct of their lives people should now assume the responsibility for timing their actions themselves.

Taken to its conclusion, this observation goes far beyond the problems arising out of the premise of an 'industrialization of time'. No longer do individuals offer resistance solely to the time pressure generated by the economy, which might appear to them to be exaggerated, artificial and hazardous to their health. They also fall under the influence of a super system time which demands that they accept personal responsibility for time management. This super system time recognizes no 'good turns', remains oblivious to the fact that time means money, and refuses to reveal how much time is required for 'living', etc. This abstract time is neutral towards that which occurs within it, thus facilitating the development and characterization of individual and specific local times.

The second observation concerns the relationship between temporal individualization, on the one hand, and the organizational arrangement of time, on the other. The way in which people conducted their lives was once largely determined by the social class or stratum to which they belonged. By contrast, modern conduct of life is influenced both by functional systems and by individual decisions, aspirations and interests, etc. which undergo structural evaluation. In consequence, it should not only be assumed that lifestyles enjoy more diversification and a greater degree of subtlety, but also that they suffer the loss of overall social obligations relating to issues affecting the conduct of life, such as those which emanate from a class- and stratum-based social system. Via the organizations, the existence of a large number of demands upon social time comes to light, demands which are constantly synchronized with functional requirements and laid at the door of the individual.

(3) The third time reference of lifestyle is *subjective* time. This encompasses individual experience of time; it has a synchronous dimension, everyday time, and a diachronous dimension, lifetime from the cradle to the grave. Subjective time is based upon the biographically unique perception of time, notwithstanding the fact that it is of inter-subjective construction, and entails a perspectivity which is oriented towards the various social and socially relevant time structures and time systems. It lends structure to experience of time, which has close ties with the development of meaningful orders and social time categories. In

effecting allocations of time, the time reference of subjective time also measures time in that, for example, it establishes how usefully and constructively it has been spent, how well it has been synchronized and allocated, or how quickly it has passed. Our observations below are based on a sociological analysis of the constitution of subjective time which has primarily been developed from the field of philosophical phenomenology.

Subjective time proper is deemed to be inner duration. It is the automatically progressive flow of experience in the consciousness of the individual which remains in a state of continual flux: every present becomes a 'just-has-been', and then a 'was'. Every current phase of an experience constitutes at one and the same time the boundary phase of continuous retentions and protentions, of past and future horizons (see Schütz and Luckmann 1975: 67; Luckmann 1983, 1986). The past horizon consists of the evanescent phases, the future horizon, of the anticipated, typified experiences. This continuous sequence of experiences constitutes the fundamental temporal structuring of human experience; its flow is continuous and unbroken, but it is structured by its close links with the meaning of experience.

The rhythms of inner duration, in other words, the volume of the temporal experiences, vary due to subjectively motivated categories of attention, that is to say, due to specific experiential styles which are linked to different themes, meaning schemata or concatenations of activity. These in turn can be subjected to excessive formative influence by physical conditions and enforced changes (institutional controls, different reality areas with a closed meaning structure, and various situational requirements) (Schütz and Luckmann 1975: 70). Thus temporal experiences are structured by meaning, and specific experiential styles which are linked to corresponding meaning structures determine the subjective experiences of time.

The acquisition of various time references is closely linked to temporal ascriptions of meaning. The characteristic pace, decelerations and accelerations of the experiential rhythm of inner duration do not enter consciousness as such; they are first registered reflexively, particularly in linguistically objectified categories of the everyday lifeworld. The categories for various temporal ranges of the meaning of past experiences and activities are employed as associational and comparative variables for the purpose of interpreting experiences and anticipating activities. In consequence of the widespread routinization of the requirements of daily life, linguistic time categories remain largely confined within the thematic environment of activities and experiences and thus they seldom penetrate their thematic core.

Linguistic, socially objectified *time categories* provide immediate interactions with a temporal background situated outside the inner duration of whoever is engaged in activity. Their interactive function is utilized for the purpose of synchronizing common activity. The mediatory function of social categories of time lies in the subdivision of experiences into intersubjectively recognizable segmentations (beginnings, duration and ends of typical experiences and activities) for the purpose of social action (Luckmann 1986: 153ff). The characterization of social categories of time which are based on the concrete world of the activity and experience of the members of society find correlation and legitimation in the corresponding socio-historical perception of time (see Luckmann 1986: 156). The prevailing perception of time exercises a crucial formative influence upon the temporal interpretive schemata of the members of society, and thus also upon the ways of articulating opportunities and experiencing subjective time.

The time structures of lifestyle develop as an overlap between and a unique combination of the following three salient time references: social time, sub-system times and subjective times. Lifestyle time is a typical complex structure of time system schemata entailing these associations. It weaves the threads of various time systems into a specific pattern.

1.4 Flexibilization in the context of working time policy

Our study focuses on special forms of working time arrangements, namely, shorter and flexible working hours. As new time references in the working environment, these special forms of working time arrangements arouse expectations of changes in the way that people organize their lives in general. Our basic theory is that lifestyles which embrace the reference factor of working time in its special form of shorter and flexible working hours also incorporate lifetime. However, it is essential that any analysis of flexible working time should also afford consideration to flexibilization within the context of working time policy.

Since the beginning of the 1970s, the term 'flexible working time' has been endowed with emancipatory overtones. In an era of accelerated change, flexible working time is presented as a desirable and necessary option which provides individuals with scope for shaping their own lives. This is supposed to facilitate the improvement of the social acceptability of working life and the enhancement of the subjective quality of life. In this social-reform context, the time dimension attains overriding importance. It is discovered that time is a 'central resource' and a 'valuable commodity', and from this discovery 'a policy of time sovereignty is derived' (Teriet 1978, 1984: 41).

The objective of the 'new working time policy' is the creation of arrangements for individual options, whereas 'traditional working time policy' is oriented towards general, universal standards which are equally binding on everyone. The origin of this difference lies in the fact that during the debate conducted in the Federal Republic of Germany on the subject of mass unemployment, attention was also focused on working time as an instrument for reducing unemployment and redistributing work. On the one hand, the reassessment of standard working time is under discussion, initiated by the trade union demand for a 35-hour week, and on the other, the 'new working time policy' is putting the case for individual, flexible working time arrangements involving a significant amount of dispositional scope for employees. When, as a counter-strategy to the trade union demand for the across-the-board introduction of a 35-hour week, the employers began talking in terms of a flexibilization of working time, they adopted the emancipatory aspirations of the committed advocates of flexibilization, though they quickly misused and devalued such aspirations (Wiesenthal 1985). The objective of individual dispositional scope for the flexible organization of working time was transformed into company strategies for the flexible arrangement of employment policy and manpower management.

The 'new working time policy' promises individual employees a greater degree of 'time sovereignty', in other words, the augmentation of their individual dispositional scope for the qualitative and quantitative organization of time utilization both in various areas of life and in their lives as a whole (Olk et al. 1979: 24). The objectives of such a 'policy of temporal sovereignty', whether based on grounds of social, humanization, educational, family or health policy, are first and foremost reducing unemployment, incorporating further groups of people into working life, exercising positive effects upon production output, attaining a superior level of compatibility between family and job, reducing the strain on the health of employees, demystifying attendance discipline and rectifying the temporal demands placed upon the infrastructures.[4]

In relation to collectively agreed arrangements, such flexible forms of working time are at odds with previous trade union policy.[5] For a long time, the trade unions were opposed to such flexibilization models. It is only during the course of their collective negotiations on the subject of shorter working time in recent years that they have been compelled to make some compromises which also make provision for so-called flexibilization arrangements. Only within a narrowly defined and collectively agreed framework do these compromises permit agreements on the 'flexibilization' of working time, within the scope of which only company-specific variations are possible. The general rejection on the part of the trade unions of individual working time arrangements is primarily based on the fear that such individual arrangements would weaken their collective bargaining position. The central objection of the trade unions to such flexibilization arrangements is that individualized forms of working time undermine trade union policy on the organization of working time, and particularly the strategy of solidarity which is pursued for the implementation of the 35-hour week. However, this objection cannot be fully understood unless it is considered in connection with the origin and function of the standard working day (Deutschmann 1985: 32–45). After all, the history of the labour struggle is the history of the simultaneous standardization and reduction of the working day. It was standardization, the establishment of the standard working day, alone which brought about the gradual reduction of working time to 40 hours and less per week (Hegner and Landenberger 1988; Kevelaer and Hinrichs 1985; Schneider 1984). It is not possible to understand the reasons behind the negative attitude adopted by the trade unions towards forms of working time which pose a threat to the institution of the standard working day unless it is clear that the origin of the standard working day constitutes an enforced compromise whose price was the dissociation of 'work from living'. Given the fact that the consequences of the erosion of the standard working day would issue in greater access on the part of employers to the time of their employees,[6] and in the loss of trade union bargaining power, from the standpoint of the trade unions, such consequences carry considerable implications (Hinrichs and Wiesenthal 1984; Vobruba 1982; Wiesenthal 1985: 15).

The central objection to this trade union position is that, to a large extent, the negative consequences of flexible working time are primarily attributable to trade union non-activity. The trade unions allow employers regulation-free scope for unilateral utilization. They fail to exploit the increase in productivity which the introduction of flexible working time brings in its train by means of, for example, the introduction of collectively agreed surcharges for certain forms of working time. It would undoubtedly be possible to prevent the de-solidarization of the workforce by means of a collective bargaining policy which lent support to differentiated working time arrangements. Trade union policy affords scant consideration to the fact that the individual reduction of working time need not necessarily result from an involuntary decision on the part of employees. The trade unions appear to display little interest in supporting the freedom of choice of individual employees with regard to the determination of their working time, or in restricting the dispositional freedom of company deployment scheduling to the benefit of individual working time preferences. The inactivity of the trade unions with regard to flexible working time arrangements leads to the accumulation of negative consequences and risks for individual employees.

In contrast to the trade unions, the employers' associations have incorporated flexible working hours into their collective bargaining policy, albeit primarily as a strategy with which to counter trade union demands, and to divorce factory/office hours from working hours. In the absence of any stance in opposition to that of the employers on the issue of the managerial organization of individual working time at the level of collectively agreed arrangements, flexible working time falls under the overwhelming organizational influence of the employers. *Vis-à-vis* individual employees, employers clearly have the upper hand.

However, below the level of working time flexibilization arrangements on offer from employers, there is a plurality of ways in which individuals are able to secure flexible working time which hitherto have attracted scant attention, let alone any legal or contractual structural assistance. They are restricted to direct negotiations between employees and their immediate superiors. This implies the individualization of working time agreements and the personalization of the risks which such agreements entail.

In explicitly investigating cases of working time flexibilization arrangements secured on a non-contractual, individual basis, we encounter two problems. First, a glance at existing working time arrangements reveals that such cases are excluded from interest group policy. Secondly, the research situation demonstrates that hitherto the individual securement of flexible working time has attracted scant academic interest. Thus our study affords a hearing to a group of people whom the discussion concerning working time policy has badly neglected.[7]

Overall, previous empirical studies into the introduction of shorter and flexible working hours have been restricted to particular aspects of the complex of problems involved. Their main areas of research are concentrated *firstly* upon the effects of the management of working time on the job and personal contentment of employees. The problems and advantages which flexible working time entails for employees are identified. In addition, examination is afforded to the question of the extent to which new forms of working time can facilitate the creation of more humane and family-friendly working and private lives.[8]

Secondly, in addition to this set of questions based on humanistic considerations, the operational significance of changes to 'classic' working time in favour of a 'greater degree of flexibilization' is examined. Many of these studies investigate the avenues which flexible working time opens up for work scheduling and personnel policy. The fundamental question concerns increases and decreases in company efficiency, and the possibilities and limitations of enhancing efficiency by means of working time management.[9]

A *third* group of studies transcends the narrow confines of issues concerning company and employee interests, and thematizes the reduction and flexibilization of working time from the standpoint of labour market policy. These studies address the question of the extent to which new forms of working time can, if not solve, then at least alleviate, the structural problem of the labour market.[10]

Lastly, a *fourth* group of studies addresses the issue of the special regulatory problems associated with the management of flexible working time within the framework of company and inter-company working time policy.[11]

In contrast to these studies, our specific perspective is that of the constitution of time within the framework of lifestyle as a whole. By means of the temporal characteristics of lifestyle, our objective is to investigate associations with structural changes in society – which also include changes in social time structures – beyond the confines of the working time issue. This problem orientation is based on the hypothesis that the current working time question is indicative of a qualitatively new stage in the working time struggle. A new generation of employees is appearing on the scene whose working time demands, temporal aspirations and relationship with time cannot be grasped unless the problems associated with the constitution of time form the fundamental point of departure for the study.

E. P. Thompson (1991: 390) provides a pointed summary of the historical changes which the working time struggle has hitherto undergone:

The first generation of factory workers were taught by their masters the importance of time; the second generation formed their short-time committees in the ten-hour movement; the third generation struck for overtime or time-and-a-half. They had accepted the categories of their employers and learned to fight back within them. They had learned their lesson, that time is money, only too well.

On the horizon of the fully developed industrial society, there now appears a new type of worker who gives a remarkable new twist to the logic of the working time dispute. The specific arrangement to which employees had been more or less forced to become accustomed – namely, that freedom in time can only be achieved through paid work, that only work can generate freedom since work facilitates the earning of money which provides dispositional scope and creates opportunities for postponing now decisions which affect the future – widespread though it may be, is no longer accepted without question. The new form of working time dispute has a tendency to undermine the temporal structure of the organization of work, and thus to effect the simultaneous redefinition of the categories of work, money and time, and to orient them firmly towards personal aspirations of a 'good life'.

This fourth generation of workers has completely overcome the impotence and lack of awareness of the first generation; their representatives very consciously and deliberately seize the initiative and determine their personal working time in accordance with their own interests. They distinguish themselves from the second generation by not seeking fixed forms of working time standardization, and endeavouring to secure individual, flexible working time schemes. And finally, they undermine the premise underlying the actions of the third generation of increasing their earnings through overtime, and take the decision to accept a drop in income in favour of more free time and the dispositional scope offered by flexible working time.

We intend to show that this new generation spawns specific lifestyles which lay claim to and interpret both self-determined and flexible working time, and the temporal organization of the conduct of life. We focus our interest on the lifestyle of this fourth generation in order to establish where and how the dominant time structures of the working environment are forfeiting their definitional authority, and if this authority is undergoing moderation, subversion and radical change, or simply being deployed as a tool in the service of lifestyle.

There is a tendency to apply the vogue word 'flexibilization' to all variations of working time. 'Flexibilization' functions both as a battle cry and as the topical problem-solving formula for finding a way out of the labour market crisis. Originally, the flexibilization of working time referred to flexitime, break regulations and part-time work. However, during the course of the discussion surrounding the reorganization of working time, the term soon assumed amorphous dimensions (Wiesenthal 1985). Its meaning was extended and subjected to ideological loading. Power political disputes therefore hinge on the question of who is able to attach which permanent implications to this term. The result is the emergence of different and sometimes contradictory definitions and loaded meanings: what is presented to one party as the dream of alternatives for realization causes the other party nightmares. For employers, the term flexibilization within the context of a vision of entrepreneurial concepts and strategies carries positive connotations. For the organized representatives of workers' interests, the flexibilization of working time constitutes a capitalist threat to the protective rights of workers which have been laboriously acquired during the course of the historical process (Rossmann 1987: 7f).

What is to be understood by the term flexible working time is closely related to the particular socio-historical context of its meaning. In the discussion surrounding working time, the term assumes vague dimensions owing to the fact that the various associations connected with flexibilization are not clearly addressed and identified. For example, for the trade unions, flexible working time encompasses any variation of working time, as a result of which the company-specific implementation of the 38.5-hour week is also registered as a manifestation of flexibilization. For employers, the term flexible working time carries connotations of a high degree of variability and the abolition of previous working time arrangements, and is thus placed within the context of the flexibilization and 'deregulation' of employment (see Adamy 1988).

Ultimately, the term flexible working time is used to describe any changes to working time, no matter how insignificant the actual changes or the ensuing degree of flexibility are. Flexible working time becomes a collective term for any and every alternative to rigid working time arrangements.[12] It is also frequently used as a synonym for 'variable', 'dynamic' and 'individualized' working time.

Working time is defined as flexibilized if it varies in both its chronological and its chronometric dimensions (thus, in both duration and location), is considerably shorter than standard working time and, in addition, if employees have a relatively wide range of possible options for determining the location and the duration of their working time. Our study is based on this definition. It facilitates the analysis of how the way in which people organize their lives accommodates changed working time, and of how such working time generates changes in time structures.

The definition of 'flexibilization' hinges on one bench mark: our definition of flexible working time is predicated upon its deviation from institutionally regulated schemata of full, fixed, standardized working time. In a society in which the 40- or 38.5-hour week applies to those in paid employment, employees who for personal reasons reduce and flexibilize their hours of work do not conform to the schema of standard working time. They deviate from a standard schema which is regarded as something 'completely normal', and whose artificial, socio-historical character largely recedes into the background or fades from view altogether.

The influence of this standard schema is particularly noticeable in cases of non-compliance. People who work and are seen at home during working hours are inevitably asked whether they have the day off, are sick or no longer work. Modern parlance also documents how 'normal' the 40-hour week has become. It is described as 'full' working time, whereas working time arrangements providing for fewer hours are usually classed as 'part-time work'. The designation 'part-time work' takes the standard schema as its point of reference: it only constitutes a proportion of 'full' working time. Part-time employees work a proportion of the norm. The 40-hour week is the norm to which other working time arrangements are compared. 'Overtime' is working time 'over and above' the norm; it is performed in addition to the level which can be justifiably expected. Those on 'short-time working' work fewer hours than those on standard working time. Negative semantic comparisons are made between all these working time regulations and standard working time. It would be equally possible to speak in terms of a 20-hour employment contract, or a 30-hour job instead of in terms of part-time or half-time work.

Given that working full time is accepted as a fact of life, individual employees are barely aware of the 'artificiality' of the social institution of standard working time, which is also known as normal or regular working time. In general, standard working time is not subject to negotiation between individual employees and their employers. At the level of individual contracts of employment, its negotiatory character remains concealed from view, with the result that employees regard full-time employment as an entirely natural phenomenon requiring no further justification.

The standard working time negotiated between employers and employees at the collective level is presented to employees as a finished package. In consequence of the fact that the length of working time continually comes up for discussion and modification in the form of a 48-, 40-, 38.5- and 35-hour week, the collectively negotiated character of standard working time is clearly obvious, but what is at issue is always 'full' working time. Although the length of working time prescribed by the norm might change over the course of the years, this does not mean that the norm of working full-time follows suit.[13]

Thus two important components of the standard schema have now been mentioned: firstly, the natural character of the length of working time, and secondly, the factitiousness of a standard, the norm of full working time. Both are prerequisites for obtaining a complete grasp of the standard schema, though on their own they are insufficient. It is at this juncture that the majority of analyses of working time arrangements come to a halt, in that, for example, they focus exclusively upon the question of the length of standard working time, or, in the face of the plurality of exceptional arrangements, upon the length of time it has formally been in existence.

In contrast, we thematize shorter and flexibilized working time against the backdrop of the standard schema in an altogether more radical fashion. When we speak in terms of the current standard schema, this implies more than the existence of the working time standard. To treat them as synonymous would mean restricting ourselves to purely quantitative details, or to formal working time arrangements. In contrast, the standard schema transcends the merely quantitative aspects of working time, targeting fundamental meaning and interpretive schemata in respect of work, time, and the conduct of life which characterize and govern the behaviour of employees far beyond the sphere of work. Thus our study continually bears in mind the fact that large-scale displacements in meaning and interpretive schemata are the issue at stake, and not merely a change in the form which time arrangements take.

A glance at these meaning complexes underlying the standard schema facilitates the identification of the distinctive feature of shorter and flexibilized working time arrangements in relation to 'classic' forms of changes in working time. Short-time working, part-time work, overtime, half-time work and, obviously, flexitime, are all merely modulations of standard working time. They represent forms of working time which do not relinquish their explicit associations with the standard working day. It is not until they are regarded in relation to the length of standard working time that it becomes possible to identify their purpose. As exceptional arrangements, they underpin standard working time.

In contrast, the flexible working time upon which our study focuses is fundamentally different from the standard schema. It lies *outside* the standard schema. 'Do we really have to work 40 hours a week? It's just not normal' is a question which explicitly thematizes the previously unquestioned standard schema. The call on the part of employees for the right to determine their own working time in line with their individual interests is interpreted more as an attack upon the validity of the standard schema itself than as exceptional arrangements for a specific group of employees. Given that the barriers and difficulties which flexible forms of working time encounter constitute a manifestation of the standard schema in which it is revealed in its 'true' colours, analysing the manner in which the standard schema is questioned within the framework of the cultural paradigm of the employment society provides an insight into the operational method of the standard schema itself.

1.5 The research group of 'time pioneers'

The criteria for selecting the research group at the centre of this study were predetermined by the research objective of identifying new forms of time utilization on the part of employees via the specific problems associated with flexible working time. We endeavoured to locate people whose working arrangements deviate from standard working time in the following specific ways:

- Both the chronological and the chronometric dimensions of the forms of working time adopted by our interviewees deviate from those of standard working time.

This stipulation excludes other variations of working time such as flexitime and shift work. Although both these forms of working time do deviate from standard working time, they merely constitute modulations of location (chronological dimension), not of duration (chronometric dimension). In the case of shift work, 'normal' working hours are simply displaced, and similarly, with flexitime, employees are merely able to displace their working time within certain prescribed limits.

- The employees in our research group have relatively broad selective scope with regard to the determination of their working time.

In the absence of selective scope with regard to the duration and location of their working time, employees are unable to improve the effectiveness with which they champion their personal interests, and develop modified time utilization techniques via the introduction of their working time preferences. In contrast, in the case of capacity-oriented variable working time (CAPOVAT) and short-time working, deviation from 'normal' working time is determined exclusively by the interests of the employer. In view of the fact that these variations allow employees no selective scope for determining their working time, they are excluded from the purview of this study. Both sets of working time regulations are characterized by an extreme form of the subordination of employees to the time hegemony of the employer. Working time is dictated by the volume of orders accruing. The CAPOVAT regulation in particular is a classic case of 'on-tap' manpower utilization, since both chronological dimension and chronometric flexibilization are determined by the employer.

- The employees falling within the compass of this study work between 20 and 32 hours per week.

Fixing the upper limit at 32 hours per week is intended to ensure that shorter hours bring lengthy blocks of free time in their train. The objective of the lower limit of a minimum of 20 hours per week is the exclusion from the study of employees who are not liable for social insurance payments.

- In our study, shorter working time is related to the reference period of weekly working time.

This permits a large degree of scope for the development of new, every-day time utilization techniques on the part of employees. Reductions in annual working time in the form of sabbaticals or retirement regulations are excluded.

- Our interviewees have been on modified working time for a minimum of six months, and flexibilization is in force for an indefinite period of time.

This focuses attention on life circumstances in which to some extent, in the form of a 'new normality', flexible working time has already become part and parcel of everyday life. Those for whom flexible working time is nothing more than a short-term arrangement for a clearly limited period of time, such as jobbers, are excluded. On the other hand, the assumption is not made that flexible working time is a lifelong alternative to full-time working; it is simply a stipulation that, in the eyes of the employee in question, flexible working time should not be regarded as a transitional or makeshift arrangement.

- Our interviewees are dependent employees in the formal employment sector.

Freelancers, the self-employed and employees working in the informal sector are excluded on the grounds that the standard working day as a standardized working time arrangement does not apply to them in the same way as it does to employees in the formal sector. Freelancers and the self-employed have always been able to deviate downward, or more frequently upward, from the norm, since they have always been both able and compelled to assume the responsibility for planning and organizing their work, and thus their working time, to a much greater degree than those in dependent employment.

- Our interviewees are pursuing their primary source of employment.

Anyone earning supplementary income from part-time work which they pursue alongside their primary source of employment, while undergoing a period of training, or while drawing a pension, is excluded.

- Our interviewees are sole breadwinners.

Typical secondary wage earners, in other words, spouses or family members who earn a supplementary wage, are excluded from this study on the grounds that they are not reliant upon their own income as their sole source of maintenance. On the one hand, we were anxious to avoid copying the typical structures of the part-time labour market, and on the other, there is less probability in the case of such secondary wage earners that flexible working time will be accompanied by changes in time awareness, though the possibility cannot be ruled out altogether.

We would particularly stress that in establishing these criteria it is not our intention to highlight the typical features of the trade union line of argument which is oriented towards special groups. The fact that the vast majority of part-time employees belong to 'special groups' (single mothers, older employees) is utilized by the trade unions as a strategic argument against the reduction and flexibilization of working time at the individual level. In collective negotiations, flexibilization and part-time work are treated as a special problem affecting specific groups who are irrelevant to the regular workforce. This means that the trade unions turn a blind eye to both notifications of requirements on the part of employees and to the plurality of cases of working time flexibilization which have been secured throughout the whole range of occupational and age groups. In focusing our study upon the 'regular' workforce, we highlight the fact that in contrast to the position adopted by the trade unions, we do not regard the flexibilization and individualization of working time as an issue affecting special groups.

However, this criterion also makes clear that the criteria listed above only facilitate initial research group selection, and are inadequate for the purpose of defining 'time pioneers'. Although the issue at stake is the determination of the temporality of lifestyle via working time, we were aware from the outset that the flexibilization of working time alone remains an inadequate indicator of fundamental changes in the temporality of lifestyle. Those schemata of working time which are accessible purely from the formal standpoint are of interest only insofar as they have been incorporated into lifestyle arrangements in which time is endowed with a special significance. The question concerning the organization of working time is linked to the question concerning the manner in which, in the lifestyle of the time pioneers, time is identified as a central dimension of the construction of life.

The deployment of additional, qualitative criteria is necessary in order to distinguish the inner circle of those 'time pioneers' in whom we are interested from those 'practitioners of the flexibilization of working time' who were originally located by means of external criteria. In this context, the following characteristics become evident which are explained during the course of the evaluative process. In the first place, time pioneers are characterized by a *marked sensitivity towards time* as a meaningful dimension of relevance to their everyday lives; in the second place, by *aspirations to the greatest possible degree of disposition over time and autonomous, active time allocation*; and in the third place, by a *reflexive time consciousness*. These characteristics distinguish time pioneers from a second group of practitioners of the flexibilization of working time, whom we refer to as 'time conventionalists'.

Although both time pioneers and time conventionalists came out in favour of flexible working time, nevertheless, in the interpretive schema of lifestyle, time conventionalists only utilize time as a means. They make plans in advance for the reallocation of the time which becomes free in the wake of the flexibilization of working time: paid work is superseded by an increased amount of club activities, housework and child-rearing. For the time conventionalists, time remains inextricably linked to specific objectivations (housework, child-rearing, hobbies) and their relevant meaning structures. The structural possibilities generated by their working time arrangements do not inevitably result in the development of changes in their time management techniques. No restructuring of temporal interpretive schemata occurs in the case of the time conventionalists. In contrast, the time pioneers subjectively exploit the objective opportunity: time becomes endowed with a quality in its own right which transcends its purely functional character. It becomes de-objectified and exposed, and recognized and developed as a subjective structural principle of life.

Any scrutiny of our research group for initial characterization features reveals at once that they are not pre-structured along the lines of the classic so-called 'hard' characteristics of industrial or stratification sociology such as age, sex, income level, education, occupation or position, etc.

Our selection criteria prevented the reproduction of the typical structure of the part-time labour market (Hofbauer 1981; Kurz-Scherf 1985; Büchtemann and Schupp 1986).[14] There is no major difference in the number of male (16) and female (20) interviewees. In addition, the individual age groups are fairly evenly represented. The age span ranges from 25 to 59, with the 50 to 59 age group being under-represented. In the case of those between 35 and 49 years of age, women are more heavily represented. The relatively high proportion of divorced interviewees (5) and those living apart from their spouses (9) in comparison to married interviewees (10) is indicative of biographical discontinuities and personal experiences of crises. This in itself elucidates the fact that for the interviewees the flexibilization of their working time is an expression both of biographical frictions and of a changed approach towards their life-course.

A distinctive feature of the study is the plurality of individual occupations which it comprises, the service sector being most heavily represented. The specific occupations of the interviewees are as follows:

- engineering and industrial sectors
    precision engineer, telecommunications engineer, quality con-
    troller, systems analyst, carpenter, warehouseman;
- commercial sector
    buyer, retailer, sales assistant, bank clerk, tax consultant, clerk;
- administrative sector
    administrative clerk, ministerial official, personnel manager,
    library assistant, funeral monument consultant;
- social services sector
    family/old peoples' nurse, psychologist, speech therapist, occu-
    pational therapist, nurse, social worker, social education worker;
- education sector
    teacher, academic.

In view of the fact that only some three-quarters of the interviewees
provided precise details of their net income, such details do not portray
an exact picture of the range of income level involved. According to
those net income details that were volunteered, with a few exceptions,
the net income which the interviewees earn from their reduced hours
of employment varies between around DM 1,000 and DM 3,000 per
month [Trans: 1985/6 figures]. There were only vague indications of
income levels markedly undershooting or overshooting these lower
and upper limits, with the result that the range of net income levels
of the interviewees is greater than it actually appears. In this context,
it becomes clear that a high income level is not necessarily a precondition for the flexibilization of working time. The 'luxury' of being
able to work shorter hours is not something that only the better-paid
can afford, as is so frequently assumed. The interviews which were
conducted reveal that the interviewees have no additional sources of
income from DIY or illicit work.

A glance at the household types of the interviewees reveals that far
from being restricted to single-person households, our study encompasses a wide variety of household types. Only a small proportion of
the interviewees (7) come from single-person households, the overwhelming majority coming from multi-person households, and some
also from the flat-sharing community. Over a third of the interviewees
have children under the age of majority in their care. Thus it is by
no means the case that our study concentrates solely upon people
who from the social and economic standpoint enjoy relative independence and who (living in single-person households) permit themselves
the luxury of shorter and flexible working time.

The working time of our time pioneers varies to a considerable extent. Thus, for example, there are reductions equalling 72.5, 62.5, 60 and 56.25 per cent of full-time working. Such reductions in working time go far beyond the compass of the mere halving of standard working time in the form of half-day working. In addition, our interviewees enjoy different degrees of experience of reduced and flexible forms of working time. The majority of them have been practising flexible working time for more than a year; indeed, a third of them have been on flexible working time for more than five years. Over the course of time, at least ten of the interviewees have changed the degree of working time reduction: in five cases, the length of working time was increased again (though not to full-time working), and in the remaining five cases, it was further decreased.

The flexible manipulation by the interviewees of the location of their working hours reveals a further distinctive feature of the research group. The majority of the interviewees prefer consecutive blocks of free time to an even reduction in their working day. Ultimately, the siting of the working time of the individual time pioneer should be regarded as the outcome of the process of negotiations between the individual and the employer in which a plurality of factors such as short-term, informal arrangements with colleagues, company-specific circumstances and deputization responsibilities, etc. are all contributory factors.

In the main, flexible working time arrangements are not the preserve of any specific age groups, occupational groups, household types or income groups. From this, we can deduce that 'time' exercises an autonomous discriminatory effect upon the study, rather than simply representing a dependent variable of combinations of social characteristics.

As is clear from the theoretical deliberations above, this study is based upon an approach whose conception requires the application of qualitative methods of data acquisition and evaluation. On the other hand, it would be inappropriate to deduce from these theoretical deliberations that the methodological apparatus to be employed should consist of standardized methods: such methods would produce excessively pre-structured results and hinder the discovery of new schemata. Thus, for the purpose of *data acquisition*, we employ the open interview method or, to be more precise, the method of the thematically structured interview incorporating explicitly narrative phases. Significant parts of the interview are based on the 'narrative interview',[15] though without adopting its orthodox application. In view of the fact that this type of interview bears a particularly strong resemblance to the generic communicative form of the discussion with which we are all familiar in everyday life (see Luckmann 1984), we refer to this type of interview as an 'interview-discussion'. Given the fact that, in this respect, the interviewees possess well-developed communicative competence, this is the surest method of enabling them to provide delineations which are as broad-based and detailed as possible, contain their own points of emphasis, and comprise a large amount of information.

For the purpose of the *evaluation* of the data garnered from the inter-view-discussions, we employed qualitative and interpretive methods. The interview texts are subject to methodical evaluation in two stages:

1 The first stage consists of the formal, analytical examination and sequentialization of the text which was produced during the course of the discussion (such as identifying context-switching elements, discussion units and generic forms, ascertaining the degree of indexicalization, the manner of speaking and the narrative structure, determining narrative transfers and structurally arranged oral forms of representation, and reconstructing the discussion topic).

2 The second stage comprises the hermeneutical interpretation of the meaning structures generated by the interview discussion form of communication whose objective is the reconstruction of the subjective priority structures and interpretive schemata, and the socio-cultural interpretive framework. The social scientific hermeneutics which is employed is predicated upon the deliberate deployment of the every-day hermeneutics of interacting members of society (see Soeffner 1986, 1989a, 1989b).

From the standpoint of content, the focal points of our evaluation are as follows: The first phase of the study concentrates upon the flexibilization of working time, in which context the motivations behind flexibilization, the difficulties involved in the implementation of flexible working time and the problems encountered at the work-place with flexible forms of working time are structured, brought into focus and reappraised.

During the second phase of the study, using the lifestyle of time pioneers, the spotlight is particularly focused upon the cultural changes accompanying the process of structural social change and the flexibilization of working time. Embedded in the network of struc-tural conditions, problem areas and points of departure, their sub-jective appraisal, their specific incorporation into socio-cultural meaning frameworks, and their tradition of special forms of know-ledge and approach, socio-cultural meaning structures retain their inherent meaning in the face of structural social conditions. In order to locate new orientational schemata and normality assumptions which are task-related in the truest sense of the word, and thus inter-related cultural interpretive schemata, it is necessary to adopt an investigative perspective which is based upon cultural theory. Such a perspective takes as its point of departure the socio-cultural level of the meaning structure of social reality. For the purpose of analysing this meaning structure, we employ the theory of interpretive schemata developed in the 'phenomenology of the lifeworld' (Schütz and Luckmann 1975/84). Given that this approach provides an already categorized constitutional analysis of the operations of conscious-ness, and that it is firmly based upon an extensive theoretical concept of the 'Structures of the Lifeworld',[16] this is an effective approach for analysing the consciousness and meaning structures of the time pioneers.

2 Flexible Working Time — New Perspectives and Traditional Forms of Opposition

We commence the empirical part of our study by posing the question as to which new perspectives the time pioneers pursue by flexibilizing their working time. In this context, we are particularly interested in determining the general significance which flexibilization has for the time pioneers, their underlying motives, the problems and difficulties with which they are confronted, and the forms of opposition which they encounter at the workplace during the course of their individual efforts to secure their objective.

2.1 The relevance of flexible working time to the time pioneers

In this section we determine the importance of the flexibilization of working time to the time pioneers, how they view themselves in the face of the changes which have occurred, how they assess themselves, and how they classify themselves in opposition to other employees. This process reveals the existence of fundamental differences in self-thematizations. Our differentiation between time pioneers and time conventionalists elucidates these differences and reveals that the distinction originates with the interviewees themselves.

From the interviews, it is possible to distinguish two different types of self-image of those on flexibilized working time. Right from the outset, the responses of the interviewees to our initial question demonstrate the existence of clear differences in attitude towards and assessment of their new working time arrangements. Whereas the time pioneers are more inclined to emphasize the exceptional and extraordinary character of the new arrangements, the time conventionalists stress the fact that they do not consider that shorter hours and the accompanying changes constitute anything out of the ordinary. Time and again, the time pioneers stress the singularity of their flexibilization, displaying a 'tincture of arrogance'. The fact that they are so markedly different from their full-time colleagues is a situation which they regard as a privilege. Not infrequently, this 'special situation' is expressed in the form of a platitudinously exaggerated contrast: *'When I go home at one o'clock, my colleagues know I'll be going swimming if the weather's good. When they knock off, I'll already've had a good rest and got a bit of a suntan.'*

Time conventionalists do not regard flexibilization as anything unusual. Time pioneers, on the other hand, emphasize the dramatic impact that flexibilization has had on their lives. In reply to the question as to how shorter hours were secured, in addition to stressing the fact that the achievement was the fruit of their own efforts, the time pioneers also repeatedly acknowledge 'fortuitous circumstances' as a contributory factor. In retrospect, they can hardly believe that they have successfully made the break with standard working time. One time pioneer made the following observation on securing his new working hours: *'It was due more to good luck than ability.'* The emphasis on good fortune and the use of the gambling metaphor does not imply that the achievement should be regarded as fortuitous, nor that their own efforts in securing the new working time arrangements should be underestimated. Time pioneers describe themselves as 'fortunate' in the sense that, firstly, they have succeeded in securing working hours with which they are thoroughly satisfied, and that, secondly, their own efforts and the expenditure of a great deal of energy notwithstanding, they had scarcely believed that such success was within their reach.

It is important to the time pioneers that they should be distinguished from both their full-time and their part-time colleagues. Many of the interviewees are at pains to stress that theirs is not a 'classic' instance of shorter hours, but something 'completely different'. In comparison with 'classic' part-time employment, which they subsume under the schema of standard working time, the time pioneers stress the unusual character of their working time arrangements: '*The fact of the matter is that part-time employment is something for mothers who've got no other option open to them because they've got a kid to look after. They simply can't work full-time.*'

On the whole, the cachet of shorter working hours undergoes considerable enhancement at the hands of the time pioneers. Shorter hours rather than full-time working attain privileged status, regardless of the difficulties and problems which they bring in their train. To the time pioneers, securing shorter working hours places them in an 'exposed position', the status of which derives initially from the very fact that the practice of working shorter hours is adopted by only a small number of employees. The important factor in this respect is the 'few in number' argument. It is precisely the process of deviating from the norm, of negating the customary, that generates an atmosphere in which individualization and idiosyncrasy can flourish. It is not full-time work that is acclaimed as a status symbol, but flexibilization. The question as to whether everyone should be afforded the opportunity of determining their working time on an individual basis is not explicitly thematized by the interviewees. The extent to which flexible working time as a new standard schema might be able to displace the traditional social organization of working time is an issue which at best is addressed *en passant*, more indirectly than directly, in the rejection of full-time work as generally too stressful, too exacting and on the whole, from the standpoint of lifestyle, too 'costly'.

The *time conventionalists* are completely at odds with these views. Their assessment of the change in their working time is wholly different. In contrast to the time pioneers' wellnigh euphoric assessment of their new working time arrangements, the characteristic feature of the time conventionalists is a self-assessment which underlines the fact that in their opinion, their changed working time does not constitute anything out of the ordinary or unusual. Shorter hours do not at all appear extraordinary. In the interviews which we conducted with the time conventionalists, this viewpoint even finds expression in incomprehension and bewilderment in the face of our investigative interest in shorter working time. As far as the time conventionalists are concerned, the term shorter hours has connotations which are identical to those of part-time employment, in other words, to those of conventional reductions in working time, something which is practised by a fairly large group of employees and which is prevalent throughout the employment sector.

In contrast to the passionate narrative style and detailed delineation of the problem which characterize the time pioneers, the opinions expressed by the time conventionalists on the subject are brief and lacking in substance. In their opinion, there have been no significant changes, and therefore there is little to say. Following a brief explanation of what has occurred, they remark that that is all there is to it, and ask if there are any further questions, whereupon they consider the interview to be at an end. Little information is volunteered. They assume that what they do have to say is axiomatic, that as it forms part and parcel of the standard schema, it is already a known fact. The certain minimum requirements of narrative unfamiliarity are exhausted by these reports. Following these brief comments, time conventionalists are quick to steer the conversation towards other topics, topics which though no longer relevant to the subject of working time arrangements, offer them more narrative scope.

It becomes apparent from the self-thematizations of the interviewees that the distinction which we draw between time pioneers and time conventionalists on the issue of the flexibilization of working time marks a clear differentiation. However, the question as to why the time pioneers and the time conventionalists ultimately arrive at different assessments of their working time arrangements can only be explained by considering the motivational and implementational histories of flexibilization.

2.2 The motives behind flexibilization

The question at the heart of our study is how complexes of time-related meaning factors change under the conditions of flexible and shorter working hours. In order to answer this question, it is important to establish the motivational structure which preceded the actual securement of flexibilized hours, in other words, to take as the point of departure the genesis of the desire for flexibilization. In response to our exhortation: 'Now, tell us how it all began,' every one of the interviewees related their entire motivational history as if that were the obvious approach to adopt.

Our analysis of the motives behind the desire to work flexible hours established the existence of two types of motivational species:

time conventionalists and time pioneers. Time conventionalists describe their motive for seeking flexibilization in the most literal sense, 'as if it were as plain as the nose on your face'. The motive is described in such brief phrases that it is almost as if it were self-explanatory. Dispensing with prolix explanations and collateral reasons, they adduce a single factor which stands alone as a monolith. The motivational 'history' is condensed into a central statement, such as the following: *I've got a small daughter, and so I think it's necessary that I should work less.'*

The time conventionalists restrict motivational history to the simple identification of the motive, often dispensing with any form of introduction via the conjunction 'because'. In stating their motive, they refer to everyday plausibility structures. For this reason, even without any detailed comments or explanations, they first of all cite individual circumstances, such as childcare, child-rearing, marriage, illness-induced employment restrictions, separation and the decease of a relative.

However, putting flesh on the bones is not the only factor of interest to motivational specification. Whether people reduce the number of hours they work because they have a small child or because a relative has died is not the sole decisive factor. What time conventionalists adduce as a specific cause is not that which distinguishes them from time pioneers. More crucial still is the way they present the motives which they propound as their reason for securing changed working hours. Dispensing with any further justifications, time conventionalists justify their motives against the backdrop of the prevailing 'cultural paradigm of the employment society'. The reason why they are able to define their motives with such brevity and succinctness is that they adduce socially prefabricated and recognized plausibility structures.[1] The events which are cited as a motive develop normative force. Thus, the death of a wife obliges the husband to assume the responsibility for childcare. Furthermore, these motives are depicted as extraneous occurrences, as if they had left the victim no other option. The motto is: if you're ill, you don't have to work full-time; if small children need looking after, then one parent should work less. Upon the occurrence of the event, the order of the day is to react immediately by working shorter hours. The main reason why the motivational history of the time conventionalists assumes such a high degree of plausibility is that details of how the surplus time is utilized are supplied in conjunction with the motive: *'My mother died seven years ago and I had to stay at home. As my father and my brother still lived with me, I decided to work twenty hours a week and spend the rest of the time at home doing the housework.'*

The quantum of time by which working hours are reduced is determined and occupied in advance of the actual advent of shorter hours by other responsibilities outside the sphere of employment. It immediately reassumes the character of occupied, utilized and filled time. The social obligation, the normality requirement, to work full-time is fulfilled. There is an obstacle to working full-time. The individual is unable to work full-time, despite wishing to do so. To this extent, shorter hours do not at all constitute a refusal on the part of individuals to conform to the standard schema. For the most part, they regard their inability to work full-time as a shortcoming.

As a surrogate for working time which is not wholly devoted to the pursuit of employment, reference is made to other duties. Regarded by society as quasi-essential labour, the function of these duties is to compensate for the fact that the time conventionalists work only 'part-time', indeed, to bring their working hours roughly up to the level of full-time employment. Time conventionalists reduce their working hours by exactly the amount of time which these other duties require. Reduction commences at exactly that point in time at which their labour is required elsewhere. The location of their working time is tailored to suit the time requirements of these other duties: *'When the children were older and I didn't have to look after them every minute of the day, I started working longer hours again: 50 per cent turned into 60 per cent and then into 75 per cent, and now I'm up to 80 per cent of full-time hours.'* Formally shorter working hours notwithstanding, their interpretive schemata remain rooted in the standard schema. Albeit informally, they have remained full-time employees and as a matter of principle, they endeavour to re-enter full-time employment. It should be noted that the motivational histories of time conventionalists make remarkably little reference to pressure of time, lack of time or 'more or less time'. Time remains embedded in quotidian logic in unthematized form.

The motives adduced by the time pioneers for the flexibilization of their working time are altogether different. They cannot be represented in a single sentence. The what, when and wherefore of the reorganization of their working time admit of no blanket responses. The time pioneers are unable to adduce any one event traceable to a fixed point in time which would render the flexibilization of their working time sufficiently plausible. Therefore, their motivational histories are far more complex and require far more representational scope. In response to our first question, they seek a suitable starting point for the adumbration of a complex motivational history.

As a rule, time pioneers begin their account by introducing themselves. During the course of their exposé, they forge a motivational history from relevant elements, via biographical excerpts and ergobiographical details. In contrast to the time conventionalists, they provide a comprehensive account of their previous life situation, describing the course of its development and how it came to be regarded as in need of change. They do not predicate their response upon complexes of socially prefabricated motives and interpretive schemata, but rather on their own biography. They make it plain that for them, the change in their working time by no means ensued as a matter of course. On the contrary, it was preceded by a great deal of thought which set in motion a chain of developments, the interim result of which was the decision in favour of flexibilization. They stress the importance of no longer being in thrall to full-time employment. They are not temporarily incapacitated: they distance themselves completely from the schema of standard working hours: '*You see, I had a vested interest in working shorter hours, for good, I mean.*' This break with standard working time entails the restructuring of the interpretive schemata of the time pioneers, and in consequence they are required to adduce far more justifications than the time conventionalists.

To many time pioneers, the reduction in the number of hours they work seems to have been a biographical Rubicon. During the course of the interviews, there is frequent reference to the difference between then and now. Their situation prior to the reduction in their working hours is contrasted with their current situation, not only during the course of their account of their motivational history, but throughout the entire interview. Their situation prior to the reduction in their working hours becomes a vessel of motivational force, depicted from the standpoint of various biographical perspectives, and yet with repeated occurrence of the same basic tenor. They display a desire to dissociate themselves from a way of life which to a large extent is unduly influenced, indeed dominated, by working time: '*Over the years, I noticed that it had become impossible to separate free time from work. Somehow, it suddenly reached the stage where all there was was work, and I couldn't stand it any more.*'

Time pioneers do not dissociate themselves from work *per se*, but first and foremost from the temporal organization of employment which is the rule in society and which is currently enshrined in standard working time: '*I just reckon that working the normal eight hours somehow buggers up the whole day.*' Time pioneers object to the fact that work constitutes the primary structural component of lifetime, that the rhythm of their days and lives is dictated by a time regime which is determined by the conditions of the working environment. They are no longer prepared to subjugate themselves to a socially standardized time system which precisely dictates the rhythm of their days and lives, the transition between working time and free time, and the end of work and the commencement of recuperation. They wish to be free to choose for themselves when they submit to such time constraints.

Without exception, the time pioneers adduce their specific experience of standard working time as the motivational reason behind the reorganization of their working time. To the time pioneers, a situation in which, with the exception of tedious rest periods, the day consists of nothing but work, in which they live a 'weekend life' or from one holiday to the next, is burdensome, monotonous and unsatisfactory, indeed, all things considered, not worth living. However, this rejection does not extend to work *per se*, to their actual jobs. It is by no means the case that time pioneers opt for flexibilization in consequence of a failure to place any value on their work. It is rather the case that in their experience the temporal organization of work is too 'restrictive', too 'occupied'. The negative evaluation and assessment of their former situations are conducted in a manner similar to that deployed in the extension theory of the sociology of leisure time (see Hörning and Knicker 1981: 97ff), with the difference that time pioneers primarily identify the temporal dimension of the spillover effects of the working environment.

Thus time pioneers do not reduce the number of hours they work as a result of having to assume other non-occupational responsibilities. They certainly do not 'displace' or 'transfer' their labour to another sector which is regarded as being the equivalent of employment. Time pioneers reduce and flexibilize their working hours in order to escape from the unilateral occupation of time by, and the excessive formative influence of, paid work. Their experience of standard working time, of the full working week and its implications for the way in which they organize their lives, itself becomes the motive for changing their working hours. The motivational history of the time pioneers culminates in the call for some dispositional temporal latitude of their own: '*I wanted more time for myself. It's as simple as that. From a personal point of view, I benefit from working less.*'

It is symptomatic of time pioneers that, on the one hand, they relate their entire motivational history and provide comprehensive biographical details, while on the other remaining astonishingly abstract and vague in respect of those interests and activities that occupy the hours which they have gained as a result of flexibilization. They stubbornly persist in calling vaguely for more time: '*All the time, I was just waiting for my holidays so that, at long last, I could do something again which I wanted to do and which I was interested in doing.*' This constitutes an almost vehement refusal to provide any more detailed information. Only in exceptionally vague and imprecise formulations do they provide any insinuations of or indirect references to their surrogate activities. In explaining how they occupy the additional free time, they make no mention of any specific activities, employing instead indefinite pronouns and adverbs such as 'something' and 'somehow'. Furthermore, they speak in relatively vague terms of 'a lot of interests', 'other things' and 'other areas'. Although during the further course of the discussion they do provide more specific information on their activities, in almost all cases they initially employ these terms as fillers. They reject any straightforward and unimpugned reoccupation of the time that they have (re)gained. Frequently they develop their 'other interests' only with the passage of time, long after they have made the transition to shorter hours. The emergence of 'other interests' is not necessarily connected with the reduction in the number of hours they work.

The time pioneers reject a structural social principle in accordance with which time is treated exclusively as a scarce commodity, and in accordance with which it is essential that free time should be re-expended and reoccupied as if it were a 'vacuum'. Time pioneers insist upon disposing of their time as they see fit. They wish to secure for themselves some temporal latitude which will not simply fall prey to reallocation and filling-up. It could be said that their intention is to 'disencumber' time, in other words, first and foremost, to liberate time from the clutches of the utilization imperative which society leaves unquestioned (Rinderspacher 1985: 57ff). In conclusion, it can be stated that the analyses of motivational history reveal time to be a major factor in the way in which the time pioneers organize their lives, particularly in view of the fact that time is removed from the realm of unimpugned quotidian logic and developed into the central thematic crystallization point of their lifestyle.

2.3 Obstacles to the individual implementation of flexible working time

Central to the implementation process are the endeavours of employees to reorganize their working time in accordance with their own conceptions. On the one hand, the implementation phase comprises the initiation of the new working time arrangements, in other words, the introduction of flexible hours at the workplace, and on the other, the strategies with which, following the introduction of the working hours of their 'choice', the employees concerned endeavour to assert themselves in an ergo-organizational environment and defend their specific lifestyle.

Our study is mainly concerned with forms of working time whose implementation is beset by problems.[2] These problems are attributable to the fact that in contrast to other forms of working time, in the main, the employees concerned have no recourse to any precedents and thus, from the very outset, are forced to secure the implementation of flexibilization through their own efforts. It is thus usually the case that no advance support for the reorganization of working time is forthcoming from employers in the form of an agreement. At the same time, no operational or organizational measures are introduced in preparation for such reorganization. For these reasons, the process of securing the reorganization of their working time is fraught with problems for those concerned, particularly during the phase of its initiation.

Initiatives aimed at changing well-entrenched working time schemata are not launched in a 'vacuum'. They are introduced into a normative regulatory framework, and anyone from within this framework introducing initiatives in favour of deviation and change is faced with the additional burdens of justification and implementation. However, the introduction of such initiatives primarily affects interest and power structures inhering in this regulatory framework, resulting in the emergence of the question: *cui bono*? Is flexibilization in the common interest of both employer and employee, or does flexibilization involve a clash of interests *per se*? Which power structures militate against individual employees who attempt to change their working time on their own initiative? Is this process a manifestation of the conflict between paid work and capital, and/or is it at least possible to locate some common ground? What chance does working time flexibilization stand, and what price will be exacted from the employee for the privilege?

Anyone who addresses the issue of new forms of working time initially encounters an ideologically charged field of ambivalences, contradictions and conflicts. On the one side, the results of the survey of the level of contentment and the desire for change on the part of employees in respect of their working time are extremely contradictory.[3] On the other, employers have become the spokesmen and advocates of the idea of flexibilization, which they now propagate as a possible means of reconciling their own interests with those of their employees. They undertake hasty attempts to appropriate their employees' desire for flexibilization. The trade unions regard flexibilization as the harbinger of a crisis in standard working time,[4] and justifiably caution against such precipitate harmonization overtures, though conversely, for their part, they also largely disregard the calls for change and reorganization expressed by many employees.

Below the level of the ideologically coloured positions occupied by the advocates and opponents of flexible working time, our study discovered the existence of individually secured forms of working time which have been in force for some considerable length of time. This discovery makes clear that the problems associated with the question of self-interest are so complex that it is not possible to address them by means of simply comparing the advantages and disadvantages accruing to employers and employees.[5] In many instances, such comparisons issue in a detailed redelineation of the interests of employers, and a vague and imprecise 'appendix' of those of employees. This could generate the impression that, on the whole, employers would be prepared to introduce new working time schemes if only sufficient numbers of their employees were in favour of such an initiative.

Interest in the flexibilization of employment conditions should not be seen as a completely new phenomenon; on the contrary, it has deep roots in the capitalist single-enterprise sector. However, our study of flexibilization reveals that it is by no means the case that the concepts propagated by the practitioners of flexibilization meet with a generally high level of approval at the workplace. How is it that efforts on the part of the practitioners of flexibilization meet with such difficulties, especially considering that they might reasonably assume that their flexibilization proposals are in accordance with the interests of the employer, and should thus at least find it easy to gain a hearing? Generally speaking, one answer to this question lies in the fact that the overall interests of employers do not necessarily coincide with the interests of employers at the level of individual companies. Although a whole series of general economic developments, such as the increasing internationalization of competition, structurally persistent sales fluctuations, new forms of production and the expansion of the service sector (see Bosch 1986), would appear to favour vigorous support for flexibilization at this point, it still remains the case that the effects of flexibilization vary considerably from individual employer to individual employer.

Furthermore, for the most part, flexibilization is uncharted territory. Management has by no means abandoned the practice of 'thinking in terms of standard working time', and not until new concepts are embraced on a fairly large scale will employees stand a greater chance of realizing their demands for flexible working time.

In terms of flexibilization possibilities, the advantage lies with the employers (Wotschack 1987), since they have a greater number of flexibilization dimensions at their disposal. For them, flexible working time is only one option among many. Under certain circumstances, they can impose short-time working or overtime upon the workforce, and they can also resolve discrepancies between the supply of labour and their labour requirements by variations in intensity and quantitative adjustments (Hoff 1983: 111). Not until these traditional options, which are exploited within the framework of standard working time, are exhausted will employers focus their attention on maximizing flexibilization potential.

For employers, flexibilization is not a matter of introducing an alternative to standard working time *per se*. It is much more a question of increasing their scope for introducing such changes in working time as facilitate the maximum level of coordination between working time and factory / office hours. Thus, from the standpoint of the employers, any form of flexibilization which is not geared towards meeting their specific criteria becomes less attractive. Initially, interest on the part of employers in the wishes of individual members of the workforce which are 'incompatible with the interests of the company' is limited in the extreme.

All would-be practitioners of flexibilization are faced with this problem. It is thus little wonder that flexibilization generates conflict-laden disputes much more frequently than it does agreements. The flexibilization of working time remains an ambiguous phenomenon in respect of which, depending in each case on the power and interest factors involved, the issue of unfair advantage is on the agenda. This is reflected in the following different ways of implementing flexibilization which were identified during the course of this study:

1 An employee in a strong bargaining position is more likely to meet with success. Such 'accommodation' is rare, and only occurs in cases where employees have a long period of service to their credit,

during the course of which they have to some extent become indispensable to the company, and/or they possess professional qualifications which are in relatively short supply in the labour market. In such cases, employers accede to requests for flexibilization from employees whom they have reason to suspect will otherwise leave the company.

2 Individual requests for the flexibilization of working time are in the interests of the company. The desired form of working time becomes the precursor or harbinger of working time arrangements to which the employer has long aspired. In these instances, it is possible to speak in terms of a partial convergence of interests. Thus, changed forms of working time secured by individual employees on their own initiative become an integral part of new company working time schemes.

3 The new working time arrangements requested by an employee are only granted under certain conditions advantageous to the employer. In return, the employer expects certain conditions to be accepted. Such compromises represent the most prevalent form of the implementation of flexibilization in existence. Within the framework of such a compromise, the employer is able to insist that, for example, the employee produce as much work as before, accept worse conditions of employment or forego the right to bonus pay.

4 Employers accede to individual working time requests, though only as exceptional arrangements. In emphasizing that such arrangements are 'special cases', employers are clearly indicating that they will only conclude such agreements with certain employees. In these cases, employers are underscoring the fact that the granting of such arrangements is a special privilege, thus guarding themselves against uncontrollable proliferation. In addition, such selective arrangements allow employers the scope to play one employee off against another.

2.4 Problems with flexible working time at the workplace

After securing the flexibilization of their working time, the employees concerned find themselves confronting new problems. It is upon these that our attention now devolves. The analytical perspective is focused upon the workplace, that is to say, only the repercussions of the flexibilization of working time at the shop-floor level are the subject

of initial examination. The workplace-related problems and difficulties that the flexibilization of working time brings in its train for
the employees in question are discussed. The identification of these
problems and difficulties is primarily facilitated by four thematic
complexes: the intensification of work; cooperation difficulties and
the restriction of informal contacts at the workplace; problems with
immediate superiors and their particular styles of leadership; and
difficulties in providing symbolic proof of performance as a result of
the unconventional appearance of flexible working time. Other workplace problems, such as hostility from colleagues and the reduction
in the opportunities available to the time pioneers for articulating
their interests and philosophy of life, are examined in section 3.3.
These problems are the product of the clash between two opposing
meaning horizons: in our particular case, between the life style of
the time pioneers and the 'cultural paradigm of the employment
society'.

Intensification of work

A whole series of studies on part-time employment prove that part-
time employees are more productive than their full-time colleagues,
thus contributing to the enhancement of the efficiency and performance levels of their enterprise.[6] Shorter daily hours result in fewer
lapses in concentration, reduced amounts of wasted time and reduced
levels of fatigue at the workplace. Performance is characterized by
greater commitment, a greater willingness to work and an enhanced
level of motivation. Working methods become more stringent,
performance increases and even quality standards improve. For these
reasons, our interest now particularly focuses on discovering whether
or not the performance levels of the time pioneers are similarly
enhanced.

   In this context, it should be emphasized that in line with previous
studies one of the findings of our study is that shorter hours and the
flexibilization of working time have resulted in the intensification and
compression of work. There are several reasons for this. The
majority of our interviewees secured the flexibilization of their working time through their own efforts, and in the negotiations they occupied an inferior bargaining position *vis-à-vis* their employers. For this
reason, they were able to secure flexibilization only on condition
that significant benefits ensued for their employers. Such benefits

particularly take the form of the intensification of performance levels. Additionally, the practitioners of flexibilization are frequently exposed to pressure from their colleagues, at whose hands they often encounter envy or rejection. In many cases, the latter refuse to provide any support to those of their colleagues working shorter and flexibilized hours by reducing their work load. This becomes problematic in that, in the cases that we investigated, any working time lost owing to one employee working shorter hours is not compensated for by new appointments. Thus the whole of the affected department is forced to rationalize or intensify the work load and/or the work process, or – which would appear to be the simplest solution – to devolve the problem upon the originator, in other words, upon the person working flexible time. An important factor in this respect is that all those involved in the work process are judged by the institutionalized standard of full-time work. This standard arouses suspicions of indolence and inefficiency in the employer, motivates superiors to tighten monitoring procedures, generates aloofness if nothing else on the part of colleagues, and a guilty conscience on the part of those on flexible time.

We discovered that in the experience of those employees concerned, the actual extent of the intensification resulting from the flexibilization of their working time assumed surprisingly large proportions. The work load increased considerably, doubling in some cases. Performance levels were raised in respect of all jobs which from the standpoint of the actual tasks involved were susceptible to intensification, in other words, primarily task-oriented (as opposed to person-oriented) jobs.[7] Such jobs reveal the following intensification pattern:

- Of three employees who have reduced their working time to 20 hours a week, one emphasizes that he has to do just as much work in 20 hours as he did in 40, and another that he has to do almost as much. The tasks which their jobs involve have remained virtually unchanged. The third employee in this group states that in comparison with his full-time job, he has experienced a 10 per cent reduction in his work load.
- Of the two employees working shorter hours of approximately 25 hours a week, one has exactly the same and the other almost the same work load as they had on a 40-hour week.
- Nine employees with jobs susceptible to intensification work either a 30-hour or a 32-hour week. According to their own accounts, six

of them do just as much as they did on a 40-hour week, and the remaining three approximately as much.

The *result* of this intensification pattern is as follows: in the case of those employees on flexibilized time in task-oriented jobs, the flexibilization of their working time brings in its train an extremely high degree of intensification, so much so that in terms of the volume of work which their jobs involve, their work loads remain at the same or virtually the same level as those of full-time jobs, regardless of the actual extent of the reduction in their working time.

On the one hand, in an effort to induce their employers to sanction flexible working time, it is the employees themselves who introduce into the negotiations the concessionary acceptance of the intensification principle. On the other, the employers insist that those interested in flexible working time should accept intensification as part and parcel of the package, on pain of either remaining in full-time work or of non-employment, in other words, of dismissal. This is even the case where statutory regulations on shorter hours exist (such as in the public sector), or where shorter hours have been agreed with the employer (in the form of flexible working time schemes). In the latter instance, any reduction in the volume of work appropriate to the extent of the reduction in working time is frequently circumvented by means of the continuous expansion of the amount of work or the work load which the job concerned involves, or – at least at departmental level – by the fact that no additional appointments are made, with the result that additional work is expected of the person working flexible time and/or of their colleagues. Prior to any actual appointment of additional staff or the concentration of work by their colleagues, the pressure on the person working flexible time to resume normal working intensifies. However, should they be minded to retain the status quo of their shorter hours, they have no option other than to increase their performance level. How powerful an influence this mechanism can exercise is illustrated by the following two examples:

1 In the case of one employee, this compulsive logic, triggered by a continually rising volume of work, assumed such exaggerated proportions that, in order to cope with her job assignments, she worked through the rest periods which had been collectively agreed between the works council and her employer. This state of affairs continued until her colleagues informed the works council, whereupon she was enjoined in future to observe the rest period agreements. Nevertheless, despite her obligation to observe the rest periods,

within a certain period of time she still managed to accomplish in 20 hours virtually the same volume of work as a full-time employee.

2 Although one employee in the public sector was able to invoke statutory agreements on shorter hours, his employer stipulated that he would not be permitted to reduce his working time to 30 hours a week unless he accomplished the same volume of work as he did in a 40-hour week. The extent to which this would-be practitioner of flexibilization felt that he had been forced onto the defensive can be clearly gauged by the fact that, before making this statement, he requested that the tape recorder should be switched off.

Our practitioners of flexibilization provide extremely precise accounts of the extent to which the pressure of work has intensified. The majority of them changed their working time in their existing jobs, and therefore they are in a position to make direct comparisons. Where this is not the case, they still feel that their experience in previous jobs well qualifies them to give precise details of the degree to which they are subjected to intensification. The volume of work required of them is a reliable indicator of the degree of intensification. However, this reveals nothing of the form that such intensification takes, or of the means by which it is achieved. The interviewees provide details of the following intensification strategies:

1   Job type permitting, one means of managing the work load is to locate working time to fit the volume of work. This particularly serves the employers' interest, and the realization of this interest presents little difficulty insofar as the would-be practitioners of flexibilization are far more likely to adopt a conciliatory attitude towards this arrangement than any other. At least, none of our practitioners of flexibilization withheld or attempted to withhold their cooperation on this issue.

2   It is frequently the case that extra work in the form of overtime is required. As a rule, employers will not sanction the flexibilization of working time without an agreement to work overtime. In the main, overtime is not paid, the additional hours being taken in lieu. This greatly increases flexibility in respect of the location of working time (for example, starting later in the mornings or finishing earlier in the evenings, and working longer hours in the winter and shorter hours in the summer). Although organizational structures are not usually geared towards flexible working time, nevertheless we found that particular attention is afforded to the accumulation of plus hours and that companies employ a plurality of means of registering surplus hours, such as 'time accounts', 'time sheets' and

electronic time-recording equipment. In contrast, the procedures for taking time in lieu as a *quid pro quo* for the extra hours are determined by informal internal company agreements.

3   A typical characteristic feature of such intensification is that the informal break periods (breaks in the sense of non-productive activity such as coffee or tea breaks, and gossip rounds) are either abandoned, or not taken on grounds of conscience. Flexibilized employees are often plagued by a bad conscience if they take informal breaks, and they adduce this as the main reason for dispensing with such break periods. Visits to the doctor or to local government offices, etc. are undertaken outside working hours, a feature which is also typical of part-time employment throughout the employment sector. Likewise, our practitioners of flexibiliza-tion are considerably less likely to absent themselves from work on grounds of sickness. Thus, intensification is achieved by virtue of the fact that the employer derives maximum benefit from the length and location of the time that the employee is at work, with non-productive periods of time wasting being eliminated.

4   As has already been emphasized, in terms of pace, density and intensity, the performance of the time pioneers has improved. They are under greater pressure to perform, and in their experience they face 'more stress' and greater harassment in actually completing the tasks which are required of them.

5   In order to cope with the job requirements which are imposed upon them, the time pioneers are compelled to introduce self-monitoring procedures in respect of the work process. They feel that it is incumbent upon them to improve, plan and rationalize the way in which they organize their work in order to streamline it. Some time pioneers also regard this as constituting an intensification of the pressure to perform to which they are subjected.

However, in this context, it is noticeable that our time pioneers cope with intensification and stress better than was the case when they were in full-time work. These exercise a much less detrimental effect upon the private sphere. Thus this gives rise to the contradic-tion that although the time pioneers recognize that they are experien-cing objective intensification at the workplace, from the subjective viewpoint they do not feel that this imposes any greater strain upon the organization of their daily lives. Our interviewees are only able to withstand the strain imposed by intensification, which in some cases is considerable indeed, by gearing the overall organization of their lives towards shielding them from the burdens and spillover effects of employment, and by distancing themselves from the sphere of employment.

There is a tendency for the compulsion to cope with the work load by means of the acceptance of independent rationalization to take the form of qualification in the sense that it entails the assumption of monitoring and organizational functions. The increased pressure that self-rationalization exerts on their work strengthens the reflexive attitude of flexibilized employees towards the work process, while at the same time going hand in hand with the fact that they also experience a revaluation of their competence and an increase in their independence. Thus, for example, flexibilized employees develop faculties for self-organization and rationalization, and a faculty for controlling the work process (evaluating, organizing and streamlining, etc. the work load in accordance with priority). This helps to generate a greater sense of responsibility among flexibilized employees *vis-à-vis* their own job assignments, though it also makes it more difficult for them to relinquish part or parts of their own sphere of competence at a future date, since the abnegation of any job assignments might also result in a loss of face at work.

As a rule, one of the consequences of the flexibilization of working time is an increased level of independence, competence and self-monitoring, a feature which is in complete accordance with the content-related job commitment and the high work-related aspirations of the practitioners of flexibilization. This generates the adoption of a posture of self-assurance at work, a posture which appropriates independence and which is characterized by a tendency to seek rather than to eschew conflict. Depending upon which technique of manpower management is deployed, this can result in an increased degree of independence for the practitioner of flexibilization or, if this fails to materialize, in greater potential for conflict and a higher level of dissatisfaction.

As is also the case with employees who have flexitime arrangements, employees on flexible working time are much more exposed to the punctuality risk. The practitioner of flexibilization is then required to internalize the monitoring of time utilization and allocation, and to develop a greater awareness of time utilization and time discipline. The enforcement of improved levels of cooperation and mutual agreements necessitated by the more frequent occurrence of the flexibilization of working time at the workplace also demands a greater degree of self-monitoring and responsibility on the part of flexibilized employees. In other words, the willingness to make and keep agreements. The fact that flexibilized employees are required to intensify and rationalize their work and improve the degree to which they monitor their working behaviour intensifies the pressure on them to develop an internalized awareness of working time which can foster self-discipline and increase performance levels, though this is not necessarily the case. In this respect, it can be said that the flexibilization of working time fosters the development of internalized work discipline.

Even in *person-oriented* jobs, which by virtue of the nature of the work they involve render intensification difficult to achieve, many of our flexibilized employees suffer intensification. Thus one teacher, for example, was allocated more time-consuming courses and more work to do at home. In another instance, an occupational therapist was forced to introduce more clear-cut work allocation practices and a more accurate system of time-keeping. This not only curtailed his therapy work, but also reduced the time he had available for follow-up sessions and the development of new concepts. At the same time he was also subjected to more stringent monitoring procedures, which restricted his scope for assuming the responsibility for organizing his work, thus resulting in a loss of privileges. Those whose activities involve dealing with customers and clients (shop assistants, social workers, bank cashiers and night-nurses, for example) make no mention of suffering intensification.

The individual implementation of flexible working time in particular demonstrates the fact that the ensuing intensification, which in some cases is considerable indeed, is a consequence of the fixation with regulations based on the principle of standard working time. The would-be practitioners of flexibilization are in a weaker negotiating position than their employers. In order to facilitate the acquisition of additional free time over and above that which standard working time provides and, within certain limits, the right of self-determination over the timing of their working hours, these employees are forced to make concessions. The possibility of intensifying production levels is introduced into the negotiations by both parties, the employer and the employee, though, in keeping with the power structure, from different points of departure: by the one side, it is postulated as a precondition, by the other, it is yielded as a concession.

The sole reason why the practitioners of flexibilized working time accept the disadvantages within the working environment is that these are outweighed by the advantages outside the sphere of work, in other words, the latitude for shaping the way in which they conduct their everyday lives that flexibilization provides. However, within the employment system, those employees who work flexibilized hours receive no reward for the additional energy that they are required to expend in the performance of their duties. They accept the considerable disadvantages that flexibilization brings in its train while still managing to maintain a high level of job commitment. In the absence of any statutory regulations or any agreements between employers and works councils, the implementation of a system in which individuals are able to choose their own working hours is achieved on the back of the employees, often at the cost of considerable intensification of their performance levels. Furthermore, this disadvantage is compounded by additional drawbacks such as loss of career prospects, reduced pension entitlements, and discriminatory treatment at the hands of employment and social legislation, etc.[8]

Restrictions on cooperation and communication

The intensification resulting from flexibilization eliminates periods of wasted time and slowdown, thus severely restricting the communicative and informal activities which occur at the workplace. The actual experiences of the time pioneers of the effects of this development on communication and cooperation are broadly similar.

The most frequent complaint is that the flexibilization of working time exercises a deleterious effect upon informal communication with colleagues. The lack of time for personal conversations is a serious obstacle to the maintenance of contact with colleagues, and this tends to isolate those on flexible working time, forcing them into the role of outsiders at the workplace. This is scarcely conducive to the development of social and psychological support through collegial contacts. The excessive curtailment of scope for communication entails the risk that conflicts will accumulate and might prevent the defusing of potential areas of friction among colleagues. This can result in the development of an unpleasant working atmosphere.

Less scope for communicative exchanges with colleagues makes the flow and transfer of information more difficult, one major medium of which are informal breaks and gossip rounds. The resulting social isolation of the individual which occurs in some cases is often considered to be a problem. However, at the same time, such isolation can also go hand in hand with an increase in occupational independence, which is sometimes able to compensate for poor levels of social feedback. Communicative difficulties render cooperation at the workplace somewhat more of a problem in cases where the shop-floor culture and organizational structure, which exercise a major influence on opportunities for informal contacts, are not geared towards such cooperation.

In the case of flexible working time, the individual becomes much more dependent upon the quality of formal and informal cooperation, which no longer automatically occurs through the concentration of the workforce in terms of time and space. The difficulty of establishing informal contacts, exchanges of information, and cooperation is not primarily attributable to the reduction in available conversation time in the wake of flexibilization, but rather chiefly to the level of stress to which those working flexibilized hours are subjected as a result of intensification. In contrast, the conventional working time structures of the standard working day guarantee unconcentrated periods of time which can be utilized for the purpose of exploiting informal contacts, thus at the same time fostering the enterprise's functional postulates of information, cooperation and communication.

On the whole, the consequences of flexibilization on cooperation and communication are contingent upon job type and the operational circumstances of job content. Job structures vary greatly, and this rules out the possibility of discerning any uniform effect. However, one clear result should be noted: the extent of communication and cooperation problems depends largely on the one hand on the degree to which the management organization facilitates or impedes flexible working time and, on the other, on the degree to which the working atmosphere supports or opposes flexible working time. The more positive the reaction of the company and its employees to the flexibilization of working time, the less chance there is of cooperation and information transfer problems arising, and the less the risk of social isolation.

In respect of management organization and shop-floor culture – two of the factors which exercise a crucial influence on the quality of communicative and cooperative structures – several typical findings should be noted:

1 In one case, which can be regarded as typical, the isolation resulting from insufficient contact opportunities and communication difficulties is subjectively perceived as a serious problem. The employee concerned regards himself as marginalized, both socially and from the standpoint of job content. Prejudices, envy and resentment accumulate among his colleagues, and these reinforce his isolation, creating an unpleasant working atmosphere and generating sources of conflict, which, however, are precluded from further examination by lack of time. All this rules out the development of the desired

social and motivational support at the workplace. He perceives both his social isolation and his isolation from the standpoint of job content as a deprivation.

2 In another case, the complaint is voiced that flexible working time reduces the opportunities that are available for engaging in conversation at the workplace and for gaining support. The work process assumes the form of a one-way street in which the employee himself produces output while being deprived of the socially and psychologically stabilizing feedback which he requires. The criticism is made that a trend is developing towards the objectification and depersonalization of working relations.

3 In a further typical case, social isolation is actually experienced as a pleasure in that it allows the person concerned to escape the envy of those colleagues who are out of sympathy with the flexibilization of working time. In this instance, it is those on standard working time who experience a feeling of deprivation in that they are still (perforce) at work, whereas in their mind's eye they can imagine the practitioner of flexibilization relaxing on the patio acquiring a coveted suntan.

4 In cases where flexible working time is accepted by colleagues and superiors alike, despite the fact that the management organization is not .geared towards it, our interviewees report positive experiences. There are less serious communication problems, and cooperation is characterized by understanding and mutual assistance.

5 In contrast, those (few) flexibilized employees working for companies in which relevant working time schemes were introduced some time ago and are exploited on a fairly large scale do not complain of sparse communication or reduced levels of informal contact. An organizational structure which is geared towards flexible working time fosters coordination and synchronization among the employees. Below this formal level, there has developed an informal communication structure which functions no less efficiently, creating contact opportunities for the purpose of reaching mutual accommodation. Via informal agreements and internal arrangements, mutual deputizations, exceptional arrangements and accords are reached which do not one-sidedly disadvantage those on flexibilized hours. At the same time, this informal level considerably enhances the degree of flexibilization. On the whole, the fact that the individual components offer each other mutual support generates a pleasant working atmosphere and collegial behaviour. This also requires reorientation on the part of those involved in the working process towards an organizational structure and culture which rejects models of schematically inflexible and rigidly regulated working time arrangements. Thus, for example,

it may be the case that one day, out of the blue, owing to the (previously arranged) absence of some flexibilized colleagues and to additional instances of sick leave, a 'chaotic situation' arises, which requires that the individual demonstrate situation-responsiveness and the capacity for spontaneous reorientation. It would appear that the capacity for cooperation and coexistence with flexibilized working time is greater in the case of rather more experienced employees. However, the empirical basis for this assumption is narrow, and thus such generalizations should be proffered with caution.

6 At the behest of the workforce, one organization introduced flexible working time for all employees six months ago in order to create additional jobs. From the standpoint of job content (psychological and social counselling and welfare services), one of the requirements of the organization is temporal availability for coordination and information purposes on the basis of teamwork. However, the timing of working is so enormously varied and diversified that considerable problems arise in respect of information transfer and mutual consultation. In this instance, the problem is being approached by means of the reorganization of the formal communication structure. With supervisory assistance, the organization was streamlined, communication made more effective and cooperation monitoring intensified. Thus this organization is attempting to rectify the communication problems by means of installing a superstructure for cooperation.

A sensitive point: immediate superiors

For our interviewees, the specific manner in which their immediate superiors influence the working processes and the specific nature of the attitude which they adopt towards their subordinates give rise to problems and conflicts. Under the term 'leadership style', we now focus our attention upon the problem of immediate superiors and their leadership, as typically perceived from the standpoint of those employees whom we interviewed.

The conflicting influence of two factors complicates the practice of flexible working time: on the one hand, there is the need for a greater degree of cooperation and, on the other, intensification results in a lack of opportunities for reaching mutual arrangements on an informal basis. At first glance, this contradictory structure of the flexibilization of working time would appear to be virtually insoluble. However, the more the organizational and procedural structure of a company is able to adapt to the special conditions and problem areas associated with the flexibilization of working time, the easier it is to overcome this paradoxical constellation. Cooperation is contingent upon human capabilities. Thus the establishment of flexible working time requires an organizational structure which avails itself of the scope for utilizing human capabilities such as situation-responsiveness, solidarity, the capacity to sympathize with the situation of others, independence, etc. and fosters their development. These capabilities, also utilized by participative organizational structures and in team work, are made the basis of their *modus operandi*. In contrast, they are not necessarily fostered inside organizations with strictly hierarchical structures.[9]

· The situation of flexibilized employees at the workplace is more heavily dependent upon acceptance and a willingness to cooperate on the part of their colleagues and immediate superiors than is that of those on standard working time. Our study reveals that direct superiors constitute a particular source of major conflict areas with regard to implementing flexibilization of working time. In cases where conflict does occur, those employees on flexible working time bemoan the fact that their immediate superiors display a traditional, authoritarian style of leadership based upon direct instructions and the principle of strict obedience. Those immediate superiors who adopt such an imperious style of leadership are accused of lacking the ability to create the necessary basic conditions for utilizing the human capabilities mentioned above, and for introducing an appropriate procedural structure, indeed, of actively preventing the creation of such conditions. Such conflicts over leadership styles occur with the immediate superior, that is to say, in organizations characterized by a high degree of internal differentiation, with the head of department or, in small offices, with the actual employer.[10]

Surprisingly, even within companies whose management has explicitly introduced the option of flexibilized working time, attitudinal conflicts with regard to flexible working time occur at the localized departmental level. Some employees were only able to flexibilize their working time by circumventing their departmental heads and appealing directly to the works council. The primary obstacle to the implementation of flexible working time proved to be the less than cooperative and receptive attitude on the part of departmental heads rather than the organizational concept. There are two reasons for the localization of conflicts at the level of departmental heads: on the one hand, the fact that they cleave to the traditional schemata of working culture and full-time employment, and, on the other, that they are fearful of forfeiting influence and authority. Both give rise to a specific style of leadership which is not conducive to the development of a positive attitude towards flexible working time.

A characteristic feature of conflicts at the level of departmental heads is the fact that they develop wherever leadership styles are not attuned to changed aspirations on the part of employees with flexible working time schemata. The greater level of personal organization, self-monitoring and personal responsibility, which severe instances of intensification frequently bring in their train, and the high degree of willingness to work on the part of the practitioners of flexibilization almost inevitably result in the acquisition of new skills. These new skills enhance their areas of competence and their capacity for assuming personal responsibility at the workplace, and thus generate more forceful demands for independence. The compulsion to engage in increased cooperation and reach mutual agreement on time arrangements goes hand in hand with the development of personal abilities which contribute to cooperative performance, informal arrangements and solidarity. The result of the development of these abilities is a greater claim on the part of flexibilized employees to the exercise of joint influence over the way in which their work is organized.

Where leadership styles are not geared towards the establishment of cooperation, towards communication, the settlement of conflicts by negotiation and receptiveness to argument, etc., but rather – in ideal-typical contrast – towards hierarchical authority, directive (non-content- or task-related) powers of command, increased monitoring levels, etc., the conflict potential becomes greater. Superiors who are fearful of forfeiting some of their authority, of relinquishing some of their managerial and cooperative functions to informal arrangements, and of being forced to cede some of their monitoring and control functions to the sphere of responsibility of individual subordinates endeavour to prevent the implementation of flexible working time.

Admittedly, immediate superiors enjoy the support of an organizational structure. Given the fact that full-time employees are on hand all day long and are always available to receive instructions, they are simpler and easier to manage in accordance with the established principles of organization. From this standpoint, flexible working time, in other words, deviations from standard working time, often cause havoc with the established management organization. Additional obstacles in the way of the implementation of systems of flexible working time are established norms and standards for ensuring the maintenance of working discipline. These make it difficult for immediate superiors who exercise a style of leadership based on pure supervision to adapt to one based on cooperation and communication.

Difficulties in providing symbolic proof of performance

The central legitimizing ideology in the employment society is the performance principle. The measure of performance success is reflected by income size and professional status, which map out in advance opportunities for acquiring desirable possessions. This can be seen from the visible consumerist symbols of the success which has been achieved, and from the demonstrably high standard of living resulting from such success. The converse conclusion, which is legitimately made, is that those who have lower levels of income and do not make a career are unwilling to work and lack job motivation. As a result, some of those employees whom we interviewed are faced with the difficulty of providing suitable evidence of their ability. The central issue at stake in this context is lifestyle, and how, through its power of articulation and via its physical representation by means of consumerist symbols and the value schemata which find expression in such symbols, lifestyle permits conclusions to be drawn with regard to the ethic mobilization of employees' work, and to performance achievements.

However, a more serious problem for flexibilized employees is the fact that individual proof of performance is anchored in industrial time standards. The performance principle establishes competitive conditions by which performance is gauged – in terms of higher or lower and good or bad performance levels. The compilation of generalized performance criteria requires that actual job content should be ignored. The content structure of work recedes into the background and is superseded by time structure, which, assuming the function of content structure, subsequently becomes representative of performance (see Ermert and Rinderspacher 1981; Rinderspacher 1985: 109ff; Rinderspacher and Ermert 1986). In accordance with this mechanism, obedience to the industrial time regime is a performance function *per se*.

In terms of their historical implementation process, inflexible working time arrangements and rigid time standards imposed by employers have preponderantly disciplinary functions, which can be ensured in the form of compulsory attendance based on visible and extraneously regulated control. In consequence of the exogenous displacement of controllability, unalloyed working time coincides with the time spent in attendance at the workplace, with the result that industrial work discipline is identified as attendance discipline. Furthermore, adaptability to the standard industrial time structures in the categories of punctuality, regularity, consistency, endurance and linearity of working behaviour constitutes an acknowledged integral part of overall employee performance. This has the result that attendance discipline, the punctual observance of attendance times, is elevated to the status of a general employee performance rating. The primary proof-of-performance factors are visible presence, punctuality and continuity at the workplace. It is perfectly possible for these to be deployed as substitutes for task-oriented performance factors, even if it is only a question of maintaining appearances.

Against this backdrop, some of our flexibilized employees report that, as a result of their being on shorter and flexible working hours, they experience difficulties in substantiating their willingness to work and in obtaining recognition at the workplace for their performance output. The standards traditionally employed for appraising performance are intensified rather than modified. The time criteria of continuity, consistency and endurance in particular function as yardsticks of performance appraisal, and in consequence the fact that in terms of performance flexibilized employees are unable or unwilling to adapt to these time standards counts against them. 'Unable' means that a verdict of 'laziness' is passed upon their willingness to work, and 'unwilling' means that they fall prey to the suspicion that work is not the centre of their lives, in other words, that the actual focal point of performance output is to be sought elsewhere. As a general rule our flexibilized employees are also denied the opportunity to pursue a career under the prevailing conditions. This is interpreted as indicating that they also lack performance motivation from the standpoint of longer-term orientation, that is to say, the endeavour to attain higher occupational positions. The fact that the practitioners of working time flexibilization are unable to demonstrate their willingness to work by means of adjusting to industrial time standards might be the reason why they display greater willingness to accept intensification.

Particularly in those companies in which the representational form of work takes priority over job content – a norm which is reinterpreted by the practitioners of flexibilization in particular – employees on flexible working time are branded as potentially subversive forces who could undermine industrial work values, and as troublemakers who disturb the established patterns of operational activity. According to this logic, flexibilized employees are not only forced into marginal positions; it is absolutely essential that they are stigmatized as outsiders and marginal phenomena of little social importance within the organizational structure in order not to endanger the existence of institutional standardizations and in order to avoid any potential conflict from the outset. The result is that in the case of some of our employees, flexible working time is only permitted by the employer under exceptional circumstances and is rescinded in the event of any subsequent large-scale demand. Alternatively it becomes subject to intensified levels of monitoring in order to forestall the danger that it might exercise a negative effect on their performance levels.

The claim to the exercise of authority on the part of the employer applies to the achievement of a certain performance level and the observance of certain procedural regulations, from which claims to the exercise of monitoring functions on the part of management are derived: In addition, however, it requires that employees display certain forms of behaviour and develop a sense of loyalty to the company objectives (Hörning and Bücker-Gärtner 1982: 51ff). The transgression committed by the practitioners of flexibilization against the predetermined time standards of the work process is not only interpreted as a sign of a reduced level of motivation on their part; without exception, their loyalty to the company objectives is also called into question. (This is one reason why they are refused a whole range of bonus payments, and also one reason why they are denied career opportunities.)

As a result of the temporal form taken by their work, it is often the case that those employees on flexible forms of working time are also unable to provide any symbolic proof of performance. Flexible working time does not constitute grounds for the granting of any additional bonus payments. In this context, it is also true that the difficulties which the practitioners of flexibilization experience in providing proof of performance have more serious consequences within the framework of management organizations which are less amenable towards flexible working conditions. It is not statutory regulations which prove to be a barrier to the actual implementation of flexible working time, but rather those traditional organizational principles and orientational models which, falling back upon the 'cultural paradigm of the employment society', emphasize the normative form of the integration of the workforce into the working environment.

3 The Revision of Interpretive Schemata — Commitment and Dissociation

It is common currency in contemporary studies that the employment society as it has hitherto been perceived over a long period is in the throes of structural change and has entered a period of cultural crisis. In view of this, our attention now focuses upon which routes lead out of this situation of radical upheaval. Consequently, the question which arises for us is how the adoption of flexible working time enables the time pioneers to respond to cultural schisms in the employment society.

We are particularly interested in the continuity of and the change in the cultural meaning of work. How do experiences of this situation of radical upheaval and the assimilation of the changed structural conditions assume the concrete form of specific (new) interpretive constructions, and which interpretive schemata are articulated and formulated?

Even at this stage, it may be stated that one of the results of our study is to show that the dissociation on the part of the time pioneers from the normative standards of our work-oriented culture exercises a permanent and formative influence on their interpretive schemata. They are subjected to a process of restructuring, which can be seen as a progressive retreat from the normative clutches of the working environment. The lifestyle of the time pioneers becomes dissociated from a system of values which we call the 'cultural paradigm of the employment society'. The time pioneers use this meaning schema of the employment society as a contrastive backdrop in order to render their specific lifestyle plausible.

The 'cultural paradigm of the employment society' is based upon meaning structures and background convictions which have developed historically in our society and which, as the socio-cultural form of 'employment society', constitute the dominant model of the binding activity and orientational schema. Adopting the term 'paradigm' to describe this model has the advantage that, on the one hand, it provides a categorial conceptual framework for the socio-cultural meaning of work, the configuration of central interpretive schemata, while on the other hand, it delineates central core factors of work-oriented interpretive schemata. The paradigm does not assert the uniformity or universality of central factors of interpretive schemata. It is rather the case that it highlights the orienting and model function which is its identifying feature, in spite of the existence of multi-faceted region-, class-, stratum-, branch- and occupation-specific nuances and articulative forms. We understand the 'cultural paradigm of the employment society' to signify a work-fixated orientational and value system such as that entailing full employment, growth and progressional consensus. On the basis of European traditions of employment culture over a long period of time, this paradigm has become established as a constant of social development in the Federal Republic of Germany (see Lutz 1984).

On the one hand, the paradigm refers to the employment sphere itself:[1] employees are expected to be prepared to subordinate their own formative interests and life-needs to standard manpower management regulations: standard forms of payment, the standard of life-long, full-time employment, and standardizations of job content and job performance. These conditions are enshrined in the value canon of a social character shaped by employment and which determines values of both acceptance and duty (such as the deferral of personal needs, pliancy, asceticism and the abandonment of all aspirations to personal fulfilment), and certain work values (such as diligence, reliability, competence, resilience and socio-revolutionary abstemiousness). This syndrome is connected with the ethicization and normative exaggeration of paid work,[2] by virtue of which it is transformed into a conglomerate of occupational obligations which co-determine the entire moral mobilization of manpower.

The cultural paradigm also figures the dominance of the male as the sole breadwinner and family provider who secures his personal and social identity and his life-history via his occupation. The male career man is obliged to subject himself to performance criteria, to internalize career constraints, to devote himself to his occupation and his work, by virtue of which company disciplinary strategies based on supervision and reward first come into their own. Consequently, the yardsticks of (male) success are the status criteria of income and career, which forge the retaining link in respect of the correlation between personal identity, professional identity and family identity.

On the other hand, the effects of the value system of the employment society reverberate far beyond the sphere of work: it idealizes a family model in which the husband regards occupational and economic success as attestation of his role as breadwinner, and the wife is assigned the role of 'being there for others' (Beck-Gernsheim 1983) in the guise of mother, teacher, housewife and wife. The work society's dominant type of the nuclear family is based upon a gender division of labour, and, in the face of the performance-ridden and competition-dominated chill of the sphere of employment, it serves as a zone of personal retreat.

Nevertheless, this reverse association with the private sphere as the source of meaning finds public representation via a lifestyle which is fashioned by market forces. This finds expression in consumer goods with high levels of social visibility and obligation which characterize social prestige and status. Personal success and social identity are represented via the priority status attaching to symbols of social prestige (such as home ownership, car, household furnishings and electrical household equipment, etc.) into which values such as technical progress, economic growth and performance-orientation are integrated in equal measure. Via the central legitimizing ideology of the performance principle, individual activity orientations and binding values circulate within the status system of career, income size and consumption.

Performance thinking within the schema of a full-time job dominates the evaluation of ways of life and lifestyles. In this respect, the practitioners of flexibilization regard themselves as exposed to discriminatory suspicion on many fronts through the dominance of the employment society paradigm. At the workplace, this makes it more difficult for them to provide proof of their willingness to work, makes it hard for them to explain their lifestyle, seriously reduces their articulation opportunities, generates moral discrimination and gives rise to envy and resentment on the part of their colleagues.

3.1 The time pioneers' high degree of job commitment

Their work is extremely important to the time pioneers, but it is problematized by working conditions and unreasonable demands on the part of employers. A tension develops from these two poles. This structure is held together by a thin thread from which the dead weight of the subjective experience of satisfaction hangs. Our objective now is to elaborate upon the finding that there is a convergence of different perspectives of work-cultural interpretive schemata, the relationship between which is a potential source of conflict.

However, the potential for conflict is limited by the fact that the time pioneers adopt a selective approach towards job commitment. Keeping the working environment at arm's length enables them to limit the effects of certain demands on the part of their employer upon their private lives. They find ways of managing the discrepancy between the role expectations of the employment sphere and their own adaptation problems in such a manner that they are still able to identify with their work. There thus evolves an attitude towards work which is characterized by both commitment and detachment.

In comparison with standard working time, the time pioneers have reduced and flexibilized the amount of time in which they participate in employment. However, despite this, contrary to current schemata, it is not at all the case that they regard their work as a necessary evil, the purpose of which is to secure their existence. On the contrary, the hallmarks of their approach towards employment are commitment and willingness to work, and they relate employment to the general meaning of life. The basic non-problematized orientation of the time pioneers is the interpretation of work as a form of activity whose primary purpose is to secure their livelihood and standard of living. However, over and above this general orientation towards security, their interest in employment does not extend to the maximization of income, status or career prospects; rather, they see the essential purpose of their commitment to work in the actual tasks which their job involves and in the job content itself.

Thus, a correlation is established between the quest for self-realization via the meaning experienced at work and the challenges contributing to the attainment of self-realization posed by actual job content. In consequence, the time pioneers do not interpret work as adaptation towards a given set of conditions and assimilation of occupational responsibilities, but rather as an incentive for improving their own abilities and fields of competence and for broadening their horizons. The moment of personal satisfaction, a concomitant factor of work which is regarded as meaningful, is accentuated, and the quality of their activity at work is assessed accordingly.

The practitioners of flexibilization expect their work to be interesting, enjoyable, and consist of demanding challenges to which they are able and compelled to rise. The time pioneers do not merely aspire to these expectations; on the contrary, they give rise to a reciprocal relationship: the time pioneers invest both their occupational and physical energy and their productive capacity in their work. In the event of a high level of job satisfaction failing to materialize, many practitioners of flexibilization attempt to find alternative employment, terminate their contract of employment, or change their working time arrangements. This involves accepting periods of unemployment, occupational disqualification or occupational reorientation (retraining, a course of study, a second course of study, or a change of occupation), which is an impressive demonstration of the status they ascribe to work. Purposeful activity in life accords work an exceptional intrinsic value.

The flexibilization of their working time is an attempt on the part of the time pioneers to increase the degree to which they concentrate upon the actual job, to identify the intrinsic value of their work and to cease regarding work solely from the standpoint of the restrictive influence which it exercises upon their own interests and contact opportunities. A form of flexibilization which affords individual employees a relatively large degree of freedom to determine the location and duration of their working hours means that there is a greater chance that the subject-oriented relevance of work will prevail over a performance mentality tinctured by coercion. For one employee, this post-flexibilization phenomenon is particularly present: '*Thus, the actual quality of work itself also changes. I mean, work is no longer such a big must, no longer that enormous responsibility which used to cramp my style in so many things, in many of my free time activities and in my private relationships. It's different now. The positive elements of work are coming so much more to the fore now that I can say that work is something I enjoy, and not just something which cramps my style.*' Thematic priority increasingly focuses on the actual content and tasks which the job involves, and this orientation facilitates the attainment of greater levels of job satisfaction and fulfilment. The hallmark of the time pioneers is a high degree of motivation, and although this is not solely related to employment, this is the sphere in which it is deployed with commitment. Performance motivation is focused selectively upon certain motivational inducements. Thereupon, the opportunities for identifying with work are delineated. The job situation is supposed to afford the time pioneers the opportunity of realizing their conceptions vis-à-vis job content. Their willingness to adapt to any working conditions and demands is limited.

The performance motivation of the time pioneers is removed from the traditional industrial ethos of duty, which demands conformity, the relinquishment of autonomy, and obedience. The attainment of a sense of fulfilment at work is a major requirement, which once again highlights the pre-eminent status enjoyed by work within the priority system. The motivation of the time pioneers focuses upon concrete task accomplishment during the performance of their duties. Inherent in such task-oriented performance motivation is also the generalizing mode of this willingness to work, which can be activated in a variety of different ways in other fields of activity besides that of employment (see section 4.2). This high level of motivation correlates with a self-disciplined attitude towards work and an internalized regulatory awareness, with which the challenges and demands of the job are tackled. Thus the willingness on the part of the time pioneers to effect the intensification and self-rationalization of work, and also to foster the development of self-determination and autonomy, inheres in their performance motivation: 'Well, I am under a lot of pressure. I've got jobs to do which have to be finished by a certain deadline, and I want to get them done in time. I want to keep on the right side of my customers, and keep on top of the deals because of the very fact that we never get our deadlines extended. I have no choice but to cope, but I'm not under pressure from above, I put myself under pressure. That way, it doesn't get on my nerves, and though I might be shattered when I get home, I'm satisfied.'

The fact that the time pioneers are committed to their jobs is the very reason that they experience a sense of satisfaction, self-assurance and positive achievement. However, the time pioneers are not solely concerned with achieving occupational success: they are also interested in an appropriate working atmosphere. The job-situation assessments of the time pioneers are also oriented towards the social quality of their contacts with their colleagues, and towards a pleasant atmosphere at the workplace.

This specific form of performance on the part of the time pioneers, which is geared towards job-content and task-oriented requirements, also functions as an immunization strategy against the imposition of additional and excessive demands by their employers. By concentrating on task-oriented performance, the time pioneers attempt – and this is a typical feature of their strategy – to conduct a rearguard action against the ambitions harboured by their employers of effecting the normative integration of their employees into the company activities.

External performance monitoring procedures which block the sources of performance motivation and the creation of a pleasant working atmosphere are positively detrimental to performance commitment. As far as the subjective value of work is concerned, the performance orientation of the time pioneers is geared towards the task-related, job-content elements of work, and, lending support to these components, towards the acceptance of self-monitoring, self-discipline and autonomy. For this reason, they are also prepared to subordinate themselves to the task-related consequences of work: '*I don't mind work, and when I do work, I work very intensively. I try to cope with everything that comes my way.*'

It is not the way in which the work is done which matters most, but rather the fulfilment of the task-oriented assignments which have been allocated. The more clearly they can be identified and the greater the reward they attract at work and at the workplace, the sooner the performance method of the time pioneers receives recognition. In view of the fact that this form of orientation towards work involving the exercise of self-monitoring on the basis of personal responsibility also requires independence and greater autonomy, depending upon leadership style, conflicts between the time pioneers and their immediate superiors become more frequent. In such cases, this might result in the actual performance output of the time pioneers failing to attract recognition, never mind adequate reward; on the contrary, all that does attract notice is the self-assured, seemingly arrogant behaviour of the time pioneers, which is then considered to constitute refractoriness. The example of one time pioneer who insists that his demand for subjectively meaningful work should be granted is an illustration of just such a case: '*I can't stand unnecessary work and, as a result, I very often have problems at work. I do my work and do loads of things off my own bat without anyone telling me to. In principle, it eases my work load as well if I do something right and afterwards, everything's as it should be. But on the other hand, I can't stand it when someone tells me a load of garbage either and when that happens, I often get into arguments with my superior as well.*'

Simple, monotonous work is a disincentive to performance, unable as it is to provide personal satisfaction or assume a meaningful guise. In contrast, it is often the case that time pioneers articulate demands for work entailing the highest possible levels of responsibility, variety and interest, in which they are able to utilize the professional qualifications which they have acquired and develop their skills. Time pioneers are resolutely opposed to performance in the form of 'attendance work' in which only attendance and formal working hours carry any weight. In their opinion, such 'attendance work' leads to dullness and the de-substantialization of work: '*When there's no more work to do, my colleagues often start doing some ridiculous, useless and stupid jobs or other. That's what ruins work, what makes it boring and what causes most people to lose interest in it. The upshot of it is that when it's knocking-off time, they drop everything. Their work is of absolutely no interest to them any more. At that moment, they knock off in the truest sense of the word. If you've got a positive attitude towards work, you don't mind working eight-and-a-half or nine hours once in a while. Then you're not clock-watching all the time.*'

Remaining in the same occupation with the same employer for the whole of their working lives does not form part of the time pioneers' plans. The flexible attitude adopted by the time pioneers is not focused solely upon the temporal variation of employment, but also on content variation: '*I started this job because I thought it was great to have a new challenge. I've always enjoyed taking on new challenges because I like adapting to the job in hand and then seeing how I do. When I realize that I can't contribute any more, either because I'm at a loss for ideas, or because I don't like the working conditions any more, I change my job.*' Where formative latitude exists, this also increases the willingness of the time pioneers to take the risk of varying both the way in which they organize their lives and their jobs. In this respect, we can speak in terms of the opportunity-oriented shaping of life as a suitable method of ensuring variety. The routinization of task performance bereft of any element of challenge is rejected.

The high, performance-oriented working morale of the time pioneers is also demonstrated by the fact that, as they themselves point out, they have hardly ever, or never, stayed off 'sick' without due cause. This is evidence of the existence of a 'healthy' self-confidence, which is also brought fully to bear at work. The financial demands which the time pioneers make of their employers are either reduced or, in view of the fact that they fail to provide the symbolic evidence of their conformity with the value system of the prevailing employment culture, difficult to enforce in the first place. On the other hand, given that conventional bonus systems consisting of material incentives and the bestowal of social status and prestige apply (have hitherto applied) to full-time employment, it is difficult for such systems to exercise a motivational influence on the willingness to work of the time pioneers.

3.2 Dissociation from the cultural paradigm of the employment society

In this section, our attention is focused on the aspects of the working environment from which the time pioneers dissociate themselves. Which experiences were relevant to this dissociation? What form does the process of dissociation assume, with which interpretive elements does it establish links, and from which does it distance itself?

Dissociation from the working environment is most lucidly and keenly articulated when the time pioneers address the history of their dissociation, their negative experiences with full-time employment. They are resolutely opposed to any participation in gainful activity in the form of full-time employment. Their negative experiences with full-time employment were so pronounced that they either flexibilized their working time or resigned from their jobs. This was not only a dramatic change to their previous way of life; it also resulted in the creation of a new lifestyle explicitly geared towards the avoidance of work-induced stress and the imposition of excessive demands.

In the experience of the time pioneers, the time regime of the employment system occupies their everyday lives to an extreme degree, creating a stereotyped existence and leaving them utterly at the mercy of its impositions. From their standpoint, everyday life is subject to unilateral determination and excessive regulation by the temporal requirements and stresses of employment, which define the time structure towards which the special accentuations and 'out' times are geared.

The time pioneers justify their withdrawal from full-time work with negative reference to the time schema shaped by paid work. Life, which serves as the contrastive backdrop, revolves around residual time, with the result that the predominant experience of the time pioneers is that they have reached the stage where they only exist from one weekend to the next. The period in between is regarded as 'dead time', wholly dominated by work, periods of recuperation and sleep, and the necessary mundane tasks of day-to-day living, which serve only to exacerbate time pressure still further. They are no longer able to devote any time to the pursuit and development of their own interests. The perceived costs of work far outstrip the benefits.

Everyday life appears to be at the mercy of extraneous influences and wholly occupied by work. Thus, the impression of the time pioneers that the excessive and oppressive interference of work in their way of life is unable to impart any meaning to their lives assumes concrete form: '*I found working 40 hours a week and more something of a pain, so I began wondering if that was the only type of fulfilment there actually was.*' For the time pioneers, this question as to the meaning of life is linked to their type of work. A reflexive and self-assurance process takes place *vis-à-vis* their subjective aims and activity concepts. This accelerates a reorientation of the interpretive priorities by means of which the time pioneers are better able to master the problems associated with employment. During the development of this process, there occurs a cognitive and affectual dissociation from the working environment which also facilitates the acceptance of periods of occupational interruption and discontinuity.

The meaning schemata of the time pioneers are so oriented that working time is examined from the standpoint of lifetime. The future prospect of lifelong full-time employment is not only regarded as pointless but, in extension of the dissociation process, also considered to be 'insane'. A breach is made with the perspective of full-time work, and, with regard to the current quality of their way of life, the time pioneers accentuate the reference to the present. The prospect of being compelled to place 'life' solely at the disposal of the dictates of full-time employment assumes negative connotations from which the time pioneers dissociate themselves.

In contrast, the way in which they presently fashion their lives now comes to the fore: they afford greater attention to current everyday life, and this provides them with the motivation to restructure the way in which they organize their lives. It is by no means the case that the time pioneers regard the problem of stress and the dictates of time as having been solved solely by the change in their working time. Their interpretive schemata are particularly characterized by the fact that the problematization of the relationship between working and living implies more than a change in their working time arrangements: it calls for consequences going far beyond the working environment. The thematization of the meaning horizons of the concept of life also impugns all previous normative validity standards. Thus the social expectational schemata of lifestyle are problematized, and this results in thematizing the withdrawal on the part of the time pioneers from the predetermined paths of genealogical sociation. For some of those on flexibilized working time, a typical feature of their dissociation from the working environment is that it is accompanied by their release from genealogical isolation or by an identity crisis. This goes hand in hand with the reorientation of those priority schemata which have hitherto been handed down from generation to generation.

In consequence of the stress of full-time work, which ultimately is barely able to impart a meaning to life, a gradual process of dissociation from the working environment sets in which eventually extends to the entire paradigm of the employment society. This initiates a reorientation process which co-determines the development of attitudes towards work. The socially predominant perspective of the employment cultures, which becomes particularly effective within the context of the workplace, is permanently upheld as a contrastive backdrop in the interpretive schemata of the time pioneers. However, this by no means implies a fundamental withdrawal from employment, but rather the co-inclusion of one form of a specific attitude towards work in the development of the meaning schemata of the time pioneers. In addition, there is no opposition to the social and management organization of work such as that championed by, for example, the alternative economy.

However, reorientation is not influenced solely by the time pioneers' work experiences. The essential determining factor is rather a reflexive process which adopts a critical stance towards the cultural paradigm of the employment society and plays a decisive role in fuelling the dissociation process. The factors which undergo change are the cultural reference system and the interpretive context which provide the framework for the determination of the specific attitude towards work adopted by the time pioneers. In consequence, employment ceases to be the predominant source of meaning and the focal point around which life revolves.

In the case of some of those working flexible time, the origin of the reorientation process is attributable less to their actual experiences of work than to the fact that even before they had embarked upon their working lives, they had begun distancing themselves from the working environment, though as a negative contrastive backdrop, it maintains a constant presence. As a means of illustrating their dissociation from the working environment, all our interviewees cite acquaintances, friends or parents with full-time jobs as deterrent examples who trigger affectual rejection on their part. The justification of their own attitude towards work by means of this explanatory figure requires less effort since it dispenses with any requirement for the clear delineation and the legitimation of the substance of their own interpretive schemata. Such deviation from the norm bestows a self-explicative status upon their continued maintenance of these negative images.

This changed interpretational context is also expressed in the corresponding interpretive schemata through which the working environment is viewed. The time pioneers are at pains to expose attitudes towards work based on virtues such as assiduity, conformity and trust in authority as ridiculous, indeed, even paradoxical, and to bestow rationality upon their own behaviour. In spite of all the differences of detail in the time pioneers' articulation of their interpretive schemata, the desire to fathom the socially universal core of work is common to them all. Within the context of the workplace and society, the time pioneers' treatment of the subject of employment is tinctured with latent criticism.

However, the character of the actual work is also interpreted by the time pioneers within the framework of these reference contexts and examined from the standpoint of its relevance to their lifestyle and conception of life. Dissociation is intensified wherever content- and task-oriented attitudes towards work coincide with working conditions which are felt to be de-substantializing and unsatisfactory. This loosens the time pioneers' affectual links with the workplace, though not with job content and the method of task accomplishment.

In view of the fact that employment is extremely important to the time pioneers, the organization of work at the workplace and working time assume central thematic importance. This results in a great deal of consideration to the working environment (behaviour at work), and the approval of work itself (willingness to work), but also in the relativization of working life (from the standpoint of its relevance to the time pioneers' own conception of life). This implies that the time pioneers not only change their working time, but also that they cherish ambitions of obtaining a demanding job which is commensurate with their qualifications, challenging and satisfying.

Dissociation from the working environment is intensified from both poles, that of the level of individual aspirations and that of working conditions, becoming firmly entrenched among the interpretive schemata of the time pioneers in the form of considered and critical dissociation, as demonstrated, for example, by the following comments of one time pioneer: '*I think that because I work shorter hours, it's not as easy to manipulate me as it was before. There's no way I'll work anywhere they want me to any more.*' In the wake of the change in their working time, of the increase in the amount of time at their disposal, such dissociation functions as a source of positive energy for the time pioneers. They feel less involved in events at the workplace, frictions, conflicts and stresses: the cognitive, normative and affective involvement with employment becomes less intense: *'As far as I'm concerned, I've noticed that it doesn't really bother me any more when there's friction at work, that I think I should just let them get on with it, as I'm only here in the mornings now.'*

All this creates added job value, namely, the intensification of subjective satisfaction. The conclusion drawn by the time pioneers is as follows: they derive more out of life, and they also derive much greater pleasure from going to work and approach it in a far happier frame of mind. The relief produced by the flexibilization of working time results in the liberation of the thought processes from the confined horizon of the working environment, thus facilitating their additional concentration on other areas and interests.

The time pioneers explicitly use their dissociation from the working environment as an opportunity to take stock of their own situation, to exploit impulses to fashion their own lives, and to direct the reorientation process. Distance provides them with the opportunity of seeing their own situation more clearly. This allows them to concentrate their performance output at work on its meaningful aspects, and to restrict the area of validity of the overall meaning framework of the employment society. New lifestyle priorities begin to take shape, creating for the time pioneers a new balance between working and living, and thereby circumventing the strict segregation of everyday life into periods of work and periods of free time: *'Somehow or other, I enjoy being able to combine both. I mean, on the one hand, working, having a job I like, a good job, a suitable job, and, on the other, actually achieving a high degree of fulfilment in my private life, pursuing hobbies and having the scope to engage with people.'* The flexibilization of working time increases the availability of certain formative opportunities, and these are more rigorously exploited by the time pioneers via the development of reflexive potential and subject-centred aspirations. They are thus in a position to effectuate a far greater level of reconciliation between the two issues which are of concern to them, namely, an interesting job and greater dispositional scope for organizing their free time.

3.3 Conflicts at work resulting from different cultural perspectives

Standard working time functions not only as the primary time structure, but also as a normative construct which has become an institutionalized feature of the interpretive schemata of members of society and proves considerably resistant to change. This is evident from the resistance to the introduction of flexible working time arrangements which is displayed by the workforce and the managerial staff.[3] Instances of such resistance cannot be dismissed as irrationalities, as has been done by management on some occasions. On the contrary, they are pointers towards culturally stable orientations which bar the way to changes of heart and attitude in favour of flexible forms of working time.

The question now arises as to how the champions of the cultural paradigm of the employment society react within the confines of the working environment towards the time pioneers, whose primary distinguishing feature is the unorthodox temporal form of their work. We have already shown that particularly in those companies in which the traditional work-culture value system has become institutionalized and is cemented by an appropriate organizational structure and shop-floor culture, the practitioners of the flexibilization of working time are faced with problems and difficulties (see sections 2.3 and 2.4 above). The reactions with which the time pioneers are confronted at work can thus be regarded as a test of the power and *modus operandi* of the paradigm of the employment society.

The envious and sceptical reaction of their colleagues to the flexibilization of working time is the most common theme expressed in almost identical terms by the time pioneers.[4] Many encountered more disturbing reactions, reporting that their unorthodox working time had a provocative effect, triggering resentment, confrontation and aggression. Their way of life on the basis of flexible and shorter working hours frequently meets with rejection and even overt discrimination.

Reactions such as envy on the part of the colleagues of the time pioneers touches upon a whole range of references which demonstrate the interpretive schemata which are enlisted for evaluation purposes. Envy is the expression of a relational, comparative and measuring process, and it therefore corresponds to that performance thinking which characterizes comparative evaluations. This process is initiated from a position of inferiority and is an expression of sentiments of disadvantage and non-achievement. In principle, the objective of this process is geared towards the attainment of alignment or equality. Thus, some time pioneers relate that feelings of envy are particularly awakened among those of equal status; the men are compared with their male colleagues, whereas the women can mainly expect to meet with the envy of their female colleagues.

These feelings of envy can be specified more precisely and identified by certain symbols. The champions of the cultural paradigm of the employment society are particularly sensitive towards instances of additional free time which enable the practitioners of flexibilization to manifest status symbols and forms of conduct which cannot be converted into consumer goods. Free-time symbols such as suntans obtained in summer are examples of the targets of such envy. These are adjudged to be manifestations of indolence, which is a luxury that those on standard working time cannot afford. However, the particular focus of colleagues' envy is the time pioneers' more contented and cheerful attitude towards life occasioned by their flexibilized working time: 'For example, at work, when I respond to the question "how goes it" with "fine", I can sense the envy of my colleagues. And I can also sense their envy when I turn up at work sporting a suntan, because when it gets down to it, a lot of people would love to work fewer hours but reckon they can't afford to.' The envy displayed by the colleagues of the time pioneers is the manifestation of a tense ambivalence pointing towards the phenomenon of status inconsistency: on the one hand, the relinquishment by the time pioneers of part of their earnings, of their careers, and of greater consumer opportunities, the difficulties they face in providing proof of performance, and the reduced level of their normative integration into the companies at which they are employed lead to a loss of status and prestige. However, on the other hand, the time pioneers are bearers of status symbols, access to which is governed 'under normal circumstances' by the possession of material wealth and a senior occupational position and which, regarded from this perspective, they acquire illegitimately via their specific lifestyle and temporal affluence. Since the specific attitude towards work displayed by the time pioneers clashes with the background expectations of the employment society, and their independent behaviour beyond the confines of the workplace cannot be reliably located within the framework of the social status system, which is oriented towards the maximization of income, power, possessions and consumer goods, the lifestyle of the time pioneers represents a thorn in the side of the work-culture value system.

The envy of colleagues reveals the existence of a structural ambivalence in the monoculture of the employment society which is brought into the open by the emergence of the time pioneers. This structural ambivalence relates specifically to the relationship between orientation towards material security and orientation towards free time. In the value system of the employment culture, this relationship is permanently balanced by the circulation logic of performance output – income level – consumer opportunities, in which connection, the benchmark is clearly located in the sphere of work. However, in this respect, it is possible to discern a characteristic breach in the value system of the employment society, a breach which exacerbates this ambivalence and, from the standpoint of the time pioneers, finds expression in the envy of many of their colleagues and acquaintances. It can be discerned from the fact that the orientation of the time pioneers towards the sphere of their lives outside work becomes more pronounced and assumes a potentially antagonistic stance *towards* the value hierarchy of the employment society and the extent of their temporal involvement with work. The fact that this ambivalence impinges upon limits of the value system of the employment society in which it is trapped and can be articulated is evident from the excessive degree of aggression with which it is expressed: '*At first, there was a hell of a lot of bad blood. I started in April, and then it was summer, and on my four-hour day, I could knock off at quarter past eleven. I could go swimming while the others had to work. As you can imagine, they really hated me for it.*'

Which interpretive schemata of the cultural paradigm of the employment society characterize the lifestyle of the time pioneers? The most influential and most common is the reference to the central importance of employment to securing and fashioning material existence. This reference frequently heralds the abrupt termination of any critical consideration of the flexibilization of working time without any further argument. The claim now becomes: '*I can't afford it.*' It is indicated that within the compass of the value system of the employment society no further justification is required. This reveals that material security occupies an extremely important position in the priority system of the champions of the cultural paradigm of the employment society.

This interpretive schema is oriented towards income level and income stability, and its most prominent features are material references based on quantities of money. The obvious consequence of this is that, for example, during accounts of holidays, the amount of money spent is representative of the quality of the holiday *per se*, that money is not a means to an end, but becomes an end in itself, which attracts hostility from many of those on flexible working time. Salary size functions as a status symbol, and is thus utilized as a legitimate means of self-representation, finding corresponding communicative expression. With their wholly different styles of time utilization, holiday and consumer behaviour, time pioneers do not conform to this model, and in consequence they are excluded from the ideological community of the monoculture of the employment society.

For the cultural paradigm of the employment society, life revolves around employment, as the time pioneers discover from the discrimination with which they are confronted: '*My boss accuses me of looking upon my work as a part-time job, of really having my mind on something else altogether, but that's not true.*' Many of those on flexible working time are accused of not needing to work, of, as it were, failing to grasp the *gravitas* of work and treating it as an element of fun and a pastime. Male time pioneers in particular fail in their attempts to provide a credible explanation for working shorter hours. The dominant role of work in the cultural paradigm of the employment society is most evident from the fact that it is made the gauge of the very right to exist. The champions of this dominant employment culture demonstrate that they base their lives on the guarantor of security that is represented by the benefits of the employment system, and organize their private and working lives in accordance with this logic: deferring of personal needs, reaping the rewards of their toil and moil in retirement, subjecting themselves to the standardizations of working life, and increasing their standard of living via continuous salary increases, etc. Work is evaluated in accordance with the historical, socially conventional standardizations prevailing at any one time. Against the measurable backdrop of quantifiable and objectifiable job performance, deviations from the norm are only 'permitted' in those cases where free time is utilized for the purpose of other work. Otherwise, the individual is guilty of being a sluggard, a good-for-nothing or a parasite.

In the case of male time pioneers, this generally issues in moral, and sometimes also in occupational, disqualification. According to the criterion of full-time male employment, flexible working rates as deficient. From the standpoint of time, there is a lack of any suitable male role assignations which are not devoted to the pursuit of paid employment, and in consequence, men on flexible working time are particularly denied any form of moral recognition. In contrast, the situation is less harsh for women who work flexible hours due to the existence of appropriate female role assignations in the form of housework, family responsibilities and consumption-related work.

The cultural paradigm of the employment society also prescribes time utilization techniques, in other words, it determines how and where time is to be spent constructively, and in this context time is focused exclusively upon work. The time pioneers cite this as the main reason for the problems which they encounter in communicating their way of life to their full-time colleagues at work. The time pioneers repeatedly discover that their concept of time is absent from the priority system of the dominant employment culture. Their colleagues cannot imagine what time pioneers do with 'all their free time'. One time pioneer paraphrases this inability in the following words: '*When I turn up on Tuesdays, they ask me about everything I did on the Monday. And when I knock off, they ask me what I'll be doing tomorrow.*' As for the utilization of time not spent in the pursuit of employment, in other words, the independent utilization of free time, the horizon of the employment-related background assumptions is firmly delineated. As far as this subject in particular is concerned, the work-fixated meaning system proves virtually impermeable, its normative claim to validity being firmly anchored in society. It bestows upon employment the exaggerated status of being an end in itself, and as the dominant standard schema, it remains immune to scrutiny.

The time pioneers ascribe the difficulties which they encounter with the norms of the employment culture to the stability and validity of the following *interpretive schemata*:

- that only full-time work guarantees the fulfilment of material needs and banishes existential fears; that job performance is manifested in terms of amounts of money;
- that life revolves around employment;
- that work is the measure of the right to exist;
- that overall lifestyle is characterized by employment roles;
- that the bestowal of respect and moral recognition is contingent upon full-time work;
- that the concept of free time is determined by work.

These interpretive schemata constitute the principal interpretations and background assumptions which are employed to assess the lifestyle of the time pioneers.

The standards of the cultural paradigm of the employment society particularly come into play where the issues at stake are self-representation and the articulation of the meaning horizons of the lifestyle of the time pioneers. Discussions on the subject of the lives they lead on flexible working hours provoke envy, outbursts of aggression, or a lack of understanding. The thematization constraints resulting from the plausibilization of their world-view issue in further misunderstandings and thus, rapidly and almost inevitably, in direct confrontation or, characteristically, in a breakdown in communications. The time pioneers impinge upon some of the sore points of the cultural paradigm of the employment society: '*After a while, my colleagues notice that I work shorter hours, and one day they finally reach the point of asking me what else I do besides. I've noticed that they don't understand that I only work here and haven't got a part-time job somewhere else. And because people can't grasp that fact, one day, I just started inventing things to tell them.*'

For all intents and purposes, there is no point in the time pioneers entering into discussions because their colleagues simply fail to 'grasp' the activity orientations and evaluation schemata which are at play. There is little in common between the meaning horizons and experiences of a lifestyle predicated upon the schemata of the monoculture of the employment society and those of the lifestyle of a time pioneer. The comprehension problems should be regarded as cultural communication problems: they relate to different meaning schemata and cultural priority systems. The conditions for salutary understanding, the reciprocity of perspectives and the coincidence of priority systems are difficult to create within the context of the work situation. Whenever there are serious problems in conveying the knowledge which each party is purported to possess, and whenever unimpugned background assumptions can no longer be adequately secured, communication at the workplace becomes either fraught with conflict or is abandoned altogether.

From this it can be concluded that the specific cultural interpretive schemata of the time pioneers are indications of an independent lifestyle which is considerably different from the dominant work-fixated criteria of lifestyle with which it coexists in a state of conflict-laden tension. This cultural perspective heralds the emergence of a new independent form of involvement in working life. This new form leads to a situation in which the time pioneers are unable to justify their conception of life, which also comprises their specific involvement in working life, within the traditional context of the workplace. In view of the fact that current organizational structures do not provide the means for solving such difficulties of their own accord,

the emergence of the interpretive schemata of the time pioneers constitutes the latent imposition of excessive demands upon the problem
structure of the work situation.

The expeditious abandonment at the workplace of understanding
and discussions on the subject of the lifestyle of the time pioneers is
clear evidence of the fact that the monocultural interpretive system of
the employment society is characterized by a low level of flexibility
and rigid demarcation lines. In the face of a way of life which does
not conform to the logic of full-time employment, its meaning
schemata are isolated, and, as far as the communicatory endeavours
of its own priority system are concerned, the scope of its horizons is
reduced to zero. The representatives of the cultural paradigm of the
employment society do not problematize their own interpretive
schemata within the scope of communicatory situations at the workplace; the self-explanatory is not called into question. The validity of
the interpretive system of the employment society is protected and its
inflexibility is reinforced, with the result that deviations not only
require justification from the very outset, but are also disqualified on
moral grounds. The barriers to a meaningful understanding between
time pioneers and champions of the cultural paradigm of the employment society are reinforced and therefore take a dramatic expression.

At this juncture, it is necessary to pose the following critical
questions: what are the consequences of a conflict- and tension-laden
edifice comprising representatives of different cultural perspectives,
particularly within the context of the workplace? What attitudes do
they adopt towards each other? Those concerned are under the
compulsion to tolerate each other's presence at least to the extent
that, from the standpoint of the organizational objectives, the conti-
nuance of operations is assured. Given this, attention focuses on their
mutual reactions and processes of behavioural adaptation, and on the
development of new activity orientations and strategies at the workplace. In this context, we take as our point of departure our empirical
normal scenario that the culture of the employment society has an
iron grip on the development of the organizational structure. Responsibility for securing functional postulates in line with management
concepts extending beyond the horizons of the various different
meaning schemata and cultural orientations of the workforce falls to
this structure.

In view of the fact that, within the ambit of the workplace, it is
largely the cultural paradigm of the employment society that determines which situational interpretations are appropriate and which
solutions to problems are accepted as correct, the time pioneers find

themselves on the defensive: *'If we were to behave like proselytizers and say to our colleagues: "why don't you have a go at working shorter hours like we do, you're all totally overworked", we would find ourselves out on our ears in no time. So it's just not on.'* The explicit impugnment of the prevailing assumptions of normality on the part of the time pioneers would result in their expulsion from the work-related, monocultural ideological community. The social monitoring system, which in the dichotomous structure of the interpretive system is expressed in terms of being 'in' and 'out', forecloses any impugnment of the value system of the employment society. Points of departure for a redefinition or a reinterpretation, along the lines of, for example, the argument that the normality of work in its present form could be different, are not even contemplated as a motive for changing the interpretive schemata.

Conscious and unconscious impugnments of the generally accepted value paradigm of the employment society are carefully registered and countered by means of the imposition of sanctions. In order to avoid conflicts, the time pioneers are required to maintain a quantitative check on their utterances of background convictions and their deployment of symbolic means of representation at the workplace: *'I'm very cautious. I say as little about myself as possible when I'm with my colleagues. I listen a great deal instead.'* The possible topics of conversation are therefore limited and remain at the level of the innocuous; any subjects which attract expressions of background convictions are to be avoided at all costs. Therefore, if they wish to avoid conflicts, it is necessary for the time pioneers to ensure that they are fully aware of the prevailing role expectations and behavioural monitoring procedures.

The denials of many time pioneers that they engage in any form of supplementary, illicit or intensive DIY work meet with disbelief. Thus, there is virtually no other course open to them than either consistently to avoid such topics at the workplace (which is almost impossible), or simply to lie. In order to forestall any intrusive enquiries, many time pioneers admit – untruthfully – to pursuing other activities outside the time in which they are engaged in employment, such as supposedly having to work part-time or meet considerable private commitments; in other words, as far as possible, they refer to activities for which no further justification is required.

The normality assumptions of the industrial time structures are the prime cause of the problems which the time pioneers encounter in communicating their lifestyle. The invention of supplementary work and the conscious deployment of 'lies' at the workplace have the function of removing the obligation to provide justification, and of feigning agreement with the cultural validity standards of the employment society. The fact that the time pioneers not only experience the restrictions of the cultural paradigm of the employment society at the workplace, but also endeavour to provide an explanation for them, is revealed by their reflexive attitude to the paradigm, the conditions and circumstances of which they problematize and analyse (see also section 4.3).

The time pioneers are faced with the problem of having to cope with expectations, convictions and evaluations which are not entirely compatible, particularly at the workplace. There is a gradual process of dissociation from the normative role expectations of the working environment. This dissociation provides the time pioneers with the opportunity to reject the claim to exclusivity made by the reality of the employment culture in favour of their own reality, and of placing the self above both these reality structures.[5] This involves the initiation of a process of dissociation from the general expectational structures of work, the reduction of the affective ego-achievements of role identification, and the construal of role performance which emphasizes the fulfilment of task-oriented requirements. The adequate fulfilment of the job assignments which are allocated to them functions as an area of strategic retreat for the time pioneers in the face of unreasonable demands and claims to their loyalty on the part of their employers.

The development of role distance tackles the contradictions which arise out of the differences between the role expectations of the employer and those of the time pioneers. The appearance of these conflicting perspectives is attributable to the reorientation of some of the interpretive schemata of the employment society, which have, however, not yet met with any acknowledgement within the working environment. The role-distance approach towards overcoming them is effected in the tension-laden ambivalence between commitment *to* work and dissociation *from* the working environment.

The capacity for role-distance is closely linked to the process of subject-centring whose goal is the attainment of a greater level of autonomy and independence. In order to render role dissociation tolerable, the time pioneers resort to the deployment of techniques of interpretation-related delimitation of areas of life and segmentation of value spheres. In spite of all their efforts at exercising self-control, many time pioneers are torn between these contradictions: '*It was a very stressful situation because, somehow, that meant I was living in two worlds, and I found it really awful.*' Living in two worlds requires the exercise of self-control. Given that in addition, as is the case here, the separation is symbolized by different types of clothing, this double life affects the entire disposition of this time pioneer. It is precisely the clash between different cultural perspectives that is the motivating factor behind the decision of the time pioneers to enhance the level of reconciliation between their working and private lives via the flexibilization of their working time, and to seek a job in which the clash between the contradictions of different systems is less pronounced.

In the context of the workplace, the orientation of the time pioneers between commitment and dissociation leads to irritating paradoxes. The job situation of the time pioneers is characterized by a contradictory, tension-laden relationship between a high level of job commitment and dissociation from the working environment, and from the normative expectations and meaning structures of the cultural paradigm of the employment society. The dissociation of the time pioneers finds expression in the rejection of certain incorporative demands on the part of their employers. However, the employers themselves are also guilty of exacerbating the dissociation of the time pioneers, frequently branding them as outsiders, and denying them social standing and recognition.

The contradiction inherent in the manner in which the time pioneers are incorporated into the companies at which they are employed produces the following catalogue of irritating paradoxes which characterize the situation of the time pioneers from the standpoint of the employment society:

- in spite of the fact that they suffer a loss of income, an objectively greater work load and occupational discrimination, the time pioneers are passionate and self-assured champions and practitioners of their form of flexibilized working time;
- they are fully aware of the intensification to which they are subjected, but undermine it by means of the specific form of work participation which they adopt, thus preventing the consequences of such intensification from exerting an excessive influence upon the way in which they organize their lives as a whole; their aggressive struggle for flexible working time is not accompanied by any obtrusive ambitions of changing the environment of their workplace or the character of work as such;
- they dissociate themselves from their working environment, but allow themselves to be used for company purposes and objectives;
- in so doing, they underpin the institutionalization of a form of work which does not count them among its number;

- in spite of the fact that they suffer occupational discrimination and moral disqualification, they do not place any inferior or negative interpretation upon their flexible form of employment, regarding it instead as an opportunity for fashioning their lives along more satisfactory lines.

These paradoxes are manifestations of new forms of work-related interpretive schemata and work-culture perspectives occasioned by the crisis of the value system of the employment society and lent new shape by flexible forms of working time and the specific lifestyle of the time pioneers. The particular incorporation of the time pioneers into the working environment is the result of the clash between the interpretive schemata of the time pioneers and the prevailing work-culture interpretive schema. In this connection, the development of the meaning horizon and attitudes to work of the time pioneers is not primarily attributable to the changes which the industrial employment system or the character of work have undergone; essentially, it derives from the stubbornness inhering in the character of cultural interpretive schemata.

4 The Changed Relationship between Money and Time

The group of interviewees at the centre of this study comprises sole earners in employment and, as a result, the growth in their free time and in the time that they have at their own disposal is directly reflected in a loss of income. In view of the fact that for our interviewees the flexibilization of working time entailed the 'voluntary compulsion' to relinquish part of their income,[1] the money–time relationship should be regarded as a central variable in the way in which those on flexible working time organize their lives. In relation to time gained, what role do earnings assume as the basis of material security? What are the consequences of the reduction in income suffered by the time pioneers?

The main function of the size of disposable income is to act (alongside other factors such as household type, available resources and socioeconomic environment) as the point of departure for co-determining the opportunity structure of lifestyle. However, this should not be interpreted as indicative of economic determination, but of the fact that it maps out situations in life in advance by either paving the way for or foreclosing *ab initio* certain formative opportunities. The typical characteristics of the perception and realization of these formative options bear the hallmark of the socio-economic environment, and become established as permanent possessions.

For those in dependent employment, the central source of material wealth at their individual disposal is constituted by their earnings. Money is the most common medium of association with material wealth. In modern society, the universal convertibility of money bestows upon it a high degree of social priority, and it paves the way for the universal quantification of life circumstances. According to interest or need, it can be exchanged for goods or services. In this sense, it can be said that the logic of money exercises the dominant formative social influence upon life circumstances. Individual possession of money facilitates access to social wealth and social services; as a material reserve, it affords additional protection against risks which threaten personal existence.

In accepting a reduction in income in favour of both a quantitative increase in the amount of time at their autonomous disposal and, as we shall see, a qualitative increase in their experience of time, the time pioneers give a clear indication of the high degree of relevance which additional free time has for their lifestyle. The high level of importance attached to free time is not only reflected in a reduction in income, but also in household management methods.

4.1 The complex role of reduced income

All practitioners of flexibilization are directly and immediately dependent upon earned income. Some women receive additional maintenance payments for their children, but such payments cannot be regarded as significant financial supplements to the sums of money at their individual disposal. Some can fall back upon fairly small amounts of savings, but these function as contingency reserves and do not constitute any relief from the pressure to work. Rather surprisingly, we found that the scale of reduction in working time is dependent neither upon income size in absolute terms nor upon any particular household type. Individuals requiring a greater amount of time at their autonomous disposal reduce their working time to an extent where they retain a tolerable level of financial security which will continue to safeguard their well-being, irrespective of whether they are earning full or reduced income. Thus, the amount of time by which working hours are reduced can vary greatly between one individual and another, and reduction by no means presupposes a large income.

It is common to all the time pioneers that their decision to opt for shorter working time was preceded by and predicated upon meticulous financial calculations. The problem of being forced to make shift with less money is a permanent theme in the priority structures of those working flexible time. The time pioneers adduce a plurality of examples in evidence of their perception of economical control of expenditure as a vital element of their way of life. The income which they earn after flexibilization constitutes the basic foundation upon which to finance their way of life. Although it does exercise a confiderable influence upon their way of life, it does not influence their social habits to the extent that, for example, they assume the guise of ascetics, cheeseparers or niggards. Economy is not an end in itself; rather, it is an expression of the pragmatic management of the available financial means.

A particular characteristic of the lifestyle of the time pioneers is their determined attempt not only to secure the flexibilization of their working time, but also to make economies in keeping with the reduction in their income, and to gear their housekeeping arrangements accordingly. Top priority is afforded to the flexibilization of their working time. It is frequently the case that it is not possible to foresee whether or not the reduced amount of earned income will actually suffice to meet essential requirements, and thus the first step towards working shorter hours is followed by an 'experimental phase' whose purpose is to establish the tolerable balance between the time requirements and the material aspirations of the individual. The money–time relationship, in other words, the relationship between the increase in the amount of time at the autonomous disposal of individuals and the size of their available income, is subsequently revised on the basis of these experiences. This relationship, established on the basis of subjective criteria, forms the yardstick for determining both free time requirements and the appropriate method of retrenchment.

The question now arises as to the importance of material security in the priority structures of the time pioneers for reducing existential threats and securing pension rights. Material security, the guarantee of which is a secure job (with a subjectively satisfactory level of remuneration), does not have the same degree of importance for all our interviewees. However, it is possible to identify *two types* of time pioneer whose initial distinguishing feature is the specific horizon of their experiences. The degree of subjective value which is placed upon material security depends very closely upon the specific course which the life of an individual has taken: whether it has consistently followed a secure path, or whether it has been characterized by periods of discontinuity and reorientation.

Characteristically, greatest value is placed upon the aspect of material security by those who already have a secure job, who have completed the transition from vocational training to occupational practice relatively smoothly, and who have not changed their occupation in the meantime. They take as their orientational basis the security provided by a permanent job, though, rather than absolutizing this security, they combine it with their specific task-oriented attitude towards work and relate it to the principle of variety. They recognize the basic importance of stable employment and the long-term protec- tion of their livelihood, namely, to safeguard the foundations of their existence, and that this is the only basis upon which it is possible to develop and explore interests of their own choosing. There can be no recreation without a secure foundation.

The material cushion provided by a secure job is of less existential importance to those employees who have already changed jobs several times. This attitude correlates with a pronounced cognitive dissociation from the sphere of work, a dissociation which reflects the social organization of work and relates it to the way in which over- all society functions. It is firmly rooted in relevant societal images, and relativizes existential fears about redundancy. Experience of frequent changes of job increases self-confidence and reduces affec- tual preoccupations with security-consciousness. This type of time pioneer does not feel that precarious financial security constitutes a threat: '*I like doing something different every now and again. That also explains my employment history. I mean, I've never done any- thing for more than five years, and I've always continually changed jobs. I've changed jobs for a bit more security, but I'd still change jobs even if there was a better than even chance of being made redundant. Drudgery and routine are two things I can't abide.*'

It is possible to draw a synoptical distinction between these two types of time pioneer by investigating the extent to which orientation towards material security is established in their life plans: is top priority afforded to risk reduction as an independent and affectual basic orientation, or – against the backdrop of their own empirical values and the 'tarnished' legitimacy of the value schema of the employment society – do risk acceptance and variety take pride of place in the planning hierarchy?

However, in the planning hierarchy of all the time pioneers, the money which they earn by selling their labour and their working time is of the same crucial importance in securing the independence and autonomy of their way of life. Though this should not be regarded as something which is a self-evident fact – take the typical secondary wage earners, for example – the endeavours on the part of the time pioneers to increase the amount of time at their autonomous disposal also correlate with their orientation towards financial independence: '*You see, I've always tried to avoid being a financial burden on anyone, to stay out of debt in spite of having a low income, and to do the things I want to do without any outside help.*' The interest on the part of the time pioneers in financial independence and their interest in more time at their autonomous disposal are closely inter-related. For this reason, it is necessary for the time pioneers to reduce their material aspirations, since it is highly unlikely that both these objectives can be accomplished through the obligation to work.

The high degree of importance which the time pioneers attach to time over which they enjoy autonomous rights of disposal becomes particularly apparent in the light of the fact that as a basic orienta-tion, great emphasis is placed upon a self-reliant lifestyle, and that their lifestyle is directly affected by loss of income in the form of financial restrictions, which in some cases are quite considerable. Under these circumstances, 'having more time for themselves' rather than a certain level of income becomes the fixed variable of lifestyle organization. The extent to which loss of income is able to affect the way in which the time pioneers fashion their lives also largely depends upon whether or not individuals have possessions and other resources of their own upon which to fall back. The resources in the socio-spatial environment of the time pioneers, and the opportunities available to them for accessing such resources, are the factors which primarily assume the function of a structural condition of lifestyle. The lower the income level relative to the size of the household, the more dependent is the way in which the time pioneers organize their lives on the socio-spatial infrastructure of the environment, and the more sensitive it is to structural changes. This (materially and exis-tentially) precarious arrangement of the way of life of the time pioneers is closely related to the readiness of the individual time pioneers to take risks.

More and more, the time pioneers fall back upon networks of connections among relatives and friends. This might mean, for example, borrowing a car or DIY equipment free of charge from a friend or a relative, organizing a holiday via an 'accommodation system' of acquaintances, or accepting 'neighbourhood assistance' with repairs and improvements in exchange for a symbolic considera-tion, all of which are possible ways of maintaining living expenses at a low level. The additional time which the time pioneers have on their hands in consequence of flexibilization is also utilized explicitly for the purpose of expanding and intensifying their communicative links and their contacts in social networks, as a result of which they come under increasing obligation to render reciprocal assistance. The fact that the time pioneers belong to a network of social contacts means that they have the opportunity to fall back upon a communal pool of resources. In order to provide an additional safeguard for their lifestyle and something of a cushion for their loss of income, this is an opportunity which the time pioneers frequently exploit.

Location of residence is also an important lifestyle resource for the time pioneers. Their lifestyle is distance-sensitive: location of residence in relation to the spatial removal from their place of work, to their socio-economic environment and to their social network becomes a relevant structural condition of lifestyle, from which the time pioneers develop a capacity for the strategic management of these resources.

4.2 The reorganization of household management

Upon the onset of the flexibilization of their working time, the time pioneers discover that they are also forced to reorganize their household management arrangements. We now analyse the household management routines which conflict with the changed interpretive schemata of the time pioneers. The time pioneers discover that domestic work is also in need of change and reorganization, and that under no circumstances should it be allowed to assume the function of simply occupying residual time. Thus, the performance of domestic work is increasingly determined by the basic orientation of the time pioneers, which encompasses the daily schedule, to incorporate the most flexible and disposable time structures possible into their everyday lives. In this connection, domestic work is not so much performed against the background of a reduced income level as oriented towards the generation of subjective temporal affluence.

The time pioneers attempt to reduce the extent to which daily domestic work accumulates, and to vary the times of the day in which they perform domestic work more in accordance with 'disposition and inclination'. This time structuring creates a 'better feeling', and the obligatory character of domestic work recedes. Wherever possible, household chores are not performed in compliance with the 'good housewife principle' according to some internalized, rigid schema in which tidiness and sterile cleanliness are elevated to the status of ends in themselves. The time pioneers consciously reject as supererogatory any self-sustaining increase in the quality of how domestic work is performed. It is not their intention that domestic work should perpetuate the ossified virtues of the working environment, nor that it should compensate for the reduction in the amount of time in which they are engaged in work. The consequence of this derogation from the importance of household chores is that communicative concerns and interactive associations come to the fore.

The time pioneers are at pains to perform household chores in such a manner that on the one hand, they satisfy the subjective requirements (which determine the quality of the domestic work), and that, on the other, they generate temporal affluence (which determines the amount of time spent performing the domestic work). As a result of this flexible approach and the reduction in the obligatory character of many household chores, there is a subjective reduction in the amount of energy expended in the performance of domestic work.

The same principle of reducing time commitment constraints is underpinned specifically by the provision of electrical household appliances. The electrical household appliances most frequently utilized are those which facilitate the improved performance of domestic work and greater household productivity, and thus also compensate for the reduction in income suffered by the time pioneers. However, the time pioneers are opposed to a particular form of consumption-related work which is based upon the automatization and capitalization of household production, and thus, if we accept the theories propounded in the relevant studies (see Becker 1965; Joerges 1981, 1983, 1985; Klein 1983), increasingly rationalizes household production. Beyond certain basic items of equipment, the time pioneers consistently reject the utilization of electrical appliances in the home. For the time pioneers, cost-intensive electrical household appliances are only afforded (limited) consideration insofar as they underpin disposable time structures, do not entail an excessive degree of time commitment, and increase the flexibility of household production (for example, a maintenance-free deep freezer as opposed to a grill requiring frequent cleaning and maintenance, etc.).

If the low aspiration level of some time pioneers renders them resistant from the outset to the 'temptation' to automate domestic work, which merely involves the commitment of more financial resources, other time pioneers adopt an extremely reflexive and discriminating attitude towards the immanent captive influence of household technology. These time pioneers attribute to household technology a great capacity for generating a certain concatenation of sequences of activity and consequential effects involving increased financial expenditure and time commitment. They recognize the danger that household technology will then no longer be utilized as a means to an end, but as an end in itself, which in their opinion, owing to the high maintenance levels involved, will entail the commitment of too much time and require a greater proportion of their income. Although these time pioneers analyse electrical household appliances in the context of their utilization, this does not mean that they have a negative attitude towards technology.

For the time pioneers, the fact that they have the opportunity of effecting disposable time management has the advantage of enabling them to improve the coordination of their consumer activities from the standpoint of time, and to pursue these activities on as anti-cyclical and asynchronous a basis as possible with regard to the prevailing peak times. In other words, they make thorough price comparisons or, for example, go shopping in the mornings when better advisory and customer services are available and they are able to select the items which they wish to purchase at leisure. This facilitates the avoidance of time shortages and the achievement of a qualitatively greater level of efficiency in less time and at less expense: '*I cope pretty well now with the fact that I've got so much free time on my hands because I've got to know the advantages. Take shopping, I mean, the fact that you can go shopping when the shops are pretty empty, and you soon find out when that is. And the fact that, for example, the underground is not as packed when you go to town.*' Increasingly, the experiential quality of consumption-related work itself also comes to the fore. The time pioneers assert that for them, this style of consumerism improves the money–time relationship.

Overall, the time pioneers are distinctly opposed to a goods- and capital-intensive style of consumerism. Their consumer strategy is geared towards the maintenance of their material standard of living and the protection of their greater level of temporal autonomy.

Given that the time pioneers do not utilize the increased amount of time at their autonomous disposal for performing more domestic and consumption-related work, nor for engaging in more DIY work in order to enhance the level of household production, the question arises whether or not they utilize the time for self-improvement purposes, for the pursuit of occupational and qualificational activities. The reason for this is that from their job-content and task-oriented attitude towards work and their consumer strategy of making cheaper purchases by means of careful selection and improved sources of information, it can be supposed that the lifestyle of the time pioneers is characterized by the expansion of qualificational activities.

The time which the time pioneers have at their autonomous disposal is preponderantly utilized for the purposes of developing and differentiating their own interests. On the one hand, more free time frequently enables individuals to pursue their interests or develop particular hobbies; on the other, this enlivens the way in which they fashion their lives. Thus the interests which are pursued often develop self-reinforcing tendencies extending beyond the activity as a hobby. On occasion, the intensification of their own interests on the part of the time pioneers assumes the character of true professionalization, by means of which skills and abilities are developed which are offered for public consumption (particularly in the field of art), or directly for sale in the open market. In this respect, they are subsequently utilized for the purposes of embarking upon a new career, or for preparing for self-employment. The achievement of this qualificational effect is due partly to the fact that the time pioneers invest subjectively valuable time in the development of their own fields of interest. Equally the specific development of the work-related interpretive schemata creates conditions which encourage the time pioneers to let themselves follow the self-reinforcing tendencies of their involvement with these fields of interest.

Some of the time pioneers pursue a certain amount of DIY work (mainly gardening). In the main, such activities are pursued where appropriate spatial conditions exist. Although in the case of one time pioneer his house in the country with a barn, a large garden and a greenhouse entails a great deal of DIY and gardening work, such work is defined as purposeful activity and, from the standpoint of time structure, it is integrated into the overall organization of his life as a contrast to the employment sphere.

Thus, the free time gained as a result of the flexibilization of working time is also utilized for the purpose of DIY work. Although this facilitates a slight reduction in living costs, from an economic and rational standpoint, the time pioneers do not systematically utilize DIY work as a substitute for earned income. However, neither is the additional free time invested in 'leisure time' in the sense of intensive or active leisure-time management, or (from the pedagogical standpoint) leisure-time management which is normatively recognized as useful. For the time pioneers, the latter would amount to nothing less than the continuation of economically coloured time structures.

At core, household management and consumption are based upon the relationship between time expenditure and (subjectively gauged) temporal affluence. The reason for this is that the free time, for the sake of which the time pioneers flexibilized their working time, seems to them to be much too precious to re-encumber with the time requirements of other forms of work. We can now establish with a greater degree of clarity that money and time are placed in a position of direct internal competition. The money–time convertibility of a plurality of activities and goods is evaluated in accordance with a subjective yardstick relating to the time expenditure involved. The level of time commitment involved in the pursuit of activities and the purchase of consumer goods is an indication of an important, implicitly activist moment in the way in which the time pioneers organize their lifestyle. Domestic and consumption-related work are geared towards a low and flexibly manageable level of time commitment. They are intended to avoid any concatenations of circumstances requiring strict time settings and rigid time-management principles. They underpin a flexible and disposable deployment of activity, and constitute an important crystallizing point of lifestyle which is a major co-determinant of household management and consumption methods.

The high value which the time pioneers place upon having more time at their own disposal in relation to their material standard of living is an expression of a specific marginal utility of the money–time relationship. Beyond the amount of time in which the time pioneers are required to engage in employment and consumption-related work in order to finance and obtain the necessities of life, there is a dramatic reduction in the use of the achieveable income level for the purpose of enhancing the quality of life. The increase in income level which can be achieved through employment rapidly loses its value in the face of the disadvantages involved. The evaluative criterion of economic activity is the attainable level of subjective temporal affluence.

Although the time gained by reducing the time spent in work is directly reflected in the reduction in income suffered by the time pioneers, the resulting subjective temporal affluence can be considerably increased by the flexible timing of work. In consequence, the lifestyle-specific marginal utility of the time pioneers permits a further reduction in their income levels. This also explains why the time pioneers do not consider that the reduction in their income level and material standard of living resulting from the flexibilization of their working time constitutes a deterioration in their situation in life.

The economic concept of 'marginal utility' also explains why reduced temporal commitment to employment is not necessarily grounded on a lower level of performance motivation. The willingness to work of the time pioneers may be equal to that of many a careerist or 'overtime fanatic', but from a certain level onwards, income growth levels are no longer any motivation for them to accept the burden of additional work. This comparison between the perceived costs of employment and the benefit gained proves to be a rational and plausible approach. As a result of the fact that in its inherent dynamism the employment sphere encounters internal limi-tative factors and exposes contradictions, to some extent, it actually destroys the validity of the value orientations which underpin it.

The lifestyle of the time pioneers produces a specific, independent and economic type of household which is out of step with the sociolo-gical prognoses. In the context of the discussion concerning the conse-quences for household management of an across-the-board reduction in working hours, many prognoses confirm that the increase in the amount of time not devoted to employment would be utilized for the purpose of meeting requirements through self-sufficiency. In other words, the reduction in income would be compensated for by increased free-time productivity in the form of more intensive levels of DIY and consumption-related work.[2] Under the conditions of high income levels, there would be a shift in activities towards consumption-related work, with the result, so the theory contends, that the increase in free time would be utilized economically for the purpose of enhancing the efficiency of household production. And it is expected that, in turn, greater levels of household production will generate a reduced inclination to engage in paid work (Klein 1983: 115).

A line of argument which is thus geared towards the calculation of the economic advantages of household production therefore supports the theory that the private spheres of life also undergo increasing rationalization. The effect of the flexibilization of working time is seen in a further intensification of the rationalization induced by the employment sphere. This rationalization generates a tendency towards the development of more purpose-specific activities in both private and working lives, and requires a greater degree of appro-priate effort, intensified economizing of resources, and improved coordination levels (Jurczyk et al. 1985: 155f). According to this theory, the temptation for people to organize their lifestyles along the lines of a commercial enterprise is intensifying and gaining ground.

However, in contrast, the lifestyle of the time pioneers reveals no affinity with the intensification of DIY work for the purpose of enhancing household productivity. The reason for this lies in the characteristic time structure upon which their lifestyle is predicated and which requires a form of economizing which does not invest the increase in the amount of time at their own disposal in some inten-sified shadow-economic activity. The time pioneers wish to reduce the reach of the long arm of work. At the same time, by means of the flexibilization of their working time, they lessen the extent of the time commitment involved in various forms of activity throughout the entire day. The change in their working time provides them with scope for pursuing other activities, the possibilities of which they both recognize and exploit. The extent to which the lifestyle of the time pioneers fails to conform to a work society way of thinking is revealed by the fact that their additional free time is not utilized to replace their loss of income, nor to redress or enhance their social status, etc., by means of appropriate free-time activities.

It is difficult to capture the lifestyle of the time pioneers using an approach based upon a rationalistic theory, since this completely overlooks the essential constitutional element of this lifestyle: specific time structuring. The fact that these sociological approaches are unable to identify the characteristic feature of the lifestyle of the time pioneers with a sufficient degree of adequacy lends credence to our analytical approach, namely, falling back upon the level of the socio-cultural construction of lifestyles, and the constitution of interpretive schemata. This explains why a whole battery of social indicators fails to identify and record the lifestyle of the time pioneers. Thus the voluntary character of the flexibilization of working time and the compulsion on the part of the time pioneers to increase the degree of self-control which they exercise over the way in which they fashion their lives invalidate any structural social or economic determinants upon which such social indicators are founded. In consequence, the lifestyle of the time pioneers remains outside the ken of traditional research; its characteristic feature as an independent lifestyle avoids detection by the indicator-based scrutiny of the social landscape, and it remains impervious to the scrutiny of the professional observers of the social world who have fixed their analytical gaze upon the permeation of almost every conceivable form of activity by economic principles and an increasingly work-like character.

4.3 Dissociation from the dominant dictates of money and time

The employment society is characterized by a specific relationship between money and time, an issue to which our time pioneers are also forced to devote some critical attention. We now investigate what role the socially dominant money–time relationship plays in the interpretive schemata of the time pioneers, and what status is assumed in the process by the universally recognized symbols of consumerism. By evaluating the attitude of the time pioneers towards symbolic consumer goods, we can obtain some information on the position of their lifestyle in the social structure. Generally speaking, the specific money–time relationship proves to be the coordinating point of internal structuring, and the time commitment quality of (symbolic) consumer goods and services proves to be the key to the normative consolidation of the lifestyle of the time pioneers. An examination of such symbols, which are an expression of achievement as the central legitimation principle of society, also reveals the extent to which individuals share the normative validity standards of this community of values.

The time pioneers view money–time convertibility from two perspectives: on the one hand, they thematize the utilization schemata and, on the other, they place particular importance upon the controlled management of money. The interpretive schemata thus become sensitized towards the relationship between time and money. In offering some carefully considered opinions upon this subject, the interviewees relate to a central social mechanism by means of which, in capitalist societies, time is exchanged for money. The money–time relationship is thematized by all time pioneers, though there are some differences in the degree of cognitive (and, to a lesser extent, normative) dissociation from this relationship.

In modern societies, the reciprocal, mutually dependent comparative relationship between time and money was initially generated by their direct convertibility ('time is money'). This relationship has since become generalized as the dominant systematic mechanism of sociation, and is now reflected throughout the whole of society as *shortage of time*.[3] It confronts individuals as an objectified relationship, a money–time dictate, and as an immanent schema whose captive influence it is difficult for them to escape.

The sociation mechanism of the direct convertibility of time and money also comprises a social relationship, since both represent scarce commodities via whose right of disposal and access arrangements power structures are developed. Money imparts influence, power and independence. On the other hand, the right of disposal over the fixing of times and the prescription of lengths of time affords those who possess this right the opportunity of determining the rhythm of their synchronization with other members of society, and of dictating specific time rhythms. Like money, time is valuable, but in terms of its character time is more specifically related to the subjective experience of time and the specific perception of time and – contingent upon this – more capable of qualitative enhancement. Time falls prey to the magnetism of money, under the supremacy of which money is able to prescribe the measure of time. A time structure which is infected with the logic of money generates a de-qualified time structure consisting of homogeneity, divisibility, predictability and linearity. The possession of money facilitates the saving and gaining of time, thus transforming time into a purchaseable commodity. Converting lifetime into working time in return for money generates financial assets which can be utilized in a multitude of ways. Conversely, they can also be utilized for saving time, since social working time is already inherent in many consumer goods, with the result that part of the purchase comprises the individual working time required for their production. In the case of those in employment, insofar as they have no other sources of income upon which to fall back, there is a direct, socially conveyed relationship between expended working time and earned income.

Time and money function as a resource and means of lifestyle determination. Depending upon whether individuals value money more highly than time, or time more highly than money, and upon whether they have one, both or neither of these resources at their free disposal, this fact finds expression in the development of different ways of life (see Klehm and Neumann 1985; Klehm et al. 1986). However, as a rule, under the conditions of the universal money–time dictate, ordinary employees have only one alternative open to them: the possession of either more time or more money.

Symbolic consumer goods represent secondary objectifications of meaning (Berger and Luckmann 1979: 88ff); they are indicative of socially recognized and universally binding meaning systems. The attitude which a lifestyle adopts towards these symbolic objects is also an expression of its legitimacy and social standing. Prestigious and symbolic consumer goods enjoying a high degree of social esteem and universal recognition function as distinguishing and demonstrative elements of social dissimilarity and inequality. Access to these consumer goods is regulated, preponderantly by means of material wealth, professional status and conventional power structures, and they define the status of social groupings. These symbolic objects are deliberately endowed with value and social associations which characterize the self-awareness and social identity of members of society, and therefore, as an element of social identity, exercise an influence upon human relationships and interaction. Thus they constitute an important aspect of self-interpretation, social status and socio-cultural identification. Their concrete employment initiates social identification and dissociation processes.

Given the fact that money is characterized by convertibility, substitutability and accumulability and is therefore an ideal instrument of power and social differentiation, the legitimacy of the logic of money also finds expression in the symbols of consumerism. The quantifiable quality of money generates an objective, non-personal relationship with activities and objects which is also reflected in the interpretive schemata of the members of society in that they absolutize prices, that is to say, they predicate their evaluations of goods on how much they cost. Price functions as a socially generalized standard, which is relatively simple to render socially visible. It is this logic of money that attracts the critical attention of the time pioneers. The practitioners of flexibilization recognize that frequently this logic exercises a captive influence which generates a certain way of life from which they must cognitively distance and distinguish themselves as a permanent contrastive backdrop – which will be maintained in the form of dissociation – in order to avoid their engulfment.

Money–time convertibility also reveals the attitude of the time pioneers towards the socially dominant role which money plays in the way of life of individuals: the specific economization and consumption methods adopted by individual time pioneers are rooted in their interpretive schemata. Their attention is focused upon certain commodities of the consumer goods industry. This is expressed with great clarity in their evaluations of certain consumer goods and strategies, in which the time pioneers reveal the difference between a lifestyle which is permeated by the logic of time rather than that of money. Thus, one time pioneer cites the example of her attempts to explain to her daughter how insufficient free time inevitably generates certain forms of expenditure: '*People who work 40 hours a week are very discontented, so they go out for slap-up meals and spend a packet. They flog themselves to death, and by way of compensation, they want to treat themselves to something special. So they play indoor tennis, and will pay 60 marks for a meal without batting an eyelid.*'

The time pioneers counter the obsession with price with the experiential quality of activities: they are more interested in 'experiencing something'.[4] One particular peg upon which to hang the distinction between their lifestyle and others is the thematization of the role of money, and how lifestyles are tailored to suit the universal social esteem enjoyed by money. The circulation logic of the value system of the employment society (work–career–income level–consumer goods as status symbols) is a particular target for criticism. These are the cachets which one time pioneer, without referring to anyone in particular, typically ascribes to society at large: '*They've got no idea how to do something useful with their time because they've never done anything useful with it and they're not used to doing anything useful with it. They see everything solely in terms of consumption or solely in terms of work. They don't believe that there is such a thing as really meaningful free-time activities.*' These comments are also an expression of the fact that the value association of the time pioneers is becoming dissociated from money symbols which function as prestige indicators. The sensitization of their interpretive schemata towards the money–time relationship emphasizes the relevance of money as a formative principle impinging upon everyday life. This thematization is an important precondition for developing different time management techniques and value associations with which to organize their lifestyle.

In changing their working time, the time pioneers attack the central social mechanism of the direct convertibility of time and money. At present, those who possess money are able to postpone decisions which affect the future, since money symbolizes the fact that individuals have an opportunity of achieving a high quality of life, status and power, and of securing provision for their old age. The time pioneers reduce this future horizon in order to lessen the structural impact of the money–time dictate on their present lives. However, they exploit and develop time as their main resource for shaping their lives. In consequence, time enters into competition with money and the implications associated with it; time is utilized as an alternative option.

The symbolic function of the value of consumer goods, which can be quantified and thus hierarchically arranged by price, is to indicate the legitimacy of society's money logic. The cognitive and normative dissociation from this cultural reference system on the part of the time pioneers is also an attempt to liberate themselves from the appropriation strategies of society which this logic induces.

In order to emancipate the way in which they fashion their lives from the money–time dictate, which is one of the central crystallizing points of their lifestyle, the time pioneers impugn the legitimacy of the dominant lifestyle characterized by the logic of money. The detached attitude of the time pioneers towards status symbols and the convertibility of money and time is a clear indication of their rejection of the social significance which these factors convey. This reveals a world-view which bestows only limited recognition upon the validity of the institutional order which these symbols represent, and which from the subjective standpoint regards the same institutional order as being of little relevance. In this context, the social position of the lifestyle of the time pioneers is located at the periphery of society rather than at its core.

In consequence of the dissociation of the time pioneers from the dominant value system of the employment society, they can only justify their lifestyle by means of a high degree of argumentational effort. The argumentational backdrop against which they seek to delineate the normative aspects of their lifestyle is provided by certain distinctive symbols which have a sound claim to legitimacy. However, insofar as the lifestyle of the time pioneers perceives and reassesses characteristic fault lines in the interpretive schemata of the employment society, the peripheral position of this lifestyle will assume a pioneering role in initiating radical changes in the employment society.

4.4 The resistance to change of ingrained consumption models

The loss of income suffered by the time pioneers in the wake of shorter working hours frequently assumes considerable proportions, and can result in a 50 per cent reduction in their gross income level in one fell swoop. Depending on the particular features of the individual situation, within a short period of time, the time pioneers experience a sharp drop in their standard of living and considerable disruption to their habitual way of life, which necessitate the revision of their usual activities. We now focus our attention on reconstructing the development of the interpretive priorities underlying the reduction in the income and the revision of the consumption schemata of the time pioneers.

If we pose the question as to how the time pioneers arrive at their lifestyle-specific form of economizing, we can distinguish two different types: those who during the course of their sociation process have adopted low material aspirations as their unimpugned basic orientation, and those who experience difficulty in effecting the revision of their consumer habits necessitated by the reduction in their income level.

It is a characteristic feature of the representatives of the first type that the interpretive schemata which developed during the sociation process do not gear their lives towards the maximization of their income level and career opportunities, or towards lavish consumer habits. They usually develop a basic attitude which is characterized by relatively low material aspirations and frugal consumer habits. In consequence, it is easier for them to effect the transition to shorter working hours, and the problems which they face as a result of the reduction in their income level do not appear especially daunting.

The problem of subsisting on a lower income is swiftly overcome: *'And I've got no financial problems either. You see, I never really developed much in the way of material aspirations, thank God.'*

In line with the other core factors of interpretive schemata, frugal money management is already firmly established in the meaning schema of the lifestyle of this type of time pioneer, and identified as self-evident. In this case, managing on low income levels was habitualized during earlier biographical phases and does not have the character of the dominant problem in life which only made its presence felt with the advent of working time flexibilization.

In the case of the representatives of the first type of time pioneer, it has been noted that their basic attitude is characterized by – wholly conscious – low material aspirations, and that their routine management technique consists of cutting their cloth accordingly. In contrast, the representatives of the second type of time pioneer encounter serious difficulties in managing on their voluntarily reduced income levels. In the face of ingrained consumer habits resistant to change, making ends meet on less income generates serious problems, even in the case of time pioneers who have already experimented with the practice of subsisting on relatively low consumption levels over a lengthy period of time.

The resistance to change of habitualized consumption schemata which are too extravagant *vis-à-vis* reduced income levels generates a negative experience which places household management techniques and consumption-related work in the thematic core zone of the priority system. Consequently, in such cases, the problem of financial expenditure looms large. For those affected, overcoming these problems represents a cognitive challenge. Representatives of this type of time pioneer provide a large amount of unequivocal information on the time commitment qualities of consumer goods and the lifestyle-specific relevance of the convertibility of money and time, since they explicitly thematize and ponder both these factors.

In this context, overcoming the problem of making ends meet on reduced income levels reveals a characteristic development schema. The reductions in their income level not only necessitate a – in some cases radical – revision of consumer behaviour on the part of the representatives of this type of time pioneer, but also a cognitive realignment of their range of consumer interests. They discover that the reorientation process involved in subsisting on less money is hampered by ingrained consumption schemata which swiftly transform financial expenditure and the controllability of such expenditure into a major problem. The typical approach to this problem can be demonstrated by the characteristic example of one time pioneer who is still in the process of revising her living habits and in whose mind the problem is still fresh: this time pioneer reduced her working time by 50 per cent, in consequence of which she incurred the penalty of being forced to manage on a net monthly income which was 1,200 marks less than before. She did not consider that this enterprise was too fraught with risks, since during the transitional period she could fall back upon her savings. She intended to compensate for the shortfall in her income by means of non-consumption.

However, this plan failed and rapidly led to a crisis, to 'depression', 'aggression', 'problems with my son'. As far as attempting to solve the crisis was concerned, time proved to be an important resource, since the members of the household were now able to hold intensive discussions on the money problem among themselves. However, a satisfactory solution to the problem of restricting expenditure proved elusive, and the problem remained acute – indeed, at one stage, there were even plans to resume working standard time. In the final analysis, the money problem was solved neither by household planning nor consumption retrenchment, but solely by adopting revised evaluative schemata. Initially, the members of the household experimented with various money management strategies (keeping a cash book, introducing specific distribution rules, conscious planning and utilizing bank overdraft facilities), but without exception they all ended in failure; at the time our research was concluded (mid-1986), the money problem had still not been resolved completely. Changing the habits of a lifetime by means of rational household management is a difficult task to accomplish.

In the wake of the financial problems, consumer habits become a matter of experiential assimilation: they are allocated an independent experiential quality. The moment that consumer expenditure management becomes a focus of emphasis, and thus, an 'experience', other relevant evaluative schemata are activated. Consumption is gradually placed in a different interpretive context, thus facilitating its initial partial reduction. On the whole, the areas of consumer interest remain unchanged: they are simply redefined, as is demonstrated by the following example: *'Before, we used to travel far and wide, but now we've started staying at home a lot during the holidays, and not looking upon it as some sort of restraint or deprivation, but noticing that just outside the town, among the coalfields, lie "Little Canada" and a bathing lake. Travelling has also changed for me. The days of spend, spend, spend and visiting lots of different countries are over. Instead, I travel to places where I've got friends and acquaintances.'*

In consequence, this time pioneer succeeds in lessening the subjective burdens imposed upon her by financial problems, indeed, on occasion, in negating them altogether. Her reduced income no longer triggers any 'alarming' axieties, no longer constitutes an existential question, and ultimately, the problem disappears from the priority focus of her way of life. The revision of consumer habits is a long and difficult process. In the final analysis, the representatives of this type of time pioneer master the problem of restricting their expenditure by revising their interpretive schemata and redefining their areas of consumer interest. This process of the internal revision of their orientational schemata thematizes various different social contexts affecting the issue of economizing, particularly the role of money in relation to autonomous time disposal, the role of consumer habits, and individual consumer goods and symbols. It is modest consumption levels which appear in a positive light, not the maximization of money through employment.

Only within the framework of a changed meaning schema does expenditure restriction cognitively cease to constitute a permanent experiential deficit. And with the passage of time, the time pioneers also succeed in reconciling the practical contrariness of ingrained consumer habits with their available expenditure budget. The realignment of their range of consumer interests is revealed as a technique for reducing this deficit. Reorientation of their holiday habits towards taking inexpensive, but more experience-intensive holidays – preferably in the form of travelling from place to place without being tied to any one location – is the most obvious and frequent manifestation of the redefinition of their fields of activity on the part of the representatives of this type of time pioneer. The revision of their evaluative schemata generates a reassuring confidence in the value of having more time at their autonomous disposal: '*It was a big risk for me because I'd always been told that money gives you peace of mind. The fact that time gives you greater peace of mind is something you've got to learn for yourself first.*'

5 The Time Structures of the New Lifestyle

The characteristic feature of social time is that although it is omni-present in everyday life, as a general rule it is non-thematic. In con-sequence of the far-reaching routinization of daily life, linguistic categories of time generally remain on the thematic fringe of activities and experiences, seldom penetrating to the thematic core. Given that time is implicitly admitted into the activity structure of everyday life, the analysis and identification of social time structures are faced with the problem of access (Fischer 1986: 356f). Direct access to the social dimension of time is facilitated by the failure, and thus the problema-tization, of time structuring techniques for the management of every-day life which are non-thematic and routinized. Time then becomes an explicit variable of experiential assimilation which can be thema-tized and raised during the course of interview-discussions. In view of the fact that a sharp reduction in and rigorous flexibilization of working hours constitute a manifest intervention in the previous routines of everyday life, thus very likely resulting in the thematiza-tion of everyday time allocation techniques, flexible working time presents us with the opportunity to conduct some initial methodical research into experiences of time.

The 'time schemata' of members of society comprise both their orientation in the social world from the standpoint of time and the time structuring techniques with which they 'time' their activities. These time schemata lend structure to experiences of time. The specific experiences of time among members of society indicate the existence of different experiential techniques which determine the lengths of internal duration and the meaning of experiences (see Schütz and Luckmann 1975: 70). The time schemata lend structure to the interpretation of a situation. They incorporate the time system created by society as an orientational guide for determining sequences of activities. The time schemata generate the practical, substantializing link between the perspectivity of subjective time and the intersubjectivity of the time system which society has created. This is reflected in the development of planning hierarchies, expectational horizons, priorities and time allocation techniques, and in the fashioning of biographical conceptions, perception of time and categories of time, etc.

In everyday life, the practical management of time structuring is effected by means of routinized time allocation techniques. These provide the practical solution to the question of 'how' to subject sequences of activity to time structuring. They should be regarded as methodical and organized activities for concluding everyday business from the standpoint of time.

Our attention now focuses on the reconstruction of the chronotope of the time pioneers' lifestyle.[1] In this chronotope, the various different subjective and intersubjective time structures are characteristically interwoven and independently layered. Firstly, we trace the reorientation of the time pioneers' interpretive schemata of time, demonstrating how this reorientation was initiated by the flexibilization of their working time. We then reconstruct the characteristic techniques of time management with which the time pioneers incorporate flexible and disposable time structures into the organization of their everyday lives. Next, we analyse the time pioneers' perception of time; and finally, we reveal which consequences the time structures have on lifestyle development, and how these structures form the basis of a 'temporal affluence'.

5.1 Restructuring everyday time patterns

The moment that the relationship 'working time–lifetime' enters the core zone of the thematic priorities of the time pioneers, and motivates them to seek a reduction in and the flexibilization of their working time, the thematic development of their interpretive schemata in a certain direction is already mapped out. The time pioneers direct the horizon of their interpretive schemata in the direction of the thematic field of 'time' and the subjective meanings of 'working' and 'living'. During the course of this process, they begin to dissociate themselves from the employment sphere and the socially dominant expectational structures and legitimation schemata. Pride of place among their affections is assumed by time categories of lifestyle. In this section we reconstruct the typical process involved in the restructuring of the everyday time schemata typical of the time pioneers. In that the time pioneers 'want more time for themselves' and utilize their additional time as a reserve supply, they gradually acquire the ability to structure their everyday lives in accordance with changed meaning categories, and to effect their reorganization from the standpoint of time with the aid of new time management techniques.

The first consequence for the time pioneers of the reduction in their working hours is that they have more time. Additionally, the flexibilization ·of their working time affords them the opportunity to incorporate preferred time blocks into their everyday lives. For them, the most important issue is the fact they are able to determine for themselves how to utilize the time which is 'freed'. They regard having more time for themselves as the most valuable aspect of the flexibilization of their working time. This central interest of the time pioneers is constantly emphasized in almost identical terms: '*And that means that I've got more time for myself.*' The majority of the time pioneers are keen to acquire fairly large consecutive time blocks. These represent valuable and practical periods of time with which they '*can do something*'. It is this which first endows the qualitative dimension of this time with subjective value. The time pioneers considered that the excessive strain and the demands upon their time of full-time employment severely restricted their opportunities and prevented them from initiating any useful activities. In the words of one time pioneer: '*Before, I used to come home in the evening, and all I wanted was some peace and quiet. I just couldn't be bothered doing anything. Now, I do a lot more things that I think are more worthwhile than I used to. Before, I always felt that I could or really should do something, but I was just always so knackered.*'

The quantitative extent of the time which is freed by the flexibilization of their working hours plays a crucial role in enabling the time pioneers to ease the congestion of everyday life, garner reserves and gather their strength. The time pioneers make the point that they would derive no qualitatively perceptible advantages from a minor reduction in their working time. The empirical value which they cite as representative of a 'real' gain in time is a minimum reduction in their working time of eight hours (*vis-à-vis* a forty-hour week). Otherwise, they see no possibility of the evolution of a new, intrinsic quality of time experience, or the development of new time management techniques.

An analysis of the 'in order to' motive reveals that initially the time pioneers strive towards securing the possession of time in the sense of 'having time' as an intrinsic value, as an intrinsic objective of the flexibilization of their working time: *in order to have more time*. Time is not utilized as a means of pursuing activities which have been planned and precisely defined beforehand, and which already occupy a fixed position in the compass of motivational priorities. The segments of time which are freed from occupation by work are initially conceived and maintained as pools of reserves.

In contrast to the time pioneers, the time conventionalists exploit the functional purpose of the time which they gain. This functional purpose remains closely linked with certain activities which the time conventionalists have incorporated into their time. In this sense, the time which is freed is not free (free-floating) time, but pre-planned, pre-occupied and pre-allocated time. The time conventionalists reduce their working time with the intention of, for example, performing more housework, assisting their children with their homework, or commencing a part-time job, all of which activities are actually pursued upon the onset of shorter working hours. This constitutes no more than a displacement of activities, and does not change the time management techniques of the time conventionalists.

In contrast, the time pioneers reduce their working hours primarily in order to escape the captive influence of working life. They discover that a substantial reduction in their working hours and the flexibilization of their working time, largely implemented in accordance with their own preferences, lessen the effects of the strain imposed by work and faciliate improved and more rapid recuperation. In this context, time initially has a reserve function. Shorter working hours are a precondition of the experience of having more time for themselves. It is the utilization of time blocks as pools of reserves and the establishment of time buffers which first enable the time pioneers to initiate the revision of their time management techniques, in other words, to reduce the level of time pressure and precipitation to which they are subjected, and to develop a different perception of time. This also enhances the degree of compatibility between their private and working lives, and improves the level of their general well-being. The flexibilization of their working time provides a boost to the energy level of the time pioneers, which they exploit primarily for the purpose of intensifying their private interests, and for developing their network of social contacts: '*I've got a lot more time on my hands, which means I can stay down the pub until all hours now and again like I used to. But I've also got a lot more energy, and do a lot more things in my spare time. I don't sit down in front of the box, I go to the pictures, or go out with someone or other. These are all things which I used to forget about doing before.'*

At the same time, the organization of everyday life also becomes more flexible. The additional quantum of time at the disposal of the time pioneers presents them with the opportunity to free the organization of their everyday life from the discipline of an inflexible sequential schema, a plurality of outstanding tasks, and the sheer number of demands made upon their time. Instead, they are able to allocate their time in accordance with their own preferences, which are synchronized with their own inclinations and dispositions. It is precisely the experience of 'doing as they please' which generates the salutary and gratifying sensation among the time pioneers of possessing autonomous time. Underlying this sensation are the opportunity and the experience which the time pioneers have of allocating time on the basis of personal responsibility: *'I can organize things much better, do everything in a more balanced, less inflexible fashion. If the weather's nice, I can sit out on the balcony, have a sunbathe, or visit friends. And I can also make a spur-of-the-moment trip to A.'* This illuminates the fact that time management requires a particular ability on the part of the time pioneers, in other words, the ability to develop their own time allocation system and to incorporate it into the organization of their everyday lives. The ability in question is that of active time allocation. However, if such time allocation is to avoid degenerating into a 'time wasting' exercise and being stigmatized as lost time, it is imperative that it should be synchronized with the organization of everyday life.

By way of contrast, in the following case, the time pioneer concerned does not succeed in revising her time allocation routines. In consequence of the flexibilization of her working hours, she becomes even more pressed for time: *'Because you don't have the time when you've got a full-time job, you're always thinking about how God only knows how much you'd get through. And when you have got the time, you just do what you enjoy doing, and forget about everything else there is to be done. Now, I reckon that when you've got a lot to do, you do do a lot, but when you've not got much to do, you spin out what little there is needs doing. I'm terrible for doing this at times, and more than anything else, as far as the unpleasant tasks are concerned, I keep putting them off so that everything keeps dragging on for ages, with the result that I'm worse off now than I was before.*' In the absence of any restructuring of the time schemata in the direction of active time allocation, the additional free time generates no surplus of energy or time. In this instance, the consequence of the retention of familiar time allocation techniques is the de-structuring of everyday life. The loss of the time pioneer's situation-responsive time allocation routines and time categories results in a 'disintegration of time'. The elimination of a social time system encompassing the organization of everyday life means that adequate organization becomes impossible and that organization thus slides out of control.

This experience is encountered in dramatic fashion by those practitioners of flexibilization who in one fell swoop reduce their working hours to such an extent that their ingrained time allocation routines for the organization of everyday life suffer meltdown. Time passes without their achieving anything, or being able to subsume the manner in which they have passed the time under the category of the worthwhile: '*I tried to do something with all the time I had on my hands. I thought to myself that I'd now be able to do my housework properly. I began painting in 1981, and I thought I'd come home, sit myself down at the easel and start churning out paintings. But I noticed that I couldn't produce anything, nothing happened at all, it was just utter chaos. Then the complaints started coming along the lines of you've got time on your hands now, you're at home, and yet you still haven't done the cooking.*'

This involves not only the problem of the organization of everyday life and the development of new time management techniques, but also that of substantializing the time slots which are in the process of development. The result is that, paradoxically, the time which is gained appears de-substantialized. As a means of coming to terms with this unfamiliar situation, the practitioners of flexibilization engage in a more intensive horizontal interpretation of their associative schemata of time. This induces them to afford greater consideration to time utilization schemata, meaningful ascriptions of time and time structuring techniques.

In consequence, the time pioneers focus their attention on the actual experience of time, and thus, time as a dimension of the life-world penetrates ever further into the thematic core zone of their consciousness. This initiates a process among the time pioneers by virtue of which they endow the dimension of time with a genuine experiential quality. Time is stripped of its objectifications and revealed as a dimension of the construction of life, thus facilitating its utilization and improvement as an independent resource for fashioning their lives.

This process of enhanced awareness of time is supported by a revision of their time schemata on the part of the time pioneers. The meaning which the time pioneers attach to the new time structures is closely associated with the fashioning of their interpretive priorities. The reallocation of time requires the development of appropriate time categories which substantialize time expenditure and render it capable of social communication. These social categories direct the organization of everyday life, and legitimize the organizational system.

In this context, during the initial stages of the process of restructuring their time, the time pioneers are frequently confronted by the problem of lacking any designations for their time utilization techniques. Particularly during the period of recuperation following the flexibilization of their working time, when their familiar time allocation techniques begin disintegrating and, in line with the previous (and socially dominant) practice of prioritization, 'nothing [gets] done', the time pioneers are confronted by a structural problem of the categories of time prevailing within our society. In our culture, the established categories of time are closely associated with activities of recognizable substance – with the act of 'doing'. Time management techniques which deviate from this practice and which do not fall under this activistic category are immediately branded as 'idleness', and thus belittled. In such cases, nonconformist time management techniques can only be discussed with the aid of metaphors, circumlocutions and paraphrases.

The end result of the restructuring of the interpretive schemata of the time pioneers is that dead sections of time which were previously de-substantialized and which generated feelings of dissatisfaction and aggression are redefined: they are no longer regarded as problematic and are endowed with metaphorical substantialization: '*But I didn't think that simply doing nothing every now and again was pointless. It did me good. It's not simply a question of needing to do nothing, but rather that there really is some point in sitting in an armchair for two hours listening to a blackbird sing. Blackbirds have taken on a new significance.*' In this instance, the restructuring of time has already been integrated into a new meaning schema, which also identifies 'doing nothing' as legitimate and meaningful.

With the reorientation of their meaningful ascriptions of time, the time pioneers acquire abilities which enable them to control their time allocation techniques and improve their management of time problems. This ability of the time pioneers to organize time allocation on the basis of personal responsibility relates to planning, making appointments, setting deadlines, prescribing the pace of activities, determining stretches of time and preparing schedules containing inherent priority levels. In addition it entails the evaluation of the quality and intensity of periods of time and the development of a suitable time semantics. However, it also presupposes an appropriate perception of time which has been acquired during a process of reflection on the relevance of time to the problem structure of lifestyle. It additionally entails conscious practical implementation by means of time allocation techniques.

The acquisition of this time structuring ability enables the time pioneers to discontinue the practice of passively experiencing the present, manifestations of which are, for example, adapting to task-oriented sequential arrangements, and the direct acceptance of imposed time systems, and moving towards the active examination of time and time structuring. This does not imply actionism or an activistic approach in the sense that time is to be filled with activities 'come hell or high water'. Rather, it signifies that the individuals concerned are able to structure and utilize stretches of time on their own terms, and thus show them to be meaningful.

An additional consequence of this approach is that the time pioneers can lose themselves in time, abandon themselves to the passage of time or engross themselves in experiencing time, so that they let time slip by without regarding it as either a waste or a loss of time. It becomes clear that the revision of time structuring techniques requires that the time pioneers should possess both a measure of autonomous time and self-confidence. On this basis, the demonstration that time is an independent dimension of the lifeworld can be substantialized and fructified for a process of recognition.

The aspiration of the time pioneers to 'have more time for themselves' motivates them to reduce their working hours and becomes their central interpretive schema. This and their gradual endowment with autonomous time allocation ability signal the start of their campaign to reorganize their everyday life: hence their attempt to base their lifestyle upon flexible and disposable time structures.

5.2 Changed time allocation techniques

We now focus our attention on highlighting some of the characteristic time allocation techniques by means of which the time pioneers effect the temporal organization of their everyday lives following the restructuring of their time schemata. These techniques concern planning; the gaining of time; the redefinition of responsibilities; the avoidance of peak social time; the stage-management of special-purpose time and specific experiential styles; and the establishment of time buffers. These techniques are especially geared towards assisting the incorporation of flexible and disposable time structures into the organization of their lifestyles, which increases the time pioneers' chances of fashioning their lives in accordance with their own preferences.

Planning

Planning constitutes one of the most important time allocation techniques for structuring everyday life. It is a complex activity, and encompasses making provisions for measures such as scheduling, setting deadlines, determining time spans, establishing priorities, organizing sequential arrangements, determining the required pace of the individual sections, and considering synchronization possibilities, etc. Such precautionary measures are implemented routinely and determine the activity concept. However, planning not only embraces time allocation principles: it also maps out structures of expectations. For example, planned everyday time signifies that activities are geared towards future possible achievements and future expectations in accordance with a sequential schema, which also requires the minimization of the risk of failure, and the monitoring of the individual sequences.

These elements are also contained in the ideal of the dominant economic perception of time, which – and thus is it possible to expand the number of preconditions of precise planning – also requires punctuality, consistency, linearity and regularity, and implies arithmetical time management; in other words, it includes thrift, shortage of time and future orientation. Any analysis of the time allocation techniques of the time pioneers based on this economic perception of time with its quantitative, abstract and de-qualified characteristics would overlook the fact that their planning techniques are entirely different. The specific time management techniques of the time pioneers are only accessible to analyses which are predicated upon a qualitative perception of time.

The time awareness of the time pioneers consists of two time vectors for performing the activities involved in planning. The first of these entails the precise allocation of time slots, and the establishment of time markers determining the beginning, the end and the time spans of activities and areas of activities: in other words, the time pioneers localize blocks of time and divide up sections of time. Whenever they are requested to describe their daily schedules, the time pioneers arrange the individual blocks of activity in sequential order along this time vector. It then appears to them that the planning of their daily schedule is complete.

However, this situation is not experienced as such by the time pioneers. This gives rise to the assumption that the expectational structure of their daily schedule is not determined by such fixed sequential arrangements at all. This apparent contradiction is eliminated by the inclusion of the second time vector, along which not rigid but flexible time schedules are effected which are subject to spontaneous alteration. Activities are not arranged along this time vector in a rigid sequence. Rather, provision is made for eventualities, thus improving the coordination of various different fields of activity and time references. The result is the incorporation of a flexible time allocation technique into the organization of everyday life. However, this is not considered to be a planned schema. The time structures continually permit access to time slots facilitating changes of plan, or forms of time are utilized which incorporate latent scope for such changes: *'Shopping trips are basically pre-planned. Every two weeks or so, I take the car and go shopping, buying all the major things I need in various different shops. Small items I only buy every three to four days. What I do after that depends on the weather. If it's a really nice day, I'll find a couple of hours to go for a bike ride or a walk. You see, I don't need to be at home at any particular time, so if I meet any friends or acquaintances, I can go for an ice-cream and a natter with them.'* From the standpoint of this dual aspect of regulated and non-regulated expectational horizons, time pioneers regard planning as a structural process which also includes provision for the unplannable. For them, planning implies the creation of a framework in which certain priorities are established in respect of various periods of activity. However, to some extent, these priorities are kept flexible, in other words, they are not subjected to a rigid sequential schema. Flexibility is enhanced by the incorporation of a greater degree of scope for effecting changes of plan. Planning is oriented more towards the prolongation of the present, and planning horizons also tend more towards the incorporation of short-term time spans.

Techniques of gaining time

Alternating between the two time vectors allows the time pioneers greater scope for vigorously tackling the problem of shortage of time and for reducing time deficits. According to the prevailing perception of time, shortage of time is created by an enormous concentration of periods of time in which members of society are trapped by a system of different sequences of actions. The structural density of time standards generates time pressure behind which individuals lag, and which necessitate the introduction of time saving techniques such as speeding-up, routinization, and time concentration.[2] In accordance with this standpoint, it is usual sociological practice to transfer a time shortage diagnosis (time deficit, haste, speed-up) at the social and organizational level to the individual via the application of structural-determinist methods. Individuals – so it is assumed – are unable to escape the socially produced shortage of time and, at the individual level, they reproduce the modes of socio-economic time structures.

This prevailing perception of shortage of time (dense structural conditions produce a dearth of time at the autonomous disposal of the individual) fails to discern the typical time pioneer. This is due to the fact that shortage of time is generated by the collision between two time vectors: between one time vector along which it is impossible for time to become scarce in consequence of the fact that the time sequence can always be repeated, and another time vector along which scope for arbitrary repetition is restricted by a prescribed sequential system (see Srubar 1979). Time does not become scarce until the time schemata of members of society supersede the idealization 'I can do so again and again' by the notion 'I can only do so then'.

The time pioneers attempt to incorporate such recurrences ('I can do so again and again') into the organization of their everyday lives. They succeed in this attempt by developing flexible and disposable time structures and endeavouring to effect the active and autonomous allocation of their time; this also enables them to dissociate themselves from prescribed time programmes. By means of such time allocation techniques, they avoid the permanently fixed arrangement of sequences of activities, and the excessive encumbrance of their everyday schedules with a plurality of time standards. In accordance with the endeavours of the typical time pioneers to generate autonomous dispositional scope, the simultaneous representation of 'I can do so again and again' and of 'I can only do so then' is a strategy for time optimization, a subjective gain of time.

The technique deployed by the time pioneers of freeing themselves

as far as possible from the pressure of sequential arrangements generates a time cycle which turns out to be a gain of time. Once a better
'feeling' has been created, the unavoidable tasks are also accomplished
more swiftly, in other words, 'mandatory time' management becomes
easier, and in turn this issues in the availability of quantitively additional and subjectively more valuable time.

The availability of a large amount of time is insufficient: it must
also be possible to determine which points in time facilitate the creation and placement of usable units. In this respect, the time pioneers
place great emphasis upon accentuating subject-centred time structures, and endeavour to avoid the prescribed time systems. They
become sensitized towards independent time allocation and the consequences of such allocation for their well-being: '*I notice what a
pleasant experience it is and what peace of mind it gives me to hear
people suddenly come up to me and say "you've always got time", it's
great. That's very important to me.*' The time pioneers emphasize the
fact that having time and having time at their own disposal symbolize
their lifestyle; for the time pioneers, they are a stylistic means of
endowing their lifestyle with an image of its own.

The ability to wait is an essential requirement of the successful
deployment of techniques of gaining time. From the subjective standpoint, waiting is usually an expression of (structural) power scale:
those dependent on power must wait. However, in this case, waiting
is conceived as the ability of the time pioneers to transform apparently prescribed 'mandatory times' in accordance with their own
criteria. It is a question of waiting for the right moment, the right
time ('it will come'), and then of making the correct and timely
response. Instead of conceiving waiting in terms of being the consequence of a prescribed time system ('I have to wait because I have
been set a certain prescribed sequence of action'), the time pioneers
proceed in accordance with the maxim: '*I can wait until the right
moment for the right time to come.*' The time pioneers succeed in this
if they are skilled at performing task and 'mandatory time' management at the right moment in time, which they determine themselves.
This technique of gaining time is geared towards making the right
choice at the right moment in time: '*You've got to choose your time.*'

Redefining responsibilities

In order to accommodate greater levels of autonomous dispositional
scope, the time pioneers exclude certain 'mandatory times', in other

words, unavoidable tasks. This can be demonstrated by the example of one time pioneer who reduced her working time only six months previously, and thus whose impressions of the ensuing changes are still fresh in the mind, and assume drastic proportions. When she was still working full-time, she did not just have less time at her disposal, all her remaining time was also more thoroughly planned – her every waking hour was occupied with series of tasks and arranging appointments.

In contrast, the mandatory times are now in the process of being reduced, that is to say, the list of tasks to be accomplished is being shortened and the subjective value of the list is under review, and thus the tasks are deprived of the character of a purely superficial obligation.

The advantage of this time allocation strategy is manifested at two levels: firstly, a better *feeling* is created immediately; secondly, the expectational horizon of the time pioneers is freed from outstanding responsibilities. In turn, this not only generates more time at the autonomous disposal of the time pioneers, but also liberates them from having a permanently bad conscience: '*I notice that my schedule is almost as full as it was before, but – and this is the difference – my commitments don't get on top of me any more.*'

In this context, 'feeling' implies a certain experience of time which is not clearly defined and for which no socially precise linguistic categories exist, but which is nevertheless an expression of a high degree of subjective satisfaction. This 'feeling', which is characterized by relief, is exactly the opposite of the 'feeling of congestion' or of harassment, in other words, of being permanently weighed down by a mountain of outstanding tasks. The time pioneers rebel against the perception of the future as a programme of time which is replete with regenerative commitments and whose time balance is permanently in the red – a time programme which is accompanied by a set of compulsory laws (time shortages and the obligation to adapt to prescribed time structures, etc.) and sequential arrangements: '*There's a lot of things which need to be done which you've not got enough time to do.*' Such a time structure inevitably brings in its train pressure of time and harassment, and this is responsible for generating the oppressive, occasionally extremely alarming feeling of always being 'in the red'.

The outcome of the reduction in the degree of obligation is not only that the time schemata of the time pioneers are restructured and, in the light of their tasks, reinterpreted, but also that their time allocation techniques are revised, such as the technique of always effecting flexible time allocations, or that of waiting for the right moment: '*I leave the whole pile, thinking it'll get done somehow or other. Anyway, somehow, I always get round to it all again, and everything does get done eventually. But my colleagues in the office reckon you should force yourself to do it. Today's ironing day, so you've got to do the ironing. Sometimes, I've got clothes which have been waiting to get ironed for months, and I think to myself, they can wait until I can be bothered to iron them, and one day, you can be bothered.*' Such an outlook makes the future appear more uncertain, less planned and, as a result, it is less tense or oppressive and instead viewed with confidence. Thus, on the one hand, time pressures are relieved and, on the other, a flexibility potential is established which allows scope for several changes of plan – either spur-of-the-moment changes, or changes occurring in accordance with the pleasure principle.

Avoiding peak social times

Time pioneers attempt to adopt an asynchronous stance towards socially produced peak times. On the one hand, social peak times are heavily utilized and socially highly synchronized schemata for occupying time which generate time bottlenecks and create waiting time. On the other hand, they generate time advantages which are concentrated upon up-to-date commodities (fashion and technical innovations, for example) and are therefore expensive. In contrast, 'outdated' behavioural approaches such as those which have been developed by the time pioneers help to save time and money.

The time pioneers' concentration of their time schemata upon time references also furthers the development of unconventional time allocation techniques. And the dissociation from dominant time conventions on the part of the time pioneers mobilizes their willingness to incorporate asynchronous time management techniques into everyday life.

The time pioneers demonstrate great skill at avoiding time bottlenecks, such as those which occur in connection with the demand for services, infrastructural goods, and leisure-time activities. Their more intensive utilization of their scope for time management might not enable them to abolish infrastructural conditions such as the closing times of shops and the opening times of government offices, etc., but it does enable them to avoid peak times. This reduces the length of time which they are forced to wait and enables them to steer clear of congested streets and overcrowded waiting rooms, and thus to avoid mad rushes and stress. Thereby they improve the level of their synchronization and coordination with various reference times, from both the objective and the subjective standpoint. As a result they gain additional time. Equipped with their reservoir of time, the time pioneers actively occupy time lacuna simply by flexibilizing demand. Thus the time pioneers can, for example, increase the value of their leisure time by exploiting the opportunity of pursuing their leisure-time interests during the week instead of at weekends, as is usually the case: '*You get to appreciate the benefits if, for example, you take the car out for a spin somewhere on a Thursday or a Friday as opposed to the weekend when most people are off. From my point of view, I think it's great that there's so few people who do.*'

Stage-managing individual time

A further time structuring technique which is consciously applied by the time pioneers is the symbolic marking of time slots delimiting certain activity segments, each with their own specific experiential styles. Local times which are delimited in this fashion are reinforced by means of symbolic organization techniques.

The first stage in this process consists of fixing precise time markers. This is an attempt on the part of the time pioneers to delimit certain individual times and experiential styles for the purpose of stage-managing them separately from each other and strengthening their individual character. The time pioneers deliberately deploy their everyday time allocation techniques in order to reduce the influence of externally controlled time programmes: '*I start making breakfast at quarter past seven. Breakfast is a very organized affair in our house, and it goes off smoothly without any stress. It's very important to me that we can take our time over breakfast, that we can talk to each other and have a laugh. I can't stand the "quick, I'm in a hurry" approach, it's so unfriendly. That's no way to have breakfast.*' Although this does generate pressure of time (rising earlier, meeting deadlines on time, regulated sequence of activities), it is the qualitative aspect of time utilization in accordance with self-determined criteria which is emphasized in this instance.

The time pioneers do not place any intrinsic value upon the regulation and organization of daily schedules *per se*. It is rather the case that they adopt this practice in order to generate some self-controlled room for manoeuvre in the face of externally created time systems. The time pioneer quoted above emphasizes 'leisureliness', 'liveliness' and 'cheerfulness' and contrasts them with 'haste', 'stress' and 'unfriendliness'. The stage-management of experiential styles enables special times and highlights to be emphasized and defined. Thus, the existence of partial regulation notwithstanding, the time pioneers strive to introduce variety into their everyday lives as a formal principle. The individual times delimited by means of time markers create definitional scope and fields of activity to which the appropriate allocation of experiential styles and the deployment of stage-management and symbolization techniques impart a particular intensity of significance and greater substance.

This also facilitates the conferment of a semantic quality of exceptional significance upon 'doing nothing'. Characteristically, the experiential style which is assigned to these activities is closely linked to subjective time and internal duration, which conveys to the time pioneers a sense of whiling away the time. When their attention is not focused upon this experiential style (and when standard time is taken as the yardstick), the time pioneers frequently fail to realize how much time has actually elapsed: 'It's very intensive. The time passes quickly, and somehow, I seem to gain new insights and don't find such time in the least boring, but tremendously interesting and engaging.'

Success on the part of the time pioneers in introducing into their everyday lives more self-controlled periods of time replete with purpose and endowed with appropriate experiential styles increases the intensity of these experiences. The subjective individual times undergo expansion within the framework of the meanings of time, which explains why the time pioneers mention their impression of having gained additional time. And qualitatively speaking, they also have more time at their disposal which is of relevance to their subjective experience and sense of time.

Establishing time buffers

The time pioneers succeed in alternating between one individual time and another by means of noting the breaks and demarcation lines between different time structures. This establishes time buffers between different time references. The demarcation lines between experiential styles are symbolically exaggerated in order to facilitate precise differentiation between the individual fields of activity, and the creation of 'time segments'. This assists the time pioneers in alternating between different fields of activity and time structures.

The commencement and termination of participation in the institutional time systems are effected via the sequence: engage, deactivate, disengage: '*I wouldn't want to invest any more of my time in my job. After work, I can also switch off completely, I forget all about the firm. I always walk to work, I need to be able to switch off. And when I get home afterwards, that's it, work's over.*'

In conjunction with their experiential assimilation of time allocation, the time pioneers also refine their time allocation techniques in order to effect the continual improvement and potentiation of their autonomous dispositional scope.

5.3 The time pioneers' perception of time

We now turn our attention to the characteristic features of the time pioneers' perception of time. By 'perception of time', we mean the content and the internal structure of their interpretive schemata of time. Their perception of time highlights their dissociation from dominant time conventions, their self-imposed pace-restraint policy, their emphasis on present experience, and the building-in of discontinuity. From the standpoint of quality, the specific concatenation of these interpretive schemata of time fashions a time management technique of inherent value, the singularity of which is based upon a high degree of reflexive time awareness.

Dissociation from dominant time conventions

The time pioneers oppose the rigid and continual filling of time. They do not regard the time which they have gained as a result of the flexibilization of their working hours as time which should immediately be filled with other commitments. In contrast, the dominant perception is of time in terms of production time, consumption time, and time for substantializing human existence through the provision of constant activity. Everything is subordinated to the imperative of utilization, exploitation and application. Since time is scarce and valuable, so-called slack periods or enforced periods of waiting are reutilized and filled with additional 'odd jobs'. Immediately upon the detection of a brief period of unoccupied time, consideration is afforded to the matter of 'what can be done to fill it'. For the time pioneers, the order of the day is the rejection of this interpretive schema of activistic time utilization which negativizes and demonizes slack periods. Instead, they espouse the 'de-utilization' of time: '*In your free time, there's obviously plenty of other things you can do. I'm not the type for doing this or that on a regular basis. I don't do five courses at night-school all at the same time just to fill in my time again straight away, that's not my style.*'

According to the dominant interpretive schema, time is also primarily time saved, time for doing something else, something useful. Time pioneers do not regard time solely as something to be occupied by objectifications, as a means to an end. Rather, they endeavour to keep time free from schematic time utilization plans. This de-objectification affords them the opportunity to perceive and pursue the development of time as an experiential quality and a structural dimension of life. In this light, time is conceived as a reservoir of opportunity whose variability is preserved and which can be utilized in a variety of different ways.[3]

In delineating their temporal horizons, the time pioneers dissociate themselves more and more from the time programmes of social organizations and institutions. On the one hand, this dissociation has a cognitive component, that is to say, the thematic conflict between the time pioneers and the socially produced time systems, and on the other, a normative component, namely, the time pioneers' evaluation of time conventions. Their impugnment of the legitimacy of externally controlled time standards results in the emergence of subject-oriented time schemata and subject-centred time structures.

The lifestyle of the time pioneers is predicated upon flexible and disposable time structures. This is particularly evident from the fact that, *inter alia*, the time pioneers also endeavour to weaken and negate the hold exercised by fixed times and ingrained routines. They afford the validity of universal time standards only partial recognition. Strictly speaking, for the time pioneers there are no such things as washdays, clocking-off times, afternoon naps, cleaning days, or mealtimes, no fixed time schedule in the form of a permanently institutionalized and established ritual. They have only a limited appreciation of the value of a fixed timescale for daily, weekly and yearly cycles. On the contrary, they strive to break loose from conventional time standards, prevent the excessive routinization of their lives simply for the sake of orderliness, and, most of all, avoid tedium: '*Time and again, I notice that, if I stay in any one place for more than six months, I get into a rut, and I start getting bored to death all over again. Then it's time to start looking for something else to do.*' The time pioneers employ a strategy of variety to immunize themselves against the omnipresent risk of infection from routinization, and to counter habituation, invariable repetition and the unrelenting recurrence of more of the same with variety.

Overall, it is possible to distinguish a marked tendency among the time pioneers to sever the connection between temporal circumstances and commitments regulated by time conventions. With reference to their lifestyle, they call into question and, where necessary, ignore or modify rules, regulations, and ingrained habits of performing certain tasks at certain times for a certain length of time or in a certain sequence.

Self-imposed pacing

During the course of the development of societies up to the modern day, the general pace of life has increased enormously, and this has resulted in the emergence of a certain degree of independence in assessing rapidity, speed and pace, as equated with effectiveness and efficiency. Pace ideologies have acquired a universal significance for everyday life. Something which is urgent justifies its importance almost automatically. Since it is urgent, it is also relevant. There are many examples in which the time pioneers dissociate themselves from haste, urgency, nervousness and impatience, and remark upon the fact that pace has become a constant companion of life in all situations, and creates stress.

The time pioneers combine the detachment with which they comment upon other people with 'composure' in their own lives. Since the time which has been freed is not *ab initio* reoccupied with activities and fixed sequences of activity, the time pioneers can allow themselves some scope for engaging a smoother, slower pace, which exercises an anodyne, recuperative effect. This is frequently associated with the interpretive schema of 'leisureliness'.

The additional energy at the disposal of the time pioneers enables them to increase the intensity of their experiences. Initially, it is surprising that the time pioneers simply do not do more with the time which they have gained, that it is not exploited in order to initiate other undertakings, such as improving the occupation of their leisure time. This surprise stems from the fact that the socially dominant conception of time assumes that time which is no longer spent engaged in the pursuit of income is reoccupied by other activities from the field of domestic or DIY work, or by leisure-time activities. However, the time pioneers dissociate themselves from the dictate of time utilization, and revise their time management techniques. Their philosophy is neatly summed up in the words of one time pioneer: *'I've enjoyed making a detour through the public park of an afternoon, going for a walk for one-and-a-half hours, sitting in the sun, coming home and having a leisurely cup of coffee. Time used to fly by when I worked full-time, but now everything's go slow. I've done this and that, some DIY, and a bit more reading. I did everything at a more leisurely pace, and it was much more refreshing, and so I don't think I can claim that shorter working hours have encouraged me to take up loads of exotic activities, but – and this is the difference – everything I do, I do in a more relaxed frame of mind.'* The revised time management techniques practised by this time pioneer afford her the opportunity of withdrawing from the socially dictated time flow of everyday life. This results in the emergence of 'peace of mind', which she gradually recognizes as constituting an experiential quality in its own right, and which effectuates a marked improvement in her well-being.

Emphasis on experiencing the present

The time pioneers reject the notion of planning intensively for the future. They attempt to avoid placing their present-day lives at the exclusive service of safeguarding their futures. Although they do afford thorough consideration to the risks and the future adverse repercussions and disadvantages arising out of their transition to flexible working time and their resulting loss of income, at the present moment they consider that the price of safeguarding the future is too high. They do not regard the fact that shorter working hours will reduce their future material standard of living as a problem which threatens their existence.

However, this by no means implies that the time pioneers dispense with forms of planning for the future such as paying pension insurance contributions and saving, and take 'each day as it comes'. What happens is that they effect certain displacements of emphasis in their time perspective. These displacements of emphasis intensify and enhance their experience of the present, shifting the main focal point of their lives from the end product to the process of production. However, the fact that the time pioneers enhance the importance of experiencing the present does not mean that they indulge in some nervous *'fanatisme de l'actualité'* whose objective is to remain *'au parfum'*, and which desperately tries to keep abreast of all the latest trends.

The temporal interpretive schemata of the time pioneers are oriented towards keeping their future horizons open, and reducing the degree of planning to which they are subjected; the task of the present-day perspective is the restriction of future scope for variation to an absolute minimum. The present-day is, as it were, prolonged in order to facilitate the integration of any possible alterations of decisions or courses of action. Those whose time perspective is excessively oriented towards future objectives run the risk of failing to exploit the opportunities offered by the present. In the event that the latter should come to pass, the perspective is reversed: it then becomes a question of taking every possible precaution against the distortion of the future by the deeds of the present. Time pioneers recognize that the amassing of material goods entailing a strong commitment to the future entails such risks, and that any obligations into which they have entered become a 'millstone around their necks'. The fact that the time pioneers place such emphasis on experiencing the present, and thus, to some extent, effect the prolongation of the present, signifies that they deploy the present-day perspective as a means of short-circuiting the future horizon. They 'visualize' the future; in other words, they forge close links between the present-day perspective and a future perspective whose time span is thus greatly reduced.

Inclusion of discontinuity

The flexible and disposable time structures of the time pioneers' lifestyle do not apply solely to everyday time, the daily schedule, but also to biography management, life planning. The biographical structure employed by the time pioneers is geared towards integrating the different potential eventualities of life planning, and making them the point of departure for their present-day actions. This they achieve by means of the development and reinsurance of their own biographies. In addition, the time pioneers deliberately maintain the future in a state of greater uncertainty, conceiving it to be something which is variable and unpredictable. The time span of their future perspective is decisively reduced; it is situated within a prolonged present day whose objective is the maintenance of greater freedom within the activity context of the present day to take decisions in favour of several courses of life. Overall, the future horizons of the time pioneers appear in a differentiated, flexible and variable light. This weakens the ability of biographical models spanning entire lifetimes to fashion the lives of the time pioneers, and reduces the effectiveness of institutionalized standards for structuring life phases. These are superseded in importance by strategic discontinuity management: this is the attempt by the time pioneers to integrate disparate bio-graphical models and different biographical sequences with the objec-tive of preserving scope for several reactions and changes of course.

In consequence of the additional scope available to the time pio-neers, which intensifies the selective pressure on the development of their lives, the degree of subjectivity involved in the conception of life plans increases. The growing relevance of the self-association of the time pioneers to the structuring of their way of life can be seen as a process of individualization. The tasks of life planning are being increasingly assigned to individuals, who are compelled to intensify the thematization of the course of their lives.

Time not only constitutes a resource in the sense of 'having more time', it is also a multi-modal means of effecting changes to personal identity. In this case, the motive behind seeking shorter working hours is to increase the amount of time at the disposal of the proces-ses involved in personality development. In order to further such personality changes, time is utilized as a process component which is kept open. '*The time I allow myself to let something reach fruition has given me a clearer sense of direction.*' The possibilities of influen-cing the process by means of, for example, acceleration, gradation or deceleration, are withdrawn: the process is underway, and the change occurs. The time pioneers allow themselves time '*to wait and see, to observe growth*', display patience in the face of maturing processes, and hope that the process of self-change will reach its ultimate destination. In this context, it is important to the time pioneers that the process remains open-ended and is not steered in any particular direction. Their main concern is the provision of opportunities for personal development. They utilize the time which they have gained as a result of flexibilizing their working hours for a process of self-discovery.

It is also a characteristic feature of the time pioneers that they effect discontinuities and reorientation processes during the course of their life and career histories, that they experiment with various different life plans. In order to secure access to these options, they also exploit the opportunities afforded by flexibilized and reduced working time. This increases the likelihood of the occurrence of turning points and crises which bring personality changes and alterations to the orientational schemata of the time pioneers in their train. The con-sequence of this for the time pioneers is that they tend towards the 'biographization' of their lifestyle and the temporalization of their life plans, that is to say, they question the validity of their life plans, and orient them in accordance with their current objectives and interests. In consequence, 'biography management' itself becomes a problem. There are several options available for overcoming this problem. However, we were unable to identify any specific schemata typical of the time pioneers.

The time schemata of the time pioneers are option-oriented. This is not simply a matter of creating the scope for taking alternative courses of action as such. It is also a question of being able to change plans. For example, if the weather conditions are suitable for a particular activity, it should be possible to react to them accordingly. It is not so much the nature of the planned activity which comes to the fore, but rather the 'decision-making opportunity': '*If something else comes to mind on the spur of the moment which is important to me today, I ditch something else without any qualms whatsoever.*' This improves the ability of the time pioneers to coordinate their relevant activities. The development of scope for opportunity is regarded as a quality in its own right. It offers potential for the deployment of various courses of action, and affords the time pioneers the opportunity of developing calm and composure.

Reflexive time consciousness

The availability of time triggers a self-reflexive process among the time pioneers, producing, so to speak, time loops of its own: they can now take the time to reflect upon time. They turn their attention towards time systems and time constraints. Their chief concern is the constructive incorporation of the lifeworld dimension of time into a time-sensitive and reflexively controlled lifestyle. Thus, as far as the resource of time is concerned, they explicitly thematize their experiences of time and their formative ambitions.

This process involves reflecting upon the assimilation of time experience, and the deliberate reorientation of time schemata, which can be initiated as a learning process. Time becomes an object of reflection for the time pioneers: the assessment of time allocation techniques is itself conducted according to criteria of time. The problematization and thematization of time management styles initiate a reflexive process *vis-à-vis* time references, and a consciousness of time gradually develops.

The reflexive approach to time has even resulted in the emergence of an operational theory of time which questions time allocation practices and draws practical conclusions. This is evident from the attempt on the part of the time pioneers to put a stop to the 'infinitesimal utilization logic of time' (Rinderspacher 1985: 57ff), the repercussions of which they have already perceived. According to this logic, time is subjected to repeated intensive utilization right down to its smallest units, during which process any time saved (by means of pace intensification and rationalization, for example) does not remain free, but is utilized for other purposes.

In contrast, time pioneers use time as a powerful resource for shaping their lives. They deploy techniques of time utilization in which greater emphasis is placed on individual times rather than on the functional purpose of certain activities: '*I never drive the car in my private life, and I make the kids walk as well. I mean, even the time you save by taking the car you use to do something else. We're so bloody programmed. We say, I've saved time, but in fact, all we've done is save time so we can do something else. In contrast, I often do without the car, and deliberately go on foot because it gives me time to think.*' Deliberately leaving the car at home and going on foot marks a clear contrast to the time system which prevails at work and in professional life. This is done with the intention of facilitating other experiences, experiences which enable the time pioneer to dissociate himself from the employment sphere and relativize its importance.

The elevated reflective niveau at which the sensitivized time schemata of the time pioneers operate is illuminated by, for example, the observations of one time pioneer in respect of the time structures of her colleagues. In her eyes, their time management techniques are '*firmly fixed*', a source of complaints and pressure. The utilization of every last minute of time also attracts criticism. This practice only creates harassment, stress, haste and confinement. The time pioneer clearly recognizes that this technique of time management is a misguided time optimization strategy, and deliberately avoids applying it to her own lifestyle. This intensifies the reflexive and dissociative process towards the time systems of society. Emphasis is placed upon experiencing the present, the conscious sensation of the passing of time.

In order to secure the availability of scope for organizational manoeuvre in their everyday lives, the time pioneers intensify their observations of time management techniques. The yardstick for gauging the usefulness of time expenditure is based on subjective criteria. This subject-centring is intensified still further in that the repression of the influence of external constraints and the pressure of time is experienced as a relief, and furthers the process of reverse association with the self. The emergence of reflexivity *vis-à-vis* time structures and time allocation techniques should be regarded as the salient characteristic of time pioneers. The reflexive relation to time is the central distinguishing feature between time pioneers and their peers, and especially between time pioneers and time conventionalists.

5.4 The gain in temporal affluence

The time pioneers use the temporal affluence which they have acquired as the yardstick for gauging the measure of their success in 'timing' via the employment of an autonomous time management technique, and for gauging the degree of satisfaction to which they have fashioned their lives with the aid of time structuring. Temporal affluence is achieved by incorporating into everyday life a greater number of time management techniques facilitating a satisfactory level of synchronization with subjective time. In the face of the availability of self-controlled sections of time, the importance of the actual nature of each utilization of time recedes into the background. The time pioneers regard temporal affluence as a quality in its own right, in which many elements of time structuring join forces and harden into an independent sense of satisfaction.

By developing flexible time structures, the time pioneers increase their room for selective manoeuvre, both from the standpoint of structure (in the synchronic dimension) and that of process qualities (in the diachronic dimension): time is not occupied *ab initio* in accordance with fixed sequential schemata. This increases the number of alternative courses of action available to the time pioneers.

The generation of autonomous and flexible dispositional scope also enables the time pioneers to augment the number of options open to them. There is greater choice, and problems of selection now loom larger than problems of pressure of time or scheduling. The time pioneers recognize the problem, and endeavour to find a solution.

The question of how the time pioneers organize the augmentation of options and the maintenance of opportunity directs the analysis towards the consideration of the horizonal structure of their interpretive schemata of time. In this respect, it should firstly be noted that the present-oriented time perspective of the time pioneers constitutes one of the preconditions for keeping their future horizons open and not trammelling them from the outset by fixed sequences of activity. The bond between the time pioneers and one or only

certain time references is weakened, and the possibility of synchronization with other time vectors and time structures is enhanced. This
occurs in two respects: on the one hand, the time pioneers are
afforded greater scope for switching to other time structures. This is
achieved by virtue of the fact that in simultaneously maintaining
continuity and discontinuity, the time pioneers are better able to
exploit instabilities. Instabilities then no longer appear merely as
disruptions, and they can be more systematically incorporated and
integrated into the activity horizon of the time pioneers. In order to
augment the scope of the time pioneers to switch to other time
structures, the dual aspect of flexible time structures is exploited: this
not only facilitates the readjustment of the local times of individual
fields of activity in accordance with scope and situation, it also means
that they afford the time pioneers the opportunity to initiate alternative courses of action. There is greater flexibility.

On the other hand, the time pioneers enhance their opportunity to
employ other time references. The incorporation of disposable and
flexible time structures into everyday life enables them to increase the
possibility of synchronizing various different time structures. At the
same time, the bond between the time pioneers and various time
references is weakened, which facilitates the management of different
time structures. The time pioneers become more willing to employ
and remove time constraints.

This permits a better degree of coordination between areas of life
outside the employment sphere. The time pioneers exploit the opportunities which arise primarily for the purpose of nurturing their
contacts among their friends and acquaintances: in other words,
these opportunities further the development of communicative associations and the intensification of social contacts.

To the extent that the specific time schemata and time allocation
techniques of the time pioneers are representative of typical solutions
to the problems, they also embrace the socially produced problem
structure of their lifestyle. The flexible, option-oriented approach of
the time pioneers which keeps their future horizons open and integra-
tes discontinuities is their reaction to the growing dynamic of social
and cultural flux. This dynamic dents hopes of basing life planning
on continuity idealizations. The time pioneers are able to effectuate
the assimilation and productive management of upheavals in social
time structures more efficiently than their peers.

In addition, there is a wider range of choice, and access to various different fields of activity becomes easier. On the one hand, the time
pioneers establish variability of time structures and multiple co-

ordination with various different time references; on the other, they also effect the segmentation and preservation of different time structures, making provision for individual times. The time allocation techniques of the time pioneers mark an attempt on their part to undermine the influence of externally controlled time systems and external constraints on the excessive regulation of their everyday lives, and to assert their own prioritizations and time management techniques more vigorously. For this purpose, the self-imposed regulation and organization of everyday life is also permissible. The order of the day is the restructuring of everyday life.

In opposition to the dominant time conditions, the time pioneers deliberately engage a 'smoother pace'. Given that they ascribe a powerful gravitational force to these conditions, they expend a great deal of energy to avoid succumbing to it. The aversion of the time pioneers towards the time system of the 'harassed society' is a constant incentive for them to develop different time management techniques, to enhance the reflexivity of time references, and to redouble their reflexive efforts towards meaningful ascriptions of time.

The time pioneers weave the formal time principles of irregularity, change and flexibility into the arrangement of their everyday lives. These principles are pitted against the 'routinization' of everyday life. However, it is entirely possible to integrate scheduling and deadlines without necessitating the schematic prescription of time standards. In the time schemata of the time pioneers, the sequential arrangements dictated by the socially produced time system are not treated as inflexible blocks of time. This generates and iterates variety and variation – for the time pioneers, an indispensable value for their conception of life: they endeavour to subordinate chores and tasks (particularly domestic and consumption-related work, etc.) recurring on a daily basis to disposable time utilization. Thus they strive towards the achievement of flexible deadline management, go shopping when the opportunity arises, and do not, for example, wash the car unless they are so inclined. Subjective well-being is the focal point of emphasis, the recipient of priority status. The high value which the time pioneers place upon pursuing activities according to disposition and inclination also alters their evaluation criteria: they are relocated to the sphere of subjective constitution.

The increasing subject-centring of the temporal evaluation criteria of the time pioneers ('I want') also results in a greater degree of lifestyle reflexivity. The processes of self-observation, self-assurance and identity control are developed and refined. It is characteristic of the time pioneers that this involves the interlocking and mutual furtherance of two reflexive processes – one concerning the characterization of time schemata, and the other the subject-centring of lifestyle. In the reflexive process of subject-centring, time as a dimension of the construction of life is pushed more to the fore of the thematic priorities of the time pioneers. In turn, the more intensive horizonal interpretation of time which this initiates is itself related to time references (disposability, flexibility, time management techniques, and shortage of time, etc.). These two reflexive processes generate self-reinforcing tendencies which initiate an improved level of time 'maintenance' and a process of 'self-maintenance' which are mutually supportive and enhancive.

The time pioneers utilize time which is at their autonomous disposal in order to maintain clarity with regard to their personal objectives and interests. Such time affords them a greater degree of personal autonomy, thus enabling them to exercise more effective control over the 'joystick' of lifestyle development. This reveals that the time pioneers strive towards the modulation of their everyday lives in accordance with their own formative concepts. Time functions as a manipulated variable of the organization of everyday life. The temporal affluence attained by the time pioneers is an indication of the success or otherwise of the connection between the two (time-oriented and subject-centred) reflexive processes: on the one hand, subjective well-being becomes the yardstick for evaluating the time pioneers' own lifestyle and conception of life, and, on the other, subjective well-being is organized with the aid of time, and evaluated in accordance with temporal criteria.

In the lifestyle of the time pioneers, temporal affluence functions as their personal criterion of welfare improvement, which (from a certain level based on subjective criteria) is able to compete on even terms with material affluence. The concentration of this lifestyle upon the augmentation of temporal affluence means that the time pioneers' descent in terms of distributive inequality as a result of the reduction in their income levels does not exercise a determinative influence upon the way in which they organize their lives.

6 The Dynamic of the New Lifestyle

The lifestyle of the time pioneers assimilates breaches in the cultural paradigm of the employment society, providing a response which is wholly worthy of recognition as a new form of participation in paid work, and as an identifiable, independent social form. In concluding our investigation, our attention now focuses upon the dynamic which underpins the formation and development of the time pioneers' lifestyle. On the one hand, the lifestyle of the time pioneers reflects the resistance to change of cultural interpretive schemata and, on the other, the exegesis of changed structural social conditions and problem fields. This lifestyle cannot be observed statically; on the contrary, the issue at hand is the reconstruction of its inherent dynamic. To this end, we analyse the processes involved in changing interpretive schemata and adopting the lifestyle of a time pioneer.

The time pioneers themselves experience the development of their lifestyle as a fundamental transformation. Their assessment of the restructuring of how they organize their lives is so fundamentally and existentially profound – *'transformation of life'*, *'I've started to live'* – that it is entirely appropriate to speak in terms of a 'qualitative leap forward'.[1]

At a certain phase of their lives, the time pioneers problematize and thematize paid work as the structural focus of their lives. In the opinion of the time pioneers, *'work is not everything'*.

In this connection, two typical developments can be identified. In the case of the first of these, the time pioneers had already begun the process of dissociation from the sphere of employment during their

earlier sociation, or during subsequent biographical phases –
conveyed via their involvement in non-production-oriented sub-
worlds of meaning (education and vocational training establishments,
subcultures, therapy groups); therefore, from the very beginning, the
organization of their lives was set against the dominance exercised by
the world of employment over everyday life and the course of their
lives. In contrast, in the second case, it is the concrete experience of
work within the framework of full-time employment that results in
thematizing the dominant role of work in life, and in examining the
possibilities of changing it.

However, despite such developmental differences, in both cases the
nature of their criticism of a life upon which the determinative
influence is exercised by paid work is the same. It is precisely because
both types highlight the relevance of working in relation to 'life as a
whole' that they experience problems in pursuing employment on the
basis of standard working time. They examine paid work from the
standpoint of subjective well-being and purpose fulfilment.

The industrial time regime is most frequently thematized. The time
pioneers criticize its dominance in everyday life. The nascent process
of subjectivization, in the sense that the time pioneers stake individual claims to a meaningful relation with work, puts the sphere of
employment under pressure, impelling it to provide an explanation of
what work 'does for' their present-day situation, and of how it
contributes to the improvement of their subjective well-being. From
the standpoint of these claims, standard working time occupies
everyday life to such an excessive extent that in the view of the time
pioneers life becomes subjectively intolerable.

Since the respondents experience and recognize that full-time
employment imposes restrictions on everyday life to a subjectively
unacceptable extent, they endeavour to undermine the influence
exercised by the supremacy of work over the organization of their
lives. This provides them with the motivation to effect the drastic
reduction and flexibilization of their working hours, thereby offering
them an opportunity to change the organization of their lives and
initiate a process of reorientation.

In the majority of cases, the time pioneers were already characterized by a willingness to accept change. In their personal lives, this
is indicated by discontinuities in career history, mobility, employment interruptions in consequence of periods of further training, and
divorce, etc. In some cases, this willingness to accept change was
reinforced by the fact that the desire for flexibilization initiated or
necessitated a change of job, or even a change of career. Given the

importance that time pioneers attach to the incorporation of variety into their concepts of life, and their rejection of 'routinization', that they embark upon processes of reorientation is not surprising.

In consequence of the reduction in their income level following the flexibilization of their working time, the time pioneers are confronted with different points of departure and the necessity of effecting modifications to the way in which they shape their lives. They thematize methods of economizing, subjecting them to examinination from the standpoint of subjective criteria. Careful consideration is afforded to the relationship between attainable income level and achievable temporal dispositional scope. In the course of time a decision is made in favour of 'having more time for myself' – though only insofar as individuals succeed in revising those established consumption schemata which prove stubbornly resistant to change. In an experimental phase, the time pioneers endeavour to revise their ingrained expenditure and consumption schemata in line with their reduced level of income for the purpose of the subsequent re-examination of the extent of flexibilization.

The crux of this coordination process is the revision on the part of the time pioneers of their consumer habits, and thus the exercise of control over their expenditure; after all, the reduction in their income level is not compensated for by other sources of income. The time pioneers are unable to revise their consumer habits until they have effected the reorientation of their evaluative schemata. This entails conducting a critical examination of the socially dominant money–time dictate and the power of consumer symbols. The concomitant process of their dissociation from the cultural paradigm of the employment society reinforces the role of outsider which is ascribed to them at the workplace. They particularly feel press-ganged into this role when the conventional evaluative criteria of the employment society monoculture are applied to them by their employer. Such instances provide a drastic illustration of the high price which the time pioneers pay for the flexibilization of their working time over and above suffering a reduction in their income level: a considerable degree of intensification, inadequate symbolic proof of performance, fewer communicative opportunities at the workplace, moral disqualification, and career restrictions.

The interpretive priorities of the time pioneers seek to weaken the relationship between working time and living time, relieve their situation at work, revise their consumer habits, and lessen the captive influence of the money–time dictate. This reinforces their dissociation from the cultural paradigm of the employment society. The interpretive schemata of the time pioneers become increasingly detached from this context, and undergo reorientation: 'Yes, these are all re-examination processes.'

The process of reorientation is conditional upon a marked reduction in and flexibilization of working time, by means of which individuals have a larger amount of time at their disposal. Initially, this affords the time pioneers the opportunity of establishing time buffers and reserving more time for self-controlled activities, and thus, of simply having more energy available. In the longer term, this results in the time pioneers' distancing themselves from their employment. This detachment redounds to the benefit of both work, which is approached in a more cheerful frame of mind, and private life, which is freed from time commitment constraints: 'Most of all, I've achieved the degree of detachment that I actually wanted.'

The reduction in and flexibilization of working time constitute an incision into the organization of everyday life, and create a problem which cannot be solved by means of conventional time routines. In order to enable the time pioneers to reallocate time, it is necessary that time references enter the thematic core of their consciousness. The necessity of establishing new meaningful ascriptions of time initiates a process of the continual refinement of the time schemata of the time pioneers.

The satisfactory management of the change in their everyday lives remains beyond the ability of the time pioneers unless they are gradually able to acquire an independent capacity for active time structuring, which goes hand in hand with the reorientation and refinement of their time schemata. Not until they have acquired such a capacity are they in a position to exercise control over the process of adopting new time management techniques which are able to afford consideration to subjective aspirations. The time pioneers progressively develop a perception of time which stands in marked contrast to the prevailing apprehension of time.

The time pioneers deliberately utilize their revised time allocation techniques for the purpose of organizing their everyday lives. Time is exploited as an option, and revised time allocation techniques are utilized for fashioning lifestyle. In this connection, the prime concern of the time pioneers is to have more time at their individual disposal, in other words, to achieve autonomy of time.

In order to achieve this, the time pioneers predicate their lifestyle on disposable and flexible time structures, which represent the characteristic crystallization point of their lifestyle. Overall, their time management techniques are geared towards a smoother, slower pace, which inheres in those two highly prized interpretive schemata, 'composure' and 'leisureliness'. The time allocation techniques of the time pioneers are primarily an attempt on their part to integrate subject-centred elements from their conception and way of life into the organization of their lives: '*You really do get more out of life, you just do.*'

In turn, the efforts of the time pioneers to obtain a greater degree of autonomy over the development of the way in which they conduct their lives are judged in accordance with time categories, that is to say, time becomes reflexive. This generates a continuous cycle which furthers the characterization of meaningful ascriptions of time and time utilization techniques. In consequence of the intervention of the time pioneers in the way in which they conduct their lives via the dimension of time, and of their attempts to further the integration of subjective preferences and interests into the organization of their lives by means of time structuring, these two processes are mutually related. This unleashes a dynamic force which acts as a permanent spur to the lifestyle of the time pioneers.

This reorientation process is accompanied by a tendency on the part of the time pioneers to centre their lifestyle upon subjective relations. This is evident from the fact that they develop their own interests, and focus their attention on the self-discovery and self-assurance of their concept of life. This subject-centring is particularly intensified whenever the flexibilization-induced restructuring of the orientational schemata of the time pioneers culminates in a process of discovery and in a phase, open to and hungry for new experiences, which opens up new horizons and associations of meaning. The increase in the degree of self-control which the time pioneers exercise over the shaping of their lives is a major contributory factor in the sense of satisfaction which they experience. In order to bolster their other formative ambitions, the time pioneers invest some of their time in 'individual and time maintenance', that is to say, in those factors which are primarily responsible for the allowing of some scope for subject-centred lifestyle formation in the organization of their lives.

The development of the time pioneers' lifestyle is frequently accompanied by a personal awareness and clarification process. This enhances the status of fashioning lifestyle along subject-centred lines and stakes a claim to independence, which is also regarded as one of the outcomes of the reorientation process. In this case, the time at the autonomous disposal of the time pioneers is utilized for the purpose of implementing active 'identity and biography management', which in turn ultimately assists them in their efforts to attain autonomy.

The development of subject-centred abilities (and also self-observation skills), the effect of which is in turn ascribed to subjective well-being, also initiates a reflexive process in respect of the self. This process transforms subjective well-being and the conditions for its fulfilment into the yardstick by which the time pioneers evaluate their jobs, the development of their time management techniques, and the shaping of their overall lives.

The two central forces involved in reshaping the lifestyle of the time pioneers – time sensitization and the subject-centring of the conception of life – function as catalysts in the process of change. These two components are mutually permeable and interdependent; thus they enter into a relationship of reciprocal intensification, which increases the self-control impulses of the time pioneers, and their appreciation of having time at their autonomous disposal. This outcome fosters a greater degree of subject-centredness in the shaping of their lives, and assists the time pioneers in developing their own interests. It is typical of the time pioneers that they not only proclaim their intentions and reflect upon changes, but also that they implement their ideas: '*The most important thing of all is actually getting what you really want.*'

However, the reorientation of the time pioneers also involves collateral hazards and weaknesses, and entails a plurality of risks. Identity crises and recidivist phases on the part of some time pioneers show what can happen in the absence of any appropriate socio-cultural context to support the reorientation of their meaning schemata. If the self-confidence and sense of personal identity of the time pioneers are not simultaneously reinforced by a process of self-assurance, and if this results in the inability of individuals to see past the end of the self-made beds on which they are lying, their experimental quest for new meaning schemata can end in failure. The development of the time pioneers' lifestyle is accompanied by similar difficult phases if they are unsuccessful in their attempts to revise their ingrained consumer habits, or develop their own time allocation skills. An increase in their financial burden for any reason whatsoever makes it almost impossible for the time pioneers to persist with flexibilized working time.

One result of the process of change is that the restructuring of the organization of their lives on the part of the time pioneers enhances their scope for changing and implementing plans of action. The outcome is the creation of a more open panorama of opportunities which is not obscured *ab initio* by any pre-planned time utilization schemata. This facilitates synchronization on the part of the time pioneers with several different time references, the devotion of equal attention to several perspectives, and the development of a plural orientation. The time pioneers exploit these options for the purposes of, for example, developing and expanding their own interests, intensifying their social contacts, devoting more time to their children, pursuing their hobbies, or simply for reading, thinking, 'having a natter', or going for walks.

From among their newly established lifestyle priorities, the time pioneers also examine their relationship to their employment and determine their attitude towards work. At the workplace, they target their labour input towards the content- and task-oriented job assignments, as a result of which the normative requirements of the employer are only fulfilled to a limited extent. In consequence of their development of an attitude towards work whose characteristic features are *dissociation* from the world of work and *commitment* to the job, the time pioneers constitute a source of irritation and provocation to the cultural paradigm of the employment society at the workplace, and are thus forced into a contradictory position at work. In spite of all the disadvantages which this entails for the working lives of the time pioneers, they still derive a sense of fulfilment from employment. Indeed, their detachment from the sphere of paid work redounds to the benefit of the job itself, since: '*I find that I also enjoy going to work more.*'

The time pioneers systematically relate the amount of time which they devote to work to the interests and priorities of their lifestyle. Lifestyle in its entirety proves to be the systematic decision-making location in respect of specific schemata of participation in employment, and the specific relationship between working time and lifetime.[2] The reorientation process is characterized by gradual retreat from the cultural paradigm of the employment society: there is a change of perspective away from the normative predominance of the world of work and from a way of life which revolves around paid work.

The restructuring of the orientational schemata of the time pioneers and the revision of the way in which they conduct their lives create a new integrative niveau of lifestyle, a lifestyle which the time pioneers consider to constitute a 'qualitative leap forward' and an independent source for the experience of change.

The new 'quality' primarily relates to the *changed time experience* of the time pioneers, in other words, to the integration of flexibility and disposability into the basic structure of their lifestyle. The time pioneers succeed in allocating the time which they have gained as a result of the reduction in and flexibilization of their working hours in such a way as to create enlarged, consecutive and autonomous units of time and room for manoeuvre, in consequence of which quantity becomes transformed into quality. The gravitational force of the time pioneers' lifestyle is applied to the forging of links between time references and subject-centred references. This is also the area in which the benefits of the time pioneers' lifestyle are perceived to lie. This lifestyle manifests itself as 'temporal affluence', in which the effects of the changes in time management techniques become condensed. The high degree of satisfaction among the time pioneers can chiefly be ascribed to the fact that their specific conception of lifestyle gives them a fair chance of asserting the perspectivity of subjective time in the face of the demands of the socially produced time system.

The characteristic structure of their lifestyle enables the time pioneers to achieve a greater degree of compatibility between employment and the private sphere. The marked reduction in and the flexibilization of their working time are necessary preconditions for the establishment of such compatibility, but they are by no means sufficient on their own. The time pioneers are unable to effect a more satisfactory level of compatibility between work and private life until a 'new balance' has been achieved. In order to solve this problem, the time pioneers are specifically required to effect a cognitive and normative dissociation and an affectual detachment from the sphere of employment, and to exclude and preserve the local time of the individual time references. This facilitates the reduction of the spill-over effects of the dominant time structures and the normative demands of the working environment, and the undermining of general appropriation strategies of employment.

The structure of the time pioneers' lifestyle is able to absorb intensification, which, though accurately registered, subjectively speaking is not considered to constitute a greater strain. Overall, as far as the time pioneers are concerned, the advantages arising out of the flexibilization of their working time largely outweigh the disadvantages.

Furthermore by incorporating the time forms change, flexibility and irregularity into the organization of their lives, the time pioneers endow their lifestyle with a dynamic structure: '*Life has a lot more variety and verve.*' In opposition to these time forms, the time pioneers place the interpretive schema of 'daily grind' and 'deadening', with which they stigmatize the monotonous routinization of their jobs and its inevitable permeation of all aspects of life.

The 'qualitative leap forward' relates on the one hand to the reduction in the degree of external influence exercised upon the fashioning of the lives of the time pioneers and on the other, for the most part, to the liberation of the time pioneers' lifestyle from the normative clutches of employment and the industrial time regime. The time pioneers are constantly aware of the outcome of the fact that they have reorganized their lives and adopted the lifestyle of a time pioneer. Making a comparison between their present and their previous lifestyles provides them with both a negative contrast and a constant incentive to prevent any diminution in the degree of detachment which they have achieved.

7 Future Prospects

This study of the time pioneers provides an insight into a group whose lifestyle has considerable bearing upon the social flux of present-day society. The lifestyle of the time pioneers is an acute manifestation of radical changes in the social structure of time, and of changes in employment behaviour. In this respect, despite the fact that it is not currently a widespread phenomenon, it can be said to play a pioneering role in the emergence of new social developments. The remainder of this chapter concentrates on the development of this role at several different levels.

Conflict with company organizational structures and cultures

The lifestyle of the time pioneers constitutes a new and independent form of participation in employment which is responsible for the emergence of some marked non-simultaneities *vis-à-vis* the prevailing company organizational structures and cultures. Time pioneers arrange their temporal commitment to the employment sphere on a selective basis. This is an attempt to establish for themselves a new balance in the relationship between working time and lifetime. Their conception of life severs links with standard working time, and in consequence they not only separate their personal working time from normal office and factory hours, but they also introduce their own time aspirations into the process involved in the flexible development of special working hours. They 'adopt' special working hours as their own working hours, and confront their employers with their own conceptions of working time. However, it is certainly not the case that, underlying this selective approach, there is an 'instrumental' attitude towards work which orients employment solely towards private purposes: on the contrary, the participation of the time pioneers in employment is characterized by a commitment to the professional accomplishment of their job assignments. They like working, but they would prefer to make a temporally concentrated contribution in accordance with their own requirements.

However, for the most part, employers are not prepared to concede to such demands. Efforts to achieve autonomy on the part of employees are not conducive to harmonious relations. In instances where employers do agree to flexible working hours in individual cases, such agreement is preponderantly subject to conditions which for the most part redound to the disadvantage of the individual employees concerned. It is frequently the case that, despite reduced hours, employers attempt to maintain work volumes at as constant a level as possible. In spite of suffering such intensification, the time pioneers cleave to the concept of flexibilization. They afford highest priority to having time at their own disposal.

Apart from the few well-known exceptions, it still remains necessary for employees to secure such flexible forms of working time through their own efforts. The majority of flexibilization models on offer from employers impose severe restrictions upon the permitted degree of working time flexibilization (in other words, the right of employees to determine location and duration for themselves). Even in cases where individual employees do succeed in realizing their conceptions of time, they encounter a whole series of problems at the workplace – and these problems are more severe at companies whose organizational structure and shop-floor culture are not geared towards flexible working time. These problems involve not only intensification, but also restricted communicatory opportunities, negative reactions from colleagues and, most of all, opposition from their immediate superiors at departmental level. These superiors are extremely fearful of forfeiting any of their authority. After all, they are enjoined to allow the time pioneers a greater say in the process involved in the mutual coordination of work; in addition, this results in the increasing displacement of monitoring procedures away from close levels of attendance and behavioural monitoring towards results monitoring. In consequence, a prerequisite of the successful implementation of flexible working time is not only the provision of a greater degree of employee latitude, but also the abandonment of leadership styles which are inseparably wedded to the traditional standard methods of maintaining work discipline, and unable to adjust to the requirements of flexible personnel deployment scheduling (see also Frerichs et al. 1986: 657).

Hitherto, with the exception of organizational models for flexible working time which were introduced by management and have proved their worth over a period of many years, work organization has failed to accommodate the specific achievement potential of flexibilized employees. According to our findings, for the most part the world of work is stonewalling, instead of concentrating its efforts on absorbing those whom it brands as malcontents. In so doing, it is overlooking the fact that the time pioneers have a whole series of additional merits to their credit. For example, time pioneers display a high level of willingness to work, self-discipline and initiative in the wake of the rationalization and intensification necessitated by flexibilization, and they also develop additional skills such as self-organization and self-monitoring. In the main, the development of these potential assets has not just been ignored by employers, but rather actively prevented. In addition, employers fail to exploit the innovative impulse which the time pioneers could introduce into the organizational structure of their working environment in consequence of their experiencing the development potential of the medium of time.

Insofar as it is introduced on a voluntary rather than a compulsory basis, the flexibilization of working time also requires modified organizational structures which adopt a constructive approach to the working time preferences and specific abilities of flexibilized employees. The reason for this is that, in the face of changed employee attitudes towards work differentiated along increasingly socio-cultural lines, it is also necessary to modify the criteria and methods of personnel and work management. However, conventional work-organization and work-culture schemata are slow to respond to the need for such changes.

The need for a policy on working time regulations

The stark difference in the strength of the bargaining position of employers and that of individual employees with regard to agreements on flexible working time is a manifestation of the lack of a protective framework for regulating this form of working time. Given the absence of concern on the part of any representatives of the collective interest for the problems associated with the flexibilization of the working time of individual employees, it would appear that this requirement will persist, at least in the medium term. The primary orientation of trade union policy, namely the safeguarding of standard working time, fails to afford adequate consideration to flexible forms of working time. The risks associated with such arrangements continue to be borne to a large extent by individual employees.

Our interpretation of flexible working time remains something of a 'hot potato' for the trade unions. They denounce individual working time arrangements because they are wary of subversive individualization and the undermining of solidarity. In addition, they labour under the illusion that flexibilized employees are impossible to organize. It is our opinion that the trade unions underestimate the mobilization potential of flexibilized (and would-be flexibilized) employees, whom they are too ready to tar with the same brush as 'classic' part-time employees. In particular, the difficulties which these employees encounter in their efforts to secure flexibilized working time, and the length of the process involved, forge empirical schemata which the trade unions could well exploit for the purpose of collective bargaining. After all, in securing their working time arrangements, it is a characteristic feature of the time pioneers that they are fully prepared to accept conflict, and they also come 'face to face' with the imbalance of negotiating power. In addition, flexible working time enhances the cooperative ability and sense of responsibility of the time pioneers, both of which might well be required for advocating collective interests at the workplace.

It is certainly possible to identify a number of collective employee interests. Additionally, the time pioneers emphasize the fact that they regard the flexibilization of their working time as a contribution to the redistribution of work, and that they wish to make room for new appointments (even if they do express scepticism as to the actual effect). However, their role as outsiders at the workplace means that they are less likely to be entrusted with the cause of upholding collective interests.

It is here that the second and much more potent denunciation of the flexibilization of working time on the part of the trade unions comes into play. The trade unions rightly fear the erosion of central legal obligations of the welfare state to guarantee the existence of standard working conditions: de-standardization and deregulation (for which, in the latter case, employers' federations in particular are

clamouring) decisively alter not only the regulatory framework of
employment protection standards, but also the entire system of
industrial relations. Nevertheless, as flexible working time gains
ground, it is becoming increasingly important that the trade unions
should address the revision of standard working conditions. It is
essential that they incorporate the question of the individual flexibilization of working time into their working time agreements.

At present, only a small number of employees exercise the individual right to shorter hours at mutually agreed times. But such
employees are pioneers whose strategic importance for the acceleration of processes of change must not be underestimated. In the event
of flexible forms of working time entering into competition with full-
time employment, there is a danger that, without collective agreements, they could constitute a powerful rationalization potential
which would also threaten full-time jobs – particularly if the fact that
the practitioners of flexibilization display a greater willingness to
work should 'get about'.

Hitherto, there has been a lack of institutional provisions which
also afford adequate consideration to the protective requirements of
flexible working time. What is required is a working time policy
which on the one hand is geared towards the maintenance of the
protective guarantees of standard working conditions, and on the
other includes provision for variation which takes into account the
socio-cultural diversification of attitudes towards work which is
gradually becoming more and more apparent. There would then be
an opportunity to adopt schemata of employment participation
which also make allowances for the multifaceted interest of employees
in arranging their hours of employment – schemata which are in
thrall neither to the constraints of uniformity nor to the dictate of
labour-intensifying rationalization strategies.

The enduring force of standard working time

The absence of legal and political regulations is not the only reason
why flexible working time is slow in gaining ground. The main
obstacles are the resistance to change and inflexibility of the cultural
paradigm of the employment society. Our research results suggest
that in future the effectiveness of this meaning and value schema
should be the subject of closer scrutiny.

The normative validity of the construction of 'standard working time' is a vital cornerstone of the edifice of the employment culture. On the one hand, this construction is based on the results of collective bargaining which are reflected in government, collective and company regulations. On the other, it prescribes the normative standard which exercises far-reaching influence inasmuch as it stipulates criteria for employee performance appraisal, defines role obligations, identifies overtime and determines eligibility for social welfare benefits. Standard working time only makes provision for 'part-time work'. Within the present interpretive schema, this is unavoidable for those employees whose family commitments, etc., prevent them from working full-time; however, from this standpoint, part-time work is only possible at lower levels of competence. Thus standard working time exercises considerable integrational influence as a socio-political and normative lodestar for all employment behaviour. It regulates conceptions of full-time work and normal working days, and is closely connected with the social division of labour between the sexes, occupational models, and status.

It thereby addresses the issue of the cultural influence of this central institution of the employment society, which talk of the 'erosion of standard working conditions' frequently overlooks. It cannot be concluded from the massive level of opposition which the time pioneers encounter at the workplace that the socio-cultural erosion of this edifice is already complete, but rather that it has suffered some peripheral diminution. The regulative validity of this institution for the organization of working life would appear to be more intact than is generally assumed. The time pioneers complain that this practically deprives them of any opportunity to articulate their conception of life at the workplace, that social communication is restricted by these very different cultural perspectives.

The main distinctive feature of our time pioneers is their impugnment of standard working time and their attack on its dominant influence. They refuse to use this standard as a yardstick for role definition and performance appraisal. In addition, the immediate allocation of other tasks to the free time which they have gained is not part of their plans. Thus they re-evaluate the significance of the standard schema and weaken the close links between its components. This dissociation from the dominant standard provides an opportunity for the emergence of new arrangements of socio-integrational relevance, and the development of new schemata for the relationship between 'working and living' and performance appraisal, and for modified roles and status bestowals, which, however, remain firmly anchored in the core area of the employment system.

Efforts to escape the hegemony of the employment society

In comparison with opinion polls and surveys, by means of which the change in working values is recorded, our perspective is more profound, inquiring into the significance of employment for various different lifestyles. The lifestyle of the time pioneers now enables us to identify one specific schema of attitude towards work. From certain cultural rifts in the employment society, this schema moulds a specific form of employment behaviour which is characterized by both commitment and detachment. In contrast to the dominant form of incorporation into the employment society, as far as this lifestyle is concerned, employment does not constitute *the* core factor in the conception of life and the identity development of the individual. The interpretive schema predetermined by the cultural paradigm of the employment society, particularly that concerning performance and employment behaviour, is dissected and rearranged; several interpretive schemata are retained, some remodelled, and others removed.

As far as efforts to escape the crisis of the employment society are concerned, it is generally the case that earlier certainties and expectations become problematic, and legitimations of the work-culture meaning schema begin to crumble. For the purpose of retaining their own meaningful world, these dissociational efforts on the part of the time pioneers require supportive measures in order to objectify and justify their different conception of reality. The time pioneers can only justify their conception of life and their lifestyle with a great deal of effort. This is due to a specific contradiction: on the one hand, they consciously wish to achieve occupational commitment and potential realization in the core zone of the formal employment system; on the other, they wish to liberate the organization of their lives from the dominance of employment. Such gymnastics take some explaining. This is achieved primarily by means of vigorously questioning the excessive formative influence exercised upon everyday life by the employment sphere. Their aggressive dissociation from a way of life which is in thrall to the industrial time regime and the money logic of the employment society supports the time pioneers in their efforts to legitimize their lifestyle. Time pioneers have no off-the-peg, collective conceptions of society and the world upon which to fall back, such as those typically exploited by, for example, the trade union movement, the petty bourgeoisie, the alternative movement, cultural criticism, etc.

The attitudes of the time pioneers towards work are selectively geared towards the achievement of as great a sense of fulfilment as possible in their work, coupled with the highest possible level of independence from the organization of work. On the one side, it is of fundamental importance to the time pioneers that their aspirations to independence and autonomy are secured by means of employment. On the other, the standard conditions prevailing at the workplace are unable to activate their willingness to work. Time pioneers only partially accede to the unreasonable normative demands imposed upon them by their employers, and this is reflected in the treatment which they receive at the hands of the organizational structure and its proponents: they also deal with the 'apostates' on a selective basis, permitting them out-times, while excluding them from full membership of the ideological and reward community of the 'normal workforce'.

The specific attitude towards work adopted by the time pioneers, and the restructuring of the organization of their lives, enable them to effect the gradual liberation of their lifestyle from the hegemony of work, and to establish some latitude for new priorities of their own, namely, the pursuit of multifarious interests and aspirations and, most of all, the development of a new time structure for everyday life. Inevitably, their conduct is still that of pioneers of changed attitudes towards work who come into conflict with the employment system and suffer grave disadvantages. The prospects of the employment behaviour schemata of the time pioneers gaining ground will not increase until the cultural paradigm of the employment society weakens further (to which the growing demands of women for participation in skilled employment will make a decisive contribution). However, in the train of any gradual normalization process, those who follow in the footsteps of the time pioneers will then tread altogether different paths.

Accelerated pace and the struggle for the (re)appropriation of time

The implications of our research results are not restricted to the employment sphere. The consequences which result from the time pioneers' dissociation from the industrial time regime, which they are able to exploit for the purpose of shaping the way in which they organize their lives, have their origins in more far-reaching processes

of social change. This applies both to upheavals in social time relations and to processes of social individualization. The time pioneers
develop a special sensitivity towards time relations. The studies describing the condition of our social time are unanimous: social time
relations follow in the slipstream of increasing speed and the deple-
tion of time. The symbol of our times is 'time deficiency' ('harassed
society', 'society without time'), the acceleration of time is 'vertiginous'.
Even discounting Virilio's related speculations on modern society as
the 'disappearing society' (1989), it is still possible to concur with his
designation of speed as the 'goddess of the modern age'. The industrial time regime is the historical and social basis upon which fanta-
sies and ideologies of speed are founded. The credo of this regime is:
'time is money'. Given that, like money, time is scarce, this is
complemented by the maxim: 'maximum time gain by means of opti-
mum time utilization'. In consequence of this, we become 'time
economists': we are always saving time in order to gain time, but we
immediately reutilize the time we have gained, so that ultimately we
do not have any more time at our disposal at all.

Absolutizing this powerful trend makes our time pioneers appear
veritable heretics. They break with the belief in the absolute hegemony of time economy, and offend against the obligation of rational
time optimization. However, the achievement of the time pioneers is
not as outrageously and heretically beyond belief as it would appear
from the lofty heights of the social system: the assumption that the
temporal methods of the social system exercise universal influence
upon the structuring of subjective time is a structural-determinist
irrationality. Given the fact that social times lie at the interface of
multifarious time references, they must be synchronized with various
time systems; however, this requires interpretive appropriation and
processing on the part of the members of society. This focuses attention on the specific socio-cultural resources which fashion and substantialize time relations. Although the relevant interpretive schemata
now comprise the meaningful ascriptions of time of the social time
system, they also reflect the economic dictate of time expenditure.
However, it is at this juncture that the time pioneers sever a decisive
knot: they abstract the connection between time and performance
upon which the economic dictate of utilization is based, and within
which the socially dominant time system exercises a decisive connec-
tive and formative influence upon the time allocation practices of the
members of society.

Historically, time utilization and performance become consolidated
into an influential construction which determines the legitimacy of

activity schemata, from which, in turn, personal attributes are derived and character assignations effectuated, such as idler, panic merchant, 'busy bee', or slowcoach. Modern society places a high value on activistic attributes of doing. Lack of time and deadline pressure are regarded as an expression of achievement potential. 'Anyone who admits to having too much time on their hands disqualifies themselves, and is expelled from the society of those who are able to achieve, demand, and obtain something' (Luhmann 1971: 150). Work is regarded as a particularly legitimate means of utilizing time; if at all possible, work should also be performed outside formal working hours as a permanent and omnipresent demonstration of achievement potential. Time should always be utilized (productively). Anyone who has failed to internalize the constraint of substantialization through permanent activity cannot expect recognition as a full member of the achievement-oriented society.

The achievement of the time pioneers is the fact that they attack this central interpretive schema of legitimate time utilization, and re-evaluate it in their own favour. They oppose deadline pressure, harassment and actionism with a slower pace, with self-imposed pacing. They place a high value on the constitutional 'peace of mind' which they experience as a result. The additional time which they have at their autonomous disposal is not sacrificed on the altar of either part-time or supplementary work, or to the organized pursuits of the leisure industry. Under no circumstances should time pioneers be misinterpreted as free-time pioneers. Time pioneers cultivate time management techniques which declare war on pace, in which context, pace comprises the quantitative and mensurable dimension, and the subjective experience, of speed.

The endeavours of the time pioneers are geared towards moving away from enforced schemata of time utilization to the most independent possible utilization of autonomous time. Their chief concern is the 'reappropriation of time'. Flexible working time does offer some scope for achieving this, but the time pioneers know that much more is required, namely, active and autonomous time allocation ability. This recognizes the fact that, with the aid of time, it is possible to fashion and change life (time as a dimension of the structure of life); that it is essential that disposable and flexible time management practices are integrated into everyday life (time as a structural technique); that it is imperative to prise time from the grip of the dominant time conventions (deviant perception of time); and – which is the specific achievement of the time pioneers – that the orientational knowledge of time which they have acquired should in turn be related to categories of time (reflexive perception of time). Their reflexive perception of time makes the time pioneers aware of their compulsive need for ever more time for the purpose of enhancing their sensitivity towards time, and of exploiting this sensitivity for the purpose of exercising a formative influence upon their lives. The exercise of such influence represents the time pioneers' ideal, though they are fully cognizant of the fact that a plurality of everyday restrictions and problems are strewn in its path. It is with pride that the time pioneers announce that, as a result of their time structuring endeavours, they have more time; they underline the fact that accomplishing this feat is a laborious process which takes time.

The example of the time pioneers demonstrates that it is by no means the case that the members of society are helpless in the face of the excessive determination of time requirements and the structural compaction of time on the part of the socially produced time systems. The time pioneers prove capable of managing the various time requirements of the institutional part-time worlds in such a manner as to establish a more satisfactory link between these worlds and their subjective time aspirations. In the process, they succeed in creating and substantializing their own definitional scope, dissociating themselves from the normative time requirements, and thus diminishing the influence of institutional time systems.

Individualization as subject-centring

The time pioneers' demand for more time for themselves is a reaction to the radical changes affecting the whole of society, of which individualization processes are the chief manifestation. Individualization occurs in two ways: on the one hand, the time pioneers employ time as a reserve in order to have more time for 'identity management' and life planning. On the other, with the aid of the resource of time, they attempt to structure the organization of their lives, and to change the shape of their lives. The individualization process of the time pioneers is closely linked to the sensitization of their consciousness of time.

In contrast to the definition of individualization which emphasizes the individualization of life situations and life paths (in the sense of the de-traditionalization and atomization of individuals; see particularly Beck 1983), we have theorized individualization as the growing differentiation on the part of people in relation to social systems.

'Subject-centring' is a process in which the subjective component in the shaping of the way people organize their lives increases, as does their autonomous contribution towards the integration of the way they conduct their lives and their life histories. Such subject-centred processes are particularly bolstered by the weakening of the fixed link between life conception and working life – in particular in order to facilitate the development of independent life orientations and lifestyles.

Once working time has been reduced and flexibilized for the purpose of the enhanced pursuit of various interests and the improvement of the level of coordination between different areas of life, the time pioneers are faced with the problem of the integration and temporal synchronization of these fields of activity. Time pioneers tackle this problem by, on the one hand, gearing their thematic prioritizations towards time, and, on the other, subjecting the formation of their lifestyle to a greater degree of self-steering. Given that the time pioneers are particularly exposed to the individualization processes in the employment markets, during the course of which occupational risks are personalized and left to the responsibility of the individual, greater self-monitoring is inevitable. Thus the other side of the coin of the claim to self-development insists on a greater degree of rationalization of everyday life in the sense of greater reflexive potential and the need for more active self-steering. This touches upon a complex cluster of individual accomplishments whose development is generally accorded the emphatic designation 'emancipation', and whose result is frequently expressed in such highly ambitious terms as 'self-realization' and 'autonomy'.

Although it is not our intention to overlook the salient dangers and potential for crisis associated with such individualization processes, the case of the time pioneers nevertheless demonstrates a crucial prerequisite of a self-determined life: without the support of a reflexive visualization of the conception of life, greater latitude to shape lifestyle organization is of no value. It is essential that the organization of time is accompanied by a process of clarification in respect of both the reasons for and the expectations behind the change, and the objectives which determine the direction that such change should take. This clarification process entails an intensified level of self-thematization, processes of self-discovery, and research into personal identity. In order to facilitate the fulfilment of such aspirations to enhanced capacity for self-determination, a greater level of self-observation is required. Subject-centring cannot exercise a proper degree of influence upon the way in which people fashion their lives until objectives of the conception of life are clarified and self-steering skills are acquired via a greater degree of self-reflection on the part of the subject.

The time pioneers frequently seek plausible justifications for this individualization process in their own biographies. This lies in the 'biographization of the self', in other words, in the constantly updated references on the part of the time pioneers to their own histories: whence they have come, what they have become, and what they intend to become in the future. Justifications are easier for the time pioneers to find if they distance themselves from the prevailing normality assumptions and the range of standard programmes for the conduct of life. In rearranging the relationship between working time and lifetime, the time pioneers also change their biographical perspectives. Male time pioneers in particular dissociate their biographical conceptions from 'normal' professional careers, their career histories therefore becoming less predictable. The time pioneers react actively to this, incorporating biographical reorientations and lacunas in their career histories into their life planning as a means of reducing the dangers of crisis to an absolute minimum. Consequently, they focus their emphasis on experiencing the present, and endeavour to keep their future horizons more open by the adoption of option-oriented time management styles. In order not to foreclose any possibility of variational scope and reorientations in the future, they attempt to travel 'along several tracks at once', avoid any long-term conditions and commitments, and make allowances for possible biographical discontinuities. Overall, the lifestyle of the time pioneers is geared towards the incorporation of situative mobility and manoeuvrability into their general way of life. This is mainly achieved by basing everyday life upon flexible time structures.

Thus, the time pioneers adopt a very specific reaction to the increasing level of contingency experienced in modern society. In order to cope with the growing range of options at their disposal without immediately imposing restrictions upon them, the time pioneers develop a conception of time which is as option-oriented as possible. They exploit the options opened up by society by rejecting the eight-hour day. They use their revised time structuring techniques to increase their scope for alternating between and activating the various different time references. However, this also entails the reinforcement of their selection capacity, and the development of a relative time autonomy (particularly *vis-à-vis* the demands of their employers). Thus, although the time pioneers do acquire some options, they deliberately sacrifice others (at work, for example). Both these processes (the reinforcement of selection capacity and the development of a relative time economy) are mutually dependent as a consequence of the experience of contingency, and both require the time pioneers to fashion their lives along subject-centred lines.

This facilitates the acquisition of a much more accurate understanding of the trend towards individualization than is asserted in the global diagnosis of the growing atomization and isolation of the individual. By means of greater feats of self-assurance, the time pioneers attempt to remain steadfast in the face of the selective pressure of social contingency, retain their options, and refrain from the excessive limitation of the plurality of opportunity structures from the outset. The lifestyle of the time pioneers ensures that this does not degenerate into boundless caprice, culminating in an 'epoch of emptiness', in which members of society forfeit their sense of security, and sink without trace in the 'realm of the ephemeral' of constantly changing whims and sensations. As an integrative schema, it imposes typical schemata for the organization of life, and furnishes social and personal identification constructions with pillars of support. It should be regarded as an independent lifestyle establishing a specific form of participation in employment, time structuring and the re-evaluation of the money–time dictate. It comprises characteristic schemata of problem interpretations, ascriptions of meaning and activities, via which it evolves its sociation function.

Thus the lifestyle of the time pioneers does not develop its inter-subjective associations via common milieus, common subcultures, or common social interaction and communication networks, but via collective practices of interpretation and action, via which new forms of the social integration of the individual are constituted. (For a continuation of this theme, see Hörning and Michailow 1990.)

In the time pioneers, we have identified a new social type and a lifestyle which, given favourable socio-economic and socio-cultural conditions, we assume will continue to gain ground. However, it would be too easy to fall victim to wishful thinking, to overlook the continuing cultural force and legitimacy of the employment society. Although the utopia of the employment society is a spent force, there is no indication that it will become extinct in the foreseeable future. It is more likely that the employment society will be restructured, a process in which our time pioneers could play an important role. This would mean that the time pioneers would become the vehicle of a development which gauges modern society by the aspirations which it cherishes, and insists upon the recovery of concepts of 'variety', 'autonomous disposable time' and 'self-steering' from beneath the edifice of the industrial regime.

Notes

Chapter 1   Lifestyles and Time Relations in Flux

1 In modern, differentiated society, the individual becomes a part-time parti-
   cipant in various part-time worlds (see Hitzler 1988; Hitzler and Honer
   1984, 1986).

2 See Durkheim 1976: 14ff; Heinemann and Ludes 1978: 221; Sorokin and
   Merton 1937: 615.

3 Hinrichs et al. 1982; Müller-Wichmann 1987: 155; Neckel 1984; Negt
   1984; Olk et al. 1979; Rinderspacher 1985.

4 Cyba 1983; Gensior and Wolf 1980; Heinze et al. 1979; Hoff 1982; Mertens
   1979, 1982; Offe et al. 1982; Teriet 1978.

5 The criticism which flexible working time attracts from the trade unions is
   manifold (see Hoff 1982; May and Mohr 1985): flexible working time would
   lead to rationalization as a result of the comparison of work, increased
   productivity, and the intensification of work, the undermining of collective
   safety regulations, and the division of the workforce. Flexible working time
   would accustom employees to stressful working conditions hazardous to
   their health. The objective of the concept of flexible working time is said to
   be the implementation of voluntary part-time work, thus aiding and abetting
   a further round of job cuts. It is not possible to include flexible working time
   in collective agreements. Flexible working time would constitute shorter
   working time with no compensatory wage adjustment, and thus, in effect,
   unpaid short-time working. Flexible working time is associated with lower
   levels of social security provision, and would issue in the imposition of
   greater strain on the welfare net.

6 On the erosion of standard working time, see Bosch 1986; Däubler 1988;

Hinrichs 1987, 1983: 154ff; Hinrichs and Wiesenthal 1984; Mückenberger 1985; Wiesenthal 1987: 113; Zachert 1988.

7 In the wake of the discussion surrounding mass unemployment and the demand for a 35-hour week, the subject of working time flexibilization became the focal point of public interest. The media turned the spotlight on companies which had introduced flexible working time schemes. Thus, treading the path of classic industrial sociology, we initially opted to approach the subject via all those companies in which flexible working time schemes were in force. By adopting this initial approach to the subject, we expected to encounter a large pool of time pioneers. Thus, as part of the initial stage of our study, we identified a total of 34 such companies. Upon closer scrutiny, we established that only in ten companies did the flexibilization arrangements fulfil our criteria. However, even these schemes afforded employees only a very limited degree of latitude in determining their working time. In addition, in some companies the employees took very little advantage of the flexibilization schemes on offer, with the result that the flexible working time schemes were not actually implemented. In consequence, approaching this subject via companies proved unsatisfactory. It became obvious that the topical debate had overestimated the phenomenon of company flexibilization schemes, and that there were far fewer serious attempts on the part of companies to implement such flexibilization schemes than had been assumed (see section 1.5).

8 See Bäcker 1981; Gerzer et al. 1985; Hoff and Scholz 1985; Rinderspacher 1982; Rudolph et al. 1981, Schlotter 1986; Stengel 1987; Treier 1979.

9 Bielenski 1979; Bierig 1980; Bosch 1983; Frerichs et al. 1985; Fürstenberg 1987; Gabriel 1985; Gaugler 1983; Hof 1984; Hoff 1983; Landenberger 1985b, 1987c; Marr 1987; May and Mohr 1985; Sydow and Conrad 1987; Weidinger and Hoff 1988.

10 Görres 1984; Heinze et al. 1979; Kutsch and Vilmar 1983; Ministry for Labour, Health and Social Affairs of North Rhine-Westphalia 1984; Reyher et al. 1979; Rürup and Struwe 1984; Schettkat 1983; Seifert 1989; Seifert and Welzmüller 1983.

11 Bäcker and Seifert 1982; Hinrichs et al. 1982; Hinrichs and Wiesenthal 1986; Hoff 1982; Kurz-Scherf 1987; Lemm and Skolnik 1986; Mayr and Janssen 1984; Mertens 1982; Pornschlegel 1979; Scharpf and Schettkat 1984; Seifert 1986; Vobruba 1982; Weitzel and Hoff, 1981; Wiesenthal et al. 1983.

12 On the heterogeneity of the various forms of working time covered by the term 'flexible', see Beyer 1986: 67; Gensior and Wolf 1980: 108; Linnenkohl 1985.

13 There have always been deviations from standard working time, but these do not permit us to speak in terms of flexible working time. Historically speaking, the length of the working week has always been subject to legal, collective bargaining, and economic influences (Gross et al. 1987).

14 In order to locate these people, we opted to use the press and the radio. We

presented our project in several regional and national newspapers, and on radio programmes, and requested employees to contact us for an interview-discussion. As a result of these presentations, a large number of people came forward who had secured flexibilized working time as a result of their own efforts, and who fulfilled our criteria. Hitherto, this specific group of employees has been afforded insufficient attention by the research sector, and thus our efforts secured access to a large field of research which had previously remained concealed from view. This field of research suits the time pioneers, in that it addresses the issue of their high level of commitment to their form of working time. They displayed a high degree of willingness to conduct in-depth interview-discussions which were characterized by a high level of informative content and painstaking attention to detail. A total of 47 interview-discussions were conducted, of which 36 ultimately formed the analytical basis of the study. The research was conducted between the winter of 1985 and the summer of 1986 (see also n. 7. above).

15 The narrative interview was primarily developed by Schütze (1977, 1983).

16 Hitherto, empirical research has largely ignored this approach. Industrial sociology could also employ the 'phenomenology of the lifeworld' for the purpose of securing a sounder theoretical basis upon which to analyse interpretive schemata (see Lempert et al. 1979; Neuendorff 1980; Neuendorff and Sabel 1978; Oevermann 1973; Thomssen 1980).

Chapter 2 Flexible Working Time

1 On the subject of plausibility structure, see Berger and Luckmann 1979: pp. 174–82.

2 It is possible to distinguish three forms of initiative with regard to the flexibilization of working time: firstly, instances in which it is on offer as the prevailing company working time scheme or available in the form of statutory regulations, as is the case in the public services, for example, and the resulting opportunities are exploited by the members of the workforce. Secondly, instances in which employees take jobs already involving flexibilized working time. Thirdly, instances in which individual employees secure the reorganization of their working time on their own initiative (Weitzel and Hoff 1981). The remainder of this study is primarily concerned with the last of these three alternatives.

3 See Engfer et al. 1983; Gross et al. 1987; Hinrichs 1988; Landenberger 1985.

4 Bosch 1986; Däubler 1988; Hinrichs 1988: 154ff Mückenberger 1985; Wiesenthal 1987: 113; Zachert 1988.

5 Hinrichs 1987; May and Mohr 1985; Seifert 1987.

6 See Bierig 1980: 1258; Brötz 1983; Gaugler et al. 1981; Hoff and Weidinger 1985: 34.

7 A noticeable feature of this study in comparison with others on the flexibilization of working time (e.g. Bosch 1983: 248; Held and Karg 1983: 479; Held-Gemeinhardt and Kroker 1985: 114, 173) is the extent to which intensification was found to occur. There are two principal reasons for this discrepancy:

1 The detailed interview-discussions were conducted at the home of the interviewees, which created a situation of trust in which the interviewees were able to delineate their experiences, including the extent to which they were affected by intensification, without the risk of incurring sanctions from their employers.

2 Our study primarily concerns cases of individual implementation of working time flexibilization falling outside the purview of those spectacular introductions of company working time models, staged, *inter alia*, for the consumption of the general public. In such cases, intensification is easier to implement.

8 There have been a number of studies and publications on this theme. See *inter alia* Held and Karg 1983: 471; Held-Gemeinhardt and Kroker 1985: 170ff; Hoff and Weidinger 1985: 42ff; Landenberger 1985a, 1987a; Oppolzer 1985: 17; Weitzel and Hoff 1981: 144ff.

9 See Görres 1984: 160ff: 'However, supervision is only one of the effects of rigid working time. Another of its attractions for hierarchical systems might be the fact that it demands less personal responsibility and maturity on the part of those concerned, whereas generally speaking, flexible and variable arrangements necessitate and foster personal responsibility. Insofar as the stability of hierarchies is placed in jeopardy by such qualities – by virtue of the fact that, for example, they reveal the superfluity of many managerial functions (and managers) – the insistence on persevering with rigid arrangements on the part of management is only too understandable. This does not foreclose the possibility that many employees can develop a liking for systems which deny them the opportunity of exercising personal initiative – it is within the framework of such systems that the foibles of the subjects and the inclinations of the masters are most sublimely complemented and reinforced.'

10 The same observations are also made by Haller 1981: 121; Held-Gemeinhardt and Kroker 1985: 152ff, 168ff; Frerichs et al. 1986: 186.

Chapter 3 The Revision of Interpretive Schemata

1 For the assertions which follow, see Beck 1984; see also the history of ideas behind the development of German conceptions of work in Härtel et al. 1985: 7–31.

2 Initially, the specifically 'German form' of research into value change also reacted in this vein by dramatizing the transformation of work values

and interpreting it as a tragic loss with far-reaching (international and socio-political) implications. See Kmieciak 1976; Klages 1981, 1983, 1984; Klages and Kmieciak 1979; Noelle-Neumann 1978.

3 It has been revealed that flexible working time arrangements require a long introductory phase and a carefully prepared implementation phase (see Bielenski and Hegner 1985; Frerichs et al. 1986), a state of affairs which is attributable to relatively stable cultural structures.

4 In order to demonstrate the power of the monoculture of the employment society, our expositions are loaded towards characteristic problem constella-tions. The points which are raised all relate to conflicts which have occurred at the workplace but which are not evenly distributed throughout the whole gamut of cases and do not occur everywhere with the same degree of intensity. They depend upon the degree to which the cultural paradigm of the employ-ment society has become established and influential at the workplace in a dominant and rigid manner.

5 This requires a 'triangulation process', that is to say, the reciprocal relativiza-tion of the roles, and differentiation between them, recognizing the roles as roles, and internalizing this duplicity to such a degree that it becomes possible to play the roles (see Luckmann 1979: 310).

Chapter 4   The Changed Relationship between Money and Time

1 In contrast to the trade union demand for a 35-hour week without loss of pay.
2 See Becker 1965; Hegner 1983; Joerges 1981, 1983; Klein 1983.
3 See *inter alia* Heinemann 1987; Linder 1970; Müller-Wichmann 1984; Rinderspacher 1985; Simmel 1897, 1978.
4 Conversely, this is closely associated with the specific form of time experience which accentuates the experience of the present (see section 5.3)

Chapter 5   The Time Structures of the New Lifestyle

1 In the reconstruction of the process involved in the reorientation of the tem-poral interpretive schemata of the time pioneers following the flexibilization of their working time, we particularly draw upon those time pioneers for whom implicit time structures become an explicit object of experiential reflec-tion. These interview texts thematize the everyday practical mastery of the problems associated with time allocation. Time management techniques are particularly evident in those interview texts in which attention is focused on the development of time allocation techniques when the conventional routines

of time structuring for mastering everyday life fail to function, thus requiring problematization and analysis. This is the case in those interviews which revolve around the reorganization of everyday life. In this context, we cite examples of the time management techniques adopted by the time pioneers, wherever the interview texts facilitate the identification of such examples.

2 Various sociological theories of time accept this conception of time shortage (see Luhmann 1971; Müller-Wichmann 1984; Rinderspacher 1985; Schöps 1980).

3 For this reason it is inadmissible to adopt a methodical approach such as that of time budget research (see Andorka 1987; Blass 1980), which concentrates purely on the identification and recording of activities. This would entail the adoption of a quantitative, utility-oriented perception of time which would be incapable of identifying the essential qualitative trait of time structuring.

Chapter 6 The Dynamic of the New Lifestyle

1 The quotations in this chapter are cited for the sole purpose of highlighting the situation in the words of the time pioneers, and have more of an illustrative character than anything else.

2 In respect of their relevance to specific problems associated with the life situation of the time pioneers, attitude towards work, time structuring and household management are closely interconnected. This is a clear indication of the fact that in order to be able to arrive at any significant conclusions relating to trends in the realization prospects of flexible working time, and in order to be able to examine the seriousness of working time demands which are voiced, it is necessary to scrutinize every aspect of the way in which the time pioneers organize their lives, indeed, to scrutinize their very lifestyle. Anybody who continues to base his/her argument upon survey data on working time demands and preferences is completely overestimating their reliability.

Bibliography

Adamy, Wilhelm 1988: Deregulierung des Arbeitsmarktes. Zwischenbilanz des Beschäftigungsförderungsgesetzes. *WSI-Mitteilungen*, 41, 475–82.

Andorka, Rudolf 1987: Time budgets and their uses. *Annual Review of Sociology*, 13, 149–64.

Ansbacher, Heinz L. 1967: Life style: a historical and systematic review. *Journal of Individual Psychology*, 23, 191–212.

Attias-Donfut, Claudine 1978: Freizeit, Lebensablauf und Generationenbildung. In L. Rosenmayr (ed.), *Die menschlichen Lebensalter. Kontinuität und Krisen*, Munich, 354–75.

Banning, Thomas E. 1987: *Lebensstilorientierte Marketing-Theorie*. Heidelberg.

Bardmann, Theodor M. 1986: *Die missverstandene Freizeit*. Stuttgart.

Bäcker, Gerhard 1981: Teilzeitarbeit und individuelle Arbeitszeitflexibilisierung – Festschreibung der Benachteiligung von Frauen in Beruf und Familie. *WSI-Mitteilungen*, 34, 194–203.

Bäcker, Gerhard, and Seifert, Hartmut 1982: Arbeitszeitpolitische Kontroverse: Individuelle Flexibilität oder tarifvertragliches Regelsystem. In C. Offe, K. Hinrichs, and H. Wiesenthal (eds), *Arbeitszeitpolitik. Formen und Folgen einer Neuverteilung der Arbeitszeit*, Frankfurt/Main, 244–59.

Beck, Ulrich 1983: Jenseits von Stand und Klasse? Soziale Ungleichheiten, gesellschaftliche Individualisierungsprozesse und die Entstehung neuer sozialer Formationen und Identitäten. In R. Kreckel (ed.), *Soziale Ungleichheiten* (*Soziale Welt* Special Edition, 2), Göttingen, 35–74.

Beck, Ulrich 1984: Perspektiven einer kulturellen Evolution der Arbeit. *Mitteilungen aus der Arbeitsmarkt- und Berufsforschung*, 17, 52–62.

Beck-Gernsheim, Elisabeth 1983: 'Dasein für andere' zum Anspruch auf ein Stück 'eigenes Leben': Individualisierungsprozesse im weiblichen Lebenszusammenhang. *Soziale Welt*, 34, 307–40.

Becker, Gary S. 1965: A theory of the allocation of time. *Economic Journal*, 75, 493–517.

Becker, Ulrich, and Nowak, Horst 1982: Lebensweltanalyse als neue Perspektive der Meinungs- und Marketingforschung. *European Society for Opinion and Marketing Research Congress*, 2, 247–67.

Berger, Peter A. 1987: Klassen und Klassifikationen. Zur 'neuen Unübersichtlichkeit' in der soziologischen Ungleichheitsforschung. *Kölner Zeitschrift für Soziologie und Sozialpsychologie*, 39, 59–85.

Berger, Peter L., and Luckmann Thomas, 1979: *The Social Construction of Reality*. Harmondsworth.

Berger, Peter L., and Luckmann, Thomas 1983: Social Mobility and Personal Identity. In T. Luckmann, *Life-worlds and Social Realities*, London, 1983, 110–123.

Bergmann, Werner 1981: *Die Zeitstrukturen sozialer Systeme. Eine systemtheoretische Analyse*. Berlin.

Bergmann, Werner 1983: Das Problem der Zeit in der Soziologie. *Kölner Zeitschrift für Soziologie und Sozialpsychologie*, 35, 462–504.

Beyer, Horst-Tilo 1986: *Betriebliche Arbeitszeitflexibilisierung: Zwischen Utopie und Realität*. Munich.

Bielenski, Harald 1979: Barrieren gegen eine flexible Arbeitszeitgestaltung. *Mitteilungen zur Arbeitsmarkt- und Berufsforschung*, 12, 300–12.

Bielenski, Harald, and Hegner, Friedhart (eds) 1985: *Flexible Arbeitszeiten. Erfahrungen aus der Praxis*. Frankfurt/Main.

Bierig, Günter 1980: Teilzeitarbeit. Siemens-Untersuchung. *Der Arbeitgeber*, 32, 1257–60.

Bierig, Günter 1981: Flexibler durch Teilzeitarbeit? *Zeitschrift für Organisation*, 50, 361–4.

Blass, Wolf 1980: *Zeitbudget-Forschung. Eine kritische Einführung in Grundlagen und Methoden*. Frankfurt/Main.

Bosch, Gerhard 1983: Arbeitszeit und Rationalisierung – Ergebnisse betrieblicher Fallstudien. *WSI-Mitteilungen*, 36, 235–48.

Bosch, Gerhard 1986: Hat das Normalarbeitsverhältnis eine Zukunft? *WSI-Mitteilungen*, 39, 163–76.

Bourdieu, Pierre 1983: Ökonomisches Kapital, kulturelles Kapital, soziales Kapital. In R. Kreckel (ed.), *Soziale Ungleichheiten* (*Soziale Welt* Special Edition, 2), Göttingen, 183–98.

Bourdieu, Pierre 1984: *Distinction: a social critique of the judgement of taste*. London.

Brötz, Rainer 1983: Flexible Arbeitszeitregelungen am Beispiel eines multinationalen Mischkonzerns. *WSI-Mitteilungen*, 36, 480–90.

Büchtemann, Christoph, and Schupp, Jürgen 1986: Zur Sozioökonomie der Teilzeitbeschäftigung in der Bundesrepublik Deutschland. *Discussion Paper IIM/LMP 86-15*, Wissenschaftszentrum, Berlin.

Conradi, Helmut 1982: *Teilzeitarbeit. Theorie, Realität, Realisierbarkeit.* Munich.

Cyba, Eva 1983: Arbeitszeit: Probleme der Arbeitszeitflexibilisierung. *Österreichische Zeitschrift für Soziologie*, 8, 39–45.

Dahrendorf, Ralf 1980: Im Entschwinden der Arbeitsgesellschaft. Wandlungen in der sozialen Konstruktion des menschlichen Lebens. *Merkur*, 34, 749–60.

Dahrendorf, Ralf 1983: Wenn der Arbeitsgesellschaft die Arbeit ausgeht. In J. Matthes (ed.), *Krise der Arbeitsgesellschaft? Verhandlungen des 21. Deutschen Soziologentages in Bamberg 1982*, Frankfurt/Main, 25–37.

Däubler, Wolfgang 1988: Deregulierung und Flexibilisierung im Arbeitsrecht. *WSI-Mitteilungen*, 41, 449–57.

Deutsches Jugendinstitut, Munich 1984: *Anpassungsprobleme zwischen 'Familie und Arbeitswelt'. Eine empirische Untersuchung anhand des Kaufhauses 'Ludwig Beck am Rathauseck'.* Munich.

Deutschmann, Christoph 1983: Systemzeit und soziale Zeit. *Leviathan*, 11, 494–514.

Deutschmann, Christoph 1985: *Der Weg zum Normalarbeitstag. Die Entwicklung der Arbeitszeiten in der deutschen Industrie bis 1918.* Frankfurt/Main.

Durkheim, Emile 1976: *Elementary Forms of the Religious Life*, 2nd edn. London.

Eichler, Gert 1979: Spiel und Arbeit. In *Zur Theorie der Freizeit*, Stuttgart–Bad Cannstatt.

Elias, Norbert 1982: Über die Zeit. *Merkur*, 36, 841–56 and 998–1016.

Engfer, Uwe, Hinrichs, Karl, Offe, Claus, and Wiesenthal, Helmut 1983: Arbeitszeitsituation und Arbeitszeitverkürzung in der Sicht der Beschäftigten. Ergebnisse einer Arbeitnehmerumfrage. *Mitteilungen aus der Arbeitsmarkt- und Berufsforschung*, 16, 91–105.

Ermert, Axel, and Rinderspacher, Jürgen P. 1981: Alles eine Frage des Timing – Bemerkungen über den Zusammenhang von Zeit und Leistung. *Ästhetik und Kommunikation*, 12, 37–73.

Fischer, Wolfram 1986: Soziale Konstitution von Zeit in biographischen Texten und Kontexten. In Gottfried Heinemann (ed.), *Zeitbegriffe*, Freiburg, 355–77.

Frerichs, Johann, Kock, Klaus, and Ulber, Jürgen 1985: *Rahmenbedingungen betrieblicher Arbeitszeitpolitik.* Cologne.

Frerichs, Joke, Gross, Hermann, and Pekruhl, Ulrich 1986: Lernprozesse bei der betrieblichen Umsetzung der Arbeitszeit. Erfahrungen aus der Druckindustrie. *WSI-Mitteilungen*, 39, 652–61.

Fürstenberg, Friedrich 1987: Flexible Gestaltung der industriellen Arbeitsbedingungen. *Zeitschrift für Arbeitswissenschaft*, 41, 65–8.

Gabriel, Jürgen 1985: *Flexibilisierung der Arbeit. Überlegungen zur Theorie und Empirie des Beschäftigungsverhaltens von Unternehmen bei Unsicherheit.* Munich.

Gaugler, Eduard 1983: Betriebswirtschaftliche Aspekte der Arbeitszeitflexibilisierung. *Personal – Mensch und Arbeit*, 35, 334–7.

Gaugler, Eduard, Gille, Gerd, and Paul, Herwig 1981: *Teilzeitarbeit*. Mannheim.

Gensior, Sabine, and Wolf, Frieder O. 1980: Zeitsouveränität' und Normalarbeitszeit. Zur neueren Diskussion über 'Arbeitszeitpolitik'. *Leviathan*, 8, 107–19.

Gensior, Sabine, and Wolf, Frieder O. 1982: Betrieb als historischer Prozess. *Prokla*, 12, 85–102.

Gerhard, Anette, and Michailow, Matthias 1987: Veränderungen im Lebensarrangement unter der Bedingung reduzierter Arbeitszeit. In Jürgen Friedrichs (ed.), *23. Deutscher Soziologentag, Sektions- und Ad-hoc-Gruppen*, Opladen, 596–9.

Gerzer, Annemarie, Jäckel, Monika, and Sass, Jürgen 1985: Flexible Arbeitszeit – vor allem ein Frauenthema. In Thomas Schmid (ed.), *Das Ende der starren Zeit. Vorschläge zur flexiblen Arbeitszeit*, Berlin, 97–127.

Gilbert, Albin R. 1960: The concept of life-style: its background and its psychological significance. In *Jahrbuch für Psychologie, Psychotherapie und medizinische Anthropologie*, 7, Freiburg/Munich, 97–106.

Glatzer, Wolfgang, and Zapf, Wolfgang 1984: Lebensqualität in der Bundesrepublik. In W. Glatzer and W. Zapf (eds), *Lebensqualität in der Bundesrepublik. Objektive Lebensbedingungen und subjektives Wohlbefinden*, Frankfurt/Main, 391–401.

Gluchowski, Peter 1987: Lebensstile und Wandel der Wählerschaft in der Bundesrepublik Deutschland. In *Aus Politik und Zeitgeschichte* (*Supplement to the weekly Das Parlament*, B12/87), 18–32.

Görres, Peter Anselm 1984: *Die Umverteilung der Arbeit*. Frankfurt/Main.

Gross, Hermann, Pekruhl, Ulrich, and Thoben, Cornelia 1987: Arbeitszeitstrukturen im Wandel. Ergebnisse einer akuten Repräsentativumfrage zu den Arbeitszeitstrukturen in der Bundesrepublik Deutschland. In Minister for Labour, Health and Social Affairs of North Rhein-Westphalia (ed.), *Arbeitszeit '87*, Cologne, 1–99.

Guggenberger, Bernd 1982: Am Ende der Arbeitsgesellschaft – Arbeitsgesellschaft am Ende? In F. Benseler, R. G. Heinze, and A. Klönne (eds), *Zukunft der Arbeit*, Hamburg, 63–83.

Gushurst, Robin S. 1971: The technique, utility and validity of life style analysis. *Counseling Psychologist*, 3, 30–9.

Haller, Willi 1981: Optimale Betriebszeiten. Vorstellung eines Konzepts zur Verlängerung der Betriebszeit bei gleichzeitiger Verkürzung der Arbeitszeit. *Personal – Mensch und Arbeit*, 33, 119–22.

Härtel, Ulrich, Matthiesen, Ulf, and Neuendorff, Hartmut 1985: Kontrastierende Fallanalysen zum Wandel von arbeitsbezogenen Deutungsmustern und Lebensentwürfen in einer Stahlstadt, proposed project, unpublished manuscript, Dortmund.

Hegner, Friedhart 1983: Strukturen und Verhaltensorientierungen privater Haushalte als Rahmenbedingungen der Arbeitszeitpolitik. In F. W. Scharpf and M. Brockmann (eds), *Institutionelle Bedingungen der Arbeitsmarkt- und Beschäftigungspolitik*, Frankfurt/Main, 21–52.

Hegner, Friedhart 1987: Schritte zu einer abgestuften Neuverteilung der Erwerbsarbeit. *Discussion Paper IIM/LMP 87–111*, Wissenschaftszentrum Berlin.

Hegner, Friedhart, and Landenberger, Margarete 1988: *Arbeitszeit, Arbeitsmarkt und soziale Sicherung*. Opladen.

Heinemann, Klaus 1982: Arbeitslosigkeit und Zeitbewusstsein. *Soziale Welt*, 33, 87–101.

Heinemann, Klaus 1987: Soziologie des Geldes. In K. Heinemann (ed.), *Soziologie wirtschaftlichen Handelns* (*Kölner Zeitschrift für Soziologie und Sozialpsychologie* Special Edition, 28), Opladen, 322–38.

Heinemann, Klaus, and Ludes, Peter 1978: Zeitbewusstsein und Kontrolle der Zeit. In K. Hammerich and M. Klein (eds), *Soziologie des Alltags* (*Kölner Zeitschrift für Soziologie und Sozialpsychologie* Special Edition, 20), Opladen, 220–43.

Heinze, Rolf G., Hinrichs, Karl, Hohn, H.-Willy, Offe, Claus, and Olk, Thomas 1979: Arbeitszeitflexibilisierung als beschäftigungspolitisches Instrument – Wirkungen und Grenzen neuer Arbeitszeitpolitik. *Mitteilungen aus der Arbeitsmarkt- und Berufsforschung*, 12, 276–88.

Held, Leonore, and Karg; Peter W. 1983: Variable Arbeitszeit – Anspruch und Wirklichkeit. *WSI-Mitteilungen*, 36, 469–83.

Held-Gemeinhardt, Leonore, and Kroker, Sabine 1985: Teilzeitarbeit an technikintensiven Arbeitsplätzen – insbesondere in der Produktion. In H. Bielenski and F. Hegner (eds), *Flexible Arbeitszeiten. Erfahrungen aus der Praxis*, Frankfurt/Main, 71–178.

Hinrichs, Karl 1987: Arbeitszeitflexibilisierung. Zur Kompatibilität von Arbeitnehmerpräferenzen, betrieblichen Interessen und dem Ziel der Arbeitsmarktentlastung. In R. Marr (ed.), *Arbeitszeitmanagement*, Berlin, 55–72.

Hinrichs, Karl 1988: *Motive und Interessen im Arbeitszeitkonflikt. Eine Analyse der Entwicklung des Normalarbeitszeitstandards*. Frankfurt/Main.

Hinrichs, Karl, and Wiesenthal, Helmut 1982: Arbeitszeitwünsche der Beschäftigten und gesellschaftspolitische Zielvorstellungen. In C. Offe, K. Hinrichs and H. Wiesenthal (eds), *Arbeitszeitpolitik. Formen und Folgen einer Neuverteilung der Arbeitszeit*, Frankfurt/Main, 116–36.

Hinrichs, Karl, and Wiesenthal, Helmut 1984: Thesen zur Problematik nichtstandardisierter Arbeitszeiten. *Sozialer Fortschritt*, 33, 285–7.

Hinrichs, Karl, and Wiesenthal, Helmut 1986: Bestandsrationalität versus Kollektivinteresse. Gewerkschaftliche Handlungsprobleme im Arbeitszeitkonflikt 1984. *Soziale Welt*, 37, 280–96.

Hinrichs, Karl, Offe, Claus, and Wiesenthal, Helmut 1982: Der Streit um die Zeit – die Arbeitszeit im gesellschaftspolitischen und industriellen Konflikt, in C. Offe, K. Hinrichs and H. Wiesenthal (eds), *Arbeitszeitpolitik. Formen und Folgen einer Neuverteilung der Arbeitszeit*, Frankfurt/Main, 8–31.

Hitzler, Ronald 1988: *Sinnwelten*. Opladen.

Hitzler, Ronald, and Honer, Anne 1984: Lebenswelt – Milieu – Situation. Terminologische Vorschläge zur theoretischen Verständigung. *Kölner Zeitschrift für Soziologie und Sozialpsychologie*, 36, 56–74.

Hitzler, Ronald, and Honer, Anne 1986: *Zur Ethnographie kleiner Lebens-Welten* (Research Report, 2) Bamberg.

Hof, Bernd 1984: *Vorsprung durch Flexibilisierung*. Cologne.

Hofbauer, Hans 1981: Zur Struktur der Teilzeitarbeit bei Frauen. In W. Klauder and G. Kühlewind (eds), *Probleme der Messung und Vorausschätzung des Frauenerwerbspotentials*, Nuremberg, 107–19.

Hoff, Andreas 1981: Gewerkschaften und flexible Arbeitszeitregelungen. *Discussion Paper IIM/LMP 81–1*, Wissenschaftszentrum Berlin.

Hoff, Andreas 1982: Warum sind Gewerkschaften gegen flexible Arbeitszeitregelungen? In C. Offe, K. Hinrichs, H. Wiesenthal (eds), *Arbeitszeitpolitik. Formen und Folgen einer Neuverteilung der Arbeitszeit*, Frankfurt/Main, 204–18.

Hoff, Andreas 1983: *Betriebliche Arbeitszeitpolitik zwischen Arbeitszeitverkürzung und Arbeitszeitflexibilisierung*. Munich.

Hoff, Andreas, and Scholz, Joachim 1985: Späte Väter, arrivierte Umsteiger und andere Männer an der Peripherie der Arbeitsgesellschaft. In T. Schmid (ed.), *Das Ende der starren Zeit. Vorschläge zur flexiblen Arbeitszeit*, Berlin, 72–96.

Hoff, Andreas, and Weidinger, Michael 1985: *Teilzeitarbeit. Einführung, Organisation und vertragliche Gestaltung von Teilzeitarbeit*. Published by the Federal Minister of Labour and Social Affairs, Bonn.

Hörning, Karl H. 1970: *Ansätze zu einer Konsumsoziologie*. Freiburg.

Hörning, Karl H. 1989: Von ordentlichen Soziologen und unordentlicher Realität. *Soziale Welt*, 40, 76–85.

Hörning, Karl H., and Bücker-Gärtner, Heinrich 1982: *Angestellte im Grossbetrieb. Loyalität und Kontrolle im organisatorisch-technischen Wandel*. Stuttgart.

Hörning, Karl H., and Knicker, Theo 1981: *Soziologie des Berufs*, Hamburg.

Hörning, Karl H., and Michailow, Matthias 1990: Lebensstil als Vergesellschaftungsform. Zum Wandel von Sozialstruktur und sozialer Integration. In P. A. Berger and S. Hradil (eds), *Lebenslagen, Lebensläufe, Lebensstile* (*Soziale Welt* Special Edition, 7), Göttingen.

Hradil, Stefan 1987: *Sozialstrukturanalyse in einer fortgeschrittenen Gesellschaft*. Opladen.

Inglehart, Ronald 1977: *The Silent Revolution: changing values and political styles among Western publics*. Princeton.

Jahoda, Marie, Lazarsfeld, Paul F., and Zeisel, Hans 1972: *Marienthal*. London.

Joerges, Bernward 1981: Berufsarbeit, Konsumarbeit, Freizeit. Zur Sozial- und Umweltverträglichkeit einiger struktureller Veränderungen in Produktion und Konsum. *Soziale Welt*, 32, 168–95.

Joerges, Bernward 1983: Konsumarbeit – Zur Soziologie und Ökologie des 'informellen Sektors'. In J. Matthes (ed.), *Krise der Arbeitsgesellschaft? Verhandlungen des 21. Deutschen Soziologentages in Bamberg 1982*, Frankfurt/Main, 249–64.

Joerges, Bernward 1985: Eigenarbeit unter industriellen Bedingungen. In R. Brun (ed.), *Erwerb und Eigenarbeit*, Frankfurt/Main, 29–45.

Jurczyk, Karin, Treutner, Erhard, Voss, Günter, and Zettel, Ortrud 1985: 'Die Zeiten ändern sich.' Arbeitszeitspezifische Strategien und die Arbeitsteilung der Personen. In S. Hradil (ed.), *Sozialstruktur im Umbruch. Karl Bolte zum 60. Geburtstag*, Opladen, 147–63.

Kaufmann, Franz-Xaver 1970: *Sicherheit als soziologisches und sozialpolitisches Problem*. Stuttgart.

Kevelaer, Karl-Heinz von, and Hinrichs, Karl 1985: Arbeitszeit und 'Wirtschaftswunder'. Rahmenbedingungen des Übergangs zur 40-Stunden-Woche in der Bundesrepublik Deutschland. *Politische Vierteljahresschrift*, 26, 52–75.

Klages, Helmut 1981: *Überlasteter Staat – verdrossene Bürger? Zu den Dissonanzen der Wohlstandsgesellschaft*. Frankfurt/Main.

Klages, Helmut 1983: Wertwandel und Gesellschaftswandel in der sozialstaatlichen Demokratie. In J. Matthes (ed.), *Krise der Arbeitsgesellschaft? Verhandlungen des 21. Deutschen Soziologentages in Bamberg 1982*, Frankfurt/Main, 341–52.

Klages, Helmut 1984: *Wertorientierungen im Wandel*. Frankfurt/Main.

Klages, Helmut, and Kmieciak, Peter (eds) 1979: *Wertwandel und gesellschaftlicher Wandel*. Frankfurt/Main.

Klehm, Wolf R., and Neumann, Lilli 1985: Tragen die Freizeiterfahrungen der Arbeitsgesellschaft die zukünftige Freizeit? Verfügbarkeit über Zeit als Quelle neuer Ungleichheiten. In H.-W. Franz (ed.), *22. Deutscher Soziologentag 1984, Sektions- und Ad-hoc-Gruppen*, Opladen, 773–5.

Klehm, Wolf R., Neumann, Lilli, and Winkler, Klaus 1986: Freizeitprobleme durch unterschiedliche Zeitbudgets. In H.-W. Franz, W. Kruse and H.-G. Rolff (eds), *Neue alte Ungleichheiten*, Opladen, 197–212.

Klein, Thomas 1983: Die Durchsetzungschancen flexibler Arbeitszeit. Durchführbarkeit einer Massnahme zur Verringerung der Doppelbelastung in Beruf und Haushalt. *Zeitschrift für Bevölkerungswissenschaft*, 9, 104–28.

Kmieciak, Peter 1976: *Wertstruktur und Wertwandel in der Bundesrepublik Deutschland*. Göttingen.

Koselleck, Reinhart 1967: Historia magistra vitae. In H. Braun and M. Riedel (eds), *Natur und Geschichte, Festschrift für Karl Löwith zum 70. Geburtstag*, Stuttgart, 196–219.

Kössler, Richard 1984: Arbeitszeitbudgets ausgewählter privater Haushalte in Baden-Württemberg. In '*Materialien und Berichte*' *der Familienwissenschaftlichen Forschungsstelle des Statistischen Landesamtes Baden-Württemberg*, vol. 12, Stuttgart.

Kreckel, Reinhard 1983: Soziale Ungleichheit und Arbeitsmarktsegmentierung. In R. Kreckel (ed.), *Soziale Ungleichheiten*, (*Sozial Welt* Special Edition, 2), Göttingen, 137–62.

Krüsselberg, Hans-Günter, Auge, Michael, and Hilzenbecher, Manfred 1986: *Verhaltenshypothesen und Familienzeitbudgets. Die Ansatzpunkte der 'Neuen Haushaltsökonomik' für Familienpolitik*. Stuttgart.

Kurz-Scherf, Ingrid 1985: Teilzeitarbeit – ein reines Frauenproblem? In A. Kuhn and D. Appenzeller (eds), *Mehrheit ohne Macht. Frauen in der Bundesrepublik Deutschland*, Düsseldorf, 66–96.

Kurz-Scherf, Ingrid 1987: Arbeitszeit im Umbruch. Inventur des tariflichen Regelungsbestandes. *WSI-Mitteilungen*, 40, 694–713.

Kutsch, Thomas, and Vilmar, Fritz (eds) 1983: *Arbeitszeitverkürzung – Ein Weg zur Vollbeschäftigung?* Opladen.

Laermann, Klaus 1975: Alltags-Zeit. Bemerkung über die unauffälligste Form sozialen Zwangs. *Kursbuch*, 41, 87–105.

Landenberger, Margarete 1983: Abeitszeitwünsche. Vergleichende Analyse vorliegender Befragungsergebnisse. *Discussion Paper IIM/LMP 83–17*, Wissenschaftszentrum Berlin.

Landenberger, Margarete 1985a: Aktuelle sozialversicherungsrechtliche Fragen zur flexiblen Arbeitszeit und Teilzeitbeschäftigung. *Zeitschrift für Sozialreform*, 31, 321–35 and 393–415.

Landenberger, Margarete 1985b: Arbeitszeiten. Das Missverhältnis zwischen Wunsch und Wirklichkeit. In T. Schmid (ed.), *Das Ende der starren Zeit. Vorschläge zur flexiblen Arbeitszeit*, Berlin, 51–71.

Landenberger, Margarete 1987a: Soziale Sicherung bei Teilzeitbeschäftigung und flexiblen Arbeitszeitformen. In R. Marr (ed.), *Arbeitszeitmanagement*, Berlin, 283–98.

Landenberger, Margarete 1987b: Teilzeitarbeit und Alterssicherung. Sozialpolitische Flankierung einer Arbeitsumverteilungsstrategie. *Sozialer Fortschritt*, 36 196–201.

Landenberger, Margarete 1987c: Flexible Arbeitszeitformen im Spannungsfeld von ökonomischer Liberalisierung und sozialem Schutzbedaf. In *Aus Politik und Zeitgeschichte (Supplement to the weekly Das Parlament*, B21/87), 15–29.

Lemm, Rolf, and Skolnik, Miriam 1986: Arbeitszeitverkürzung und ihre betriebliche Umsetzung im Einzelhandel. *WSI-Mitteilungen*, 39, 337–47.

Lempert, Wolfgang, Hoff, Ernst, and Lappe, Lothar 1979: *Konzeptionen zur Analyse der Sozialisation durch Arbeit*. Max Planck Institute for Education Research, Berlin.

Linder, Staffan Burenstam. 1970: *The Harried Leisure Class*. New York/London.

Linnenkohl, Karl 1985: Begriff und Bedeutung der 'Arbeitszeitflexibilisierung'. *Arbeits- und Sozialrecht*, 1920–4.

Luckmann, Thomas 1979: Persönliche Identität, soziale Rolle und Rollendistanz. In O. Marquard and K. Stierle (eds), *Identität* (Poetik und Hermeneutik, 8), Munich, 293–313.

Luckmann, Thomas 1983: Lebensweltliche Zeitkategorien, Zeitstrukturen des Alltags und der Ort des historischen Bewusstseins. In B. Cerquiglini and H. U. Gumbrecht (eds), *Der Diskurs der Literatur- und Sprachhistorie. Wissenschaftsgeschichte als Innovationsvorgabe*, Frankfurt/Main, 13–28.

Luckmann, Thomas 1984: Das Gespräch. In K. Stierle and R. Warning (eds), *Das Gespräch* (Poetik und Hermeneutik, 11); Munich, 49–63.

Luckmann, Thomas 1986: Zeit und Identität: innere, soziale und historische Zeit. In F. Fürstenberg and I. Mörth (eds), *Zeit als Strukturelement von Lebenswelt und Gesellschaft*, Linz, 135–74.

Luckmann, Thomas 1987: Gelebte Zeiten – und deren Überschneidungen im Tages- und Lebenslauf. In R. Herzog and R. Koselleck (eds), *Epochenschwelle und Epochenbewusstsein* (Poetik und Hermeneutik, 12) Munich, 283–304.

Luhmann, Niklas 1971: Die Knappheit der Zeit und die Vordringlichkeit des Befristeten. In N. Luhmann (ed.), *Politische Planung. Aufsätze zur Soziologie von Politik und Verwaltung*, Opladen, 143–64.

Luhmann, Niklas 1975: Weltzeit und Systemgeschichte. In N. Luhmann (ed.), *Soziologische Aufklärung*, vol. 2, Opladen, 103–33.

Luhmann, Niklas 1976: The future cannot begin: temporal structures in modern society. *Social Research*, 43, 130–52.

Luhmann, Niklas 1977: Differentiation of society. *Canadian Journal of Sociology*, 2, 29–53.

Luhmann, Niklas 1980a: Temporalisierung von Komplexität. In N. Luhmann (ed.), *Gesellschaftsstruktur und Semantik* (Studien zur Wissenssoziologie der modernen Gesellschaft, 1), Frankfurt/Main, 235–300.

Luhmann, Niklas 1980b: Temporalstrukturen des Handlungssystems. Zum Zusammenhang von Handlungs- und Systemtheorie. In W. Schluchter (ed.), *Verhalten, Handeln und System. Talcott Parsons' Beitrag zur Entwicklung der Sozialwissenschaften*, Frankfurt/Main, 32–67.

Luhmann, Niklas 1988: *Die Wirtschaft der Gesellschaft*. Frankfurt/Main.

Lutz, Burkart 1984: *Der kurze Traum immerwährender Prosperität*. Frankfurt/Main.

Marr, Rainer 1987: Arbeitszeitmanagement: Die Nutzung der Ressource Zeit – Zur Legitimation einer bislang vernachlässigten Managementaufgabe. In R. Marr (ed.), *Arbeitszeitmanagement*, Berlin, 13–37.

May, Karl, and Mohr, Eveline 1985: *Probleme und Individualisierungschance individueller Arbeitszeitmodelle*. Munich.

Mayr, Hans, and Janssen, Hans (eds) 1984: *Perspektiven der Arbeitszeitverkürzung. Wissenschaftler und Gewerkschaftler zur 35-Stunden-Woche*. Cologne.

Mertens, Dieter 1979: Neue Arbeitszeitpolitik und Arbeitsmarkt. *Mitteilungen aus der Arbeitsmarkt- und Berufsforschung*, 12, 263–9.

Mertens, Dieter 1982: Das Steuerungspotential 'alter' und 'neuer' Arbeitszeitpolitik. In C. Offe, K. Hinrichs, and H. Wiesenthal (eds), *Arbeitszeitpolitik. Formen und Folgen einer Neuverteilung der Arbeitszeit*, Frankfurt/Main, 87–203.

Ministry for Labour, Health and Social Affairs of North Rhine-Westphalia 1984: *Modelle zur Arbeitszeitverkürzung und Arbeitsverteilung*, n.p.

Mooser, Josef 1983: Auflösung proletarischer Milieus. Klassenbildung und Individualisierung in der Arbeiterschaft vom Kaiserreich bis in die Bundesrepublik Deutschland. *Soziale Welt*, 34, 270–306.

Mückenberger, Ulrich 1985: Die Krise des Normalarbeitsverhältnisses. *Zeitschrift für Sozialreform*, 31, 415–34 and 457–75.

Müller-Wichmann, Christiane 1984: *Zeitnot. Untersuchungen zum 'Freizeitproblem' und seiner pädagogischen Zugänglichkeit*. Weinheim.

Müller-Wichmann, Christiane 1987: *Von wegen Freizeit*. Frankfurt/Main.

Neckel, Sighard 1984: Arbeitszeitregelungen und Freizeitkultur. In Kulturpolitische Gesellschaft (ed.), *Zukunft der Arbeit – Zukunft der Freizeit und Kultur*, Hagen, 232–40.

Negt, Oskar 1984: *Lebendige Arbeit, enteignete Zeit*. Frankfurt/Main.

Neuendorff, Hartmut 1980: Der Deutungsmusteransatz zur Rekonstruktion der Strukturen des Arbeiterbewusstseins. In K. H. Braun, U. Holzkamp-Osterkamp, H. Werner, and B. Wilhelmer (eds), *Kapitalistische Krise, Arbeiterbewusstsein, Persönlichkeitsentwicklung*, Cologne, 842–63.

Neuendorff, Hartmut, and Sabel, Charles 1978: Zur relativen Autonomie der Deutungsmuster. In K. M. Bolte (ed.), *Materialien aus der soziologischen Forschung. Verhandlungen des 18. Deutschen Soziologentages in Bielefeld 1976*, Darmstadt, 842–63.

Noelle-Neumann, Elisabeth 1978: *Werden wir alle Proletarier? Wertewandel in unserer Gesellschaft*. Zurich.

Oevermann, Ulrich 1973: Zur Analyse der Struktur von sozialen Deutungsmustern. University MS.

Offe, Claus 1983: Arbeit als soziologische Schlüsselkategorie? In J. Matthes (ed.), *Krise der Arbeitsgesellschaft? Verhandlungen des 21. Deutschen Soziologentages in Bamberg 1982*, Frankfurt/Main, 38–65.

Olk, Thomas, Hohn, H.-Willy, Hinrichs, Karl, Heinze, Rolf. G. 1979: Lohnarbeit und Arbeitszeit. Arbeitsmarktpolitik zwischen Requalifizierung der Zeit und kapitalistischem Zeitregime. *Leviathan*, 7, 151–73 and 376–407.

Oppolzer, Alfred 1985: Flexibilisierung: Kennzeichen einer neuen Arbeitszeitpolitik. *AFA-Informationen*, 35, 3–32.

Pornschlegel, Hans 1979: Arbeitszeitverkürzung als Gestaltungselement der Tarifpolitik zur Beeinflussung des Arbeitsvolumens. *Mitteilungen aus der Arbeits- und Berufsforschung*, 12, 373–80.

Rammstedt, Otthein 1975: Alltagsbewusstsein von Zeit. *Kölner Zeitschrift für Soziologie und Sozialpsychologie*, 27, 47–63.

Reyher, Lutz, Bach, Hans-Uwe, Kohler, Hans, and Teriet, Bernhard 1979: Arbeitszeit und Arbeitsmarkt. Volumenrechnung, Auslastungsgrad und Entlastungswirkung. *Mitteilungen aus der Arbeitsmarkt- und Berufsforschung*, 12, 381–420.

Rinderspacher, Jürgen P. 1982: Humanisierung der Arbeit durch Arbeitszeitgestaltung? In C. Offe, K. Hinrichs, H. Wiesenthal (eds), *Arbeitszeitpolitik. Formen und Folgen einer Neuverteilung der Arbeitszeit*, Frankfurt/Main, 233–43.

Rinderspacher, Jürgen P. 1985: *Gesellschaft ohne Zeit*. Frankfurt/Main.

Rinderspacher, Jürgen P. 1987a: Die ruhelose Gesellschaft. *Das Argument*, 29, 498–504.

Rinderspacher, Jürgen P. 1987b: *Am Ende der Woche. Die soziale und kulturelle Bedeutung des Wochenendes*. Bonn.

Rinderspacher, Jürgen P. 1988: Wege der Verzeitlichung. In D. Henckel (ed.), *Arbeitszeit, Betriebszeit, Freizeit. Auswirkungen auf die Raumentwicklung*, Stuttgart, 23–67.

Rinderspacher, Jürgen P., and Ermert, Axel 1986: Zeiterfahrung in der Leistungsgesellschaft. in H. Burger (ed.), *Zeit, Natur und Mensch*, Berlin, 304–24.

Rossmann, Wittich 1987: Ökonomische und politische Konturen des Arbeitszeitkonflikts 1987. *Blätter für deutsche und internationale Politik*, 32, 61–72.

Rudolph, Hedwig, Duran, Marga, Klähn, Margitta, Nassauer, Melanie, and Naumann, Jenny 1981: Chancen und Risiken neuer Arbeitszeitsysteme. Zur Situation teilzeitarbeitender Frauen im Berliner Einzelhandel. *WSI-Mitteilungen*, 34, 204–11.

Rürup, Bert, and Struwe, Jochen 1984: Arbeitszeitflexibilisierung als Instrument der Beschäftigungspolitik. *Konjunkturpolitik*, 30, 1–22.

Scharpf, Fritz W., and Schettkat, Ronald 1984: Verkürzung der Wochenarbeitszeit: Nur der Staat kann den beschäftigungspolitischen Handlungsspielraum erweitern. *Discussion Paper IIM/LMP 84–5*, Wissenschaftszentrum Berlin.

Schettkat, Ronald 1983: Auswirkungen einer generellen Arbeitszeitverkürzung auf öffentliche Haushalte, Arbeitnehmereinkommen und gesamtwirtschaftliche Nachfrage. *Discussion Paper IIM/LMP 83–15*, Wissenschaftszentrum Berlin.

Schlotter, Hans-Günther 1986: Individuelle und soziale Ziele der Arbeitszeitgestaltung. In G. Buttler, K. Oettle, and H. Winterstein (eds), *Flexible Arbeitszeit gegen starre Sozialsysteme*, Baden-Baden, 13–37.

Schneider, Michael 1984: *Streit um die Zeit. Geschichte des Kampfes um die Arbeitszeitverkürzung in Deutschland*. Cologne.

Schöps, Martina 1980: *Zeit und Gesellschaft*. Stuttgart.

Schütz, Alfred 1970: *Reflections on the Problem of Relevance*. New Haven, Conn.

Schütz, Alfred 1972: *The Phenomenology of the Social World*. London.

Schütz, Alfred, and Luckmann Thomas 1975/84: *Strukturen der Lebenswelt*. 2 vols. Neuwied; Frankfurt/Main.

Schütze, Fritz 1977: Die Technik des narrativen Interviews in Interaktionsfeldstudien – dargestellt an einem Projekt zur Erforschung von kommunalen Machtstrukturen. MS, Bielefeld.

Schütze, Fritz 1983: Biographieforschung und narratives Interview. *Neue Praxis*, 3, 283–93.

Seifert, Eberhard 1984: Arbeitszeitforschung und ihre unzugängliche statistische Basis. *Angewandte Sozialforschung*, 12, 189–202.

Seifert, Hartmut 1985: Arbeitszeitpolitik in der Bundesrepublik Deutschland. *Wirtschaft und Gesellschaft*, 11, 309–24.

Seifert, Hartmut 1986: Durchsetzungsprobleme zukünftiger Arbeitszeitgestaltung. *WSI-Mitteilungen*, 39, 216–27.

Seifert, Hartmut 1987: Variable Arbeitszeitgestaltung. Arbeitszeit nach Mass für die Betriebe oder Zeitautonomie für die Arbeitnehmer? *WSI-Mitteilungen*, 40, 727–35.

Seifert, Hartmut 1989: Beschäftigungswirkungen und Perspektiven der Arbeitszeitpolitik. *WSI-Mitteilungen*, 42, 156–63.

Seifert, Hartmut, and Welzmüller, Rudi 1983: Arbeitszeitverkürzung und Verteilung. *WSI-Mitteilungen*, 36, 217–35.

Sichtermann, Barbara 1987: *Frauen-Arbeit. Über wechselnde Tätigkeiten und die Ökonomie der Emanzipation*. Berlin.

Simmel, Georg 1897: Die Bedeutung des Geldes für das Tempo des Lebens. *Neue Deutsche Rundschau*, 8, 111–22.

Simmel, Georg 1978: *The Philosophy of Money* (1900). London.

Sobel, Michael E. 1981: *Lifestyle and Social Structure*. New York.

Soeffner, Hans-Georg 1986: Auslegung im Alltag – der Alltag der Auslegung. In J. Klein and H. D. Erlinger (eds), *Wahrheit, Richtigkeit und Exaktheit* (Siegener Studien, 40), Essen, 111–31.

Soeffner, Hans-Georg 1989a: Hermeneutik. Zur Genese einer wissenschaftlichen Einstellung durch die Praxis der Auslegung. In H.-G. Soeffner, *Auslegung des Alltags – der Alltag der Auslegung. Zur wissenssoziologischen Konzeption einer sozialwissenschaftlichen Hermeneutik*, Frankfurt/Main, 98–139.

Soeffner, Hans-Georg 1989b: Prämissen einer sozialwissenschaftlichen Hermeneutik. In H.-G. Soeffner, *Auslegung des Alltags – der Alltag der Auslegung. Zur wissenssoziologischen Konzeption einer sozialwissenschaftlichen Hermeneutik*, Frankfurt/Main, 66–97.

Sorokin, Pitirim A., and Merton, Robert K. 1937: Social time: a methodological and functional analysis. *American Journal of Sociology*, 42, 615–29.

Srubar, Ilja 1979: Die Theorie der Typenbildung bei Alfred Schütz. Ihre Bedeutung und ihre Grenzen. In W. M. Sprondel and R. Grathoff (eds), *Alfred Schütz und die Idee des Alltags in den Sozialwissenschaften*, Stuttgart, 43–64.

Stengel, Martin 1987: Einstellungen zur individuellen Arbeitszeitverkürzung. *Zeitschrift für Arbeitswissenschaft*, 41, 77–83.

Strümpel, Burkhard, Prenzel, Wolfgang, Scholz, Joachim, and Hoff, Andreas
1988: *Teilzeitarbeitende Männer und Hausmänner. Motive und Konse-
quenzen einer eingeschränkten Erwerbstätigkeit bei Männern*. Berlin.

Sydow, Jörg, and Conrad, Peter 1987: Der Einfluss flexibler Arbeitszeiten
auf das Organisationsklima. In R. Marr (ed.), *Arbeitszeitmanagement*,
Berlin, 199–211.

Teriet, Bernhard 1978: Zeitökonomie, Zeitsouveränität und Zeitmanage-
ment. *Zeitschrift für Arbeitswissenschaft*, 32, 112–18.

Teriet, Bernhard 1984: Stichwort: Flexible Arbeitszeit. *Management-
Wissen*, 11, 41–2.

Thompson, Edward P. 1991: Time, Work-Discipline and Industrial
Capitalism. Reprinted in his *Customs in Common: Studies in Traditional
Popular Culture*, New York, 352–403.

Thomssen, Wilke 1980: Deutungsmuster – eine Kategorie der Analyse von
gesellschaftlichem Bewusstsein. In A. Weymann (ed.), *Handbuch zur
Soziologie der Erwachsenenbildung*, Darmstadt, 258–373.

Tokarski, Walter, and Schmitz-Scherzer, Reinhard 1985: *Freizeit*. Stuttgart.

Tokarski, Walter, and Uttitz, Pavel 1985: Lebensstil – eine Perspektive für
die Freizeitforschung? In H.-W. Franz (ed.), *Beiträge der Sektions- und
Ad-hoc-Gruppen. 22. Deutscher Soziologentag 1984 in Dortmund*,
Opladen 519–21.

Treier, Peter 1979: Arbeitswissenschaftliche Aspekte des Arbeitszeitregimes
unter besonderer Berücksichtigung von Problemen der Arbeitszeitverkürzung. *Mitteilungen aus der Arbeitsmarkt- und Berufsforschung*, 12,
413–27.

Virilio, Paul 1989: *Der negative Horizont. Bewegung – Geschwindigkeit –
Beschleunigung*, Munich / Vienna.

Vobruba, Georg 1982: Interessendifferenzierung und Organisationseinheit.
Arbeitszeitflexibilisierung als gewerkschaftliches Organisationsproblem.
In C. Offe, K. Hinrichs, and H. Wiesenthal (eds), *Arbeitszeitpolitik.
Formen und Folgen einer Neuverteilung der Arbeitszeit*, Frankfurt / Main,
219–32.

Weidinger, Michael, and Hoff, Andreas 1988: Tendenzen der Betriebszeit-
und Arbeitszeitentwicklung. In D. Henckel (ed.), *Arbeitszeit, Betriebszeit,
Freizeit. Auswirkungen auf die Raumentwicklung*, Stuttgart, 93–133.

Weitzel, Renate, and Hoff, Andreas 1981: Möglichkeiten und Grenzen der
öffentlichen Förderung von Teilzeitarbeit – Ergebnisse einer Explorativ-
studie. *Discussion Paper IIM/LMP 81–8*, Wissenschaftszentrum Berlin.

Wendorff, Rudolf 1980: *Zeit und Kultur. Zur Geschichte des Zeitbewusst-
seins in Europa*. Opladen.

Wiesenthal, Helmut 1985: Themenraub und falsche Allgemeinheiten. In T.
Schmid (ed.), *Ende der starren Zeit. Vorschläge zur flexiblen Arbeitszeit*,
Berlin, 9–24.

Wiesenthal, Helmut 1987: *Strategie und Illusion. Rationalitätsgrenzen kollektiver Akteure am Beispiel der Arbeitszeitpolitik 1980–1985*. Frankfurt/Main.

Wiesenthal, Helmut, Offe, Claus, Hinrichs, Karl, and Engfer, Uwe 1983: Arbeitszeitflexibilisierung und gewerkschaftliche Interessenvertretung – Regelungsprobleme und Risiken individualisierter Arbeitszeiten. *WSI-Mitteilungen*, 36, 585–95.

Wotschack, Winfried 1987: Flexibilisierungskonzeptionen und ihre Auswirkungen auf Arbeitsanforderungen und Belastungen. *Discussion Paper IIVG dp 87–203*, Wissenschaftszentrum Berlin.

Zablocki, Benjamin D., and Kanter, Rosabeth Moss 1976: The differentiation of lifestyles. *Annual Review of Sociology*, 2, 269–98.

Zachert, Ulrich 1988: Entwicklung und Perspektiven des Normalarbeitsverhältnisses. *WSI-Mitteilungen*, 41, 457–66.

Zapf, Wolfgang, Breuer, Sigrid, Hampel, Jürgen, Krause, Peter, Möhr, Hans-Michael, and Wiegand, Erich 1987: *Individualisierung und Sicherheit. Untersuchungen zur Lebensqualität in der Bundesrepublik Deutschland* (Schriftenreihe des Bundeskanzlers, 4). Munich.

Zoll, Rainer 1982: Zeiterfahrung und Gesellschaftsform. *Prokla*, 12, 103–18.

Index